D1394438

**Cities Without Citizens**

Edited by Eduardo Cadava and Aaron Levy

# Cities Without Citizens

Edited by Eduardo Cadava and Aaron Levy

Contributions by: Giorgio Agamben, Arakawa + Gins, Branka Arsic, Eduardo Cadava, Joan Dayan, Gans & Jelacic Architecture, Thomas Keenan, Gregg Lambert, Aaron Levy, David Lloyd, Rafi Segal Eyal Weizman Architects, Gayatri Chakravorty Spivak.

Slought Books, Philadelphia with the Rosenbach Museum & Library
Theory Series, No. 1

This project was made possible through the Vanguard Group Foundation and the 5-County Arts Fund, a Pennsylvania Partners in the Arts program of the Pennsylvania Council on the Arts, a state agency. It is funded by the citizens of Pennsylvania through an annual legislative appropriation, and administered locally by the Greater Philadelphia Cultural Alliance. The Pennsylvania Council on the Arts is supported by the National Endowment for the Arts, a federal agency. Additional support for the 5-County Arts Fund is provided by the Delaware River Port Authority and PECO energy. We also acknowledge the financial support of the Memorial Foundation for Jewish Culture, NY for Aaron Levy's *Kloster Indersdorf* series, and the International Artists' Studio Program in Sweden (IASPIS) for Lars Wallsten's *Crimescape* series. We are grateful for the organizational and curatorial support of Bill Adair, Frank Smigiel, and Catherine Hitchens at the Rosenbach Museum, whose invitation prompted this project, and editorial assistants Jen Kollar, Joyce Sim, and Alyssa Timin at Slought Foundation.

These articles have appeared in the following publications acknowledged here:
1. Giorgio Agamben, *Means without ends: notes on politics*. Theory Out of Bounds, V. 20. University of Minnesota Press, Minnesota, 2000.
2. Gans and Jelacic Architecture and Design, Perspecta 34: *Temporary Architecture*, Yale Architecture School/ MIT 2003.

Printed in Canada on acid-free paper by Coach House Books, Ltd.
Set in 9pt Arial Narrow. Design by Sinder Design & Consulting, Philadelphia

For further information, http://slought.org/books/
SLOUGHT FOUNDATION
4017 Walnut Street
Philadelphia PA, 19104

Library of Congress Cataloging-in-Publication Data

Cities without citizens / edited by Aaron Levy and Eduardo Cadava ; contributions by Giorgio Agamben ... [et al.].
   p. cm. -- (Theory series ; no. 1)
Includes bibliographical references.
ISBN 0-9714848-4-8 (pbk. : alk. paper)
1. Human rights--Exhibitions. 2. Refugees--Exhibitions. 3. Social justice--Exhibitions. 4. Marginality, Social--Exhibitions. 5. Citizenship--Exhibitions. 6. Archives--Administration--Moral and ethical aspects. 7. Historical libraries--Exhibitions--Moral and ethical aspects. 8. Historical museums--Exhibitions--Moral and ethical aspects. 9. Rosenbach Museum & Library--Exhibitions. I. Levy, Aaron, 1977- II. Cadava, Eduardo. III. Agamben, Giorgio, 1942- IV. Rosenbach Museum & Library. V. Series: Theory series (Philadelphia, Pa.) ; no. 1.
JC585 .C497 2003
323--dc22
                                        2003022588

# CONTENTS

## I. CITIZENS and DISCIPLINE

## II. LIQUIDATION and SETTLEMENT

## III. DOCUMENTATION

Documentation for Cities Without Citizens, an installation organized by Aaron Levy, 2003 artist-in-residence, at The Rosenbach Museum & Library, July 8 through September 28, 2003

## REFERENCE MATTER

Giorgio Agamben teaches philosophy at the University of Verona. His publications include *The Community Community* (1993), *Homo Sacer: Sovereign Power and Bare Life* (1998), *Remnants of Auschwitz: The Witness and the Archive* (1998), *The Man Without Content* (1999), *The End of the Poem* (1999), and *Potentialities: Collected Essays in Philosophy* (1999).

Arakawa and Madeline Gins started collaborating in 1963. Their collaborative work, *The Mechanism of Meaning,* was published in 1971, and a sequel to that, *To Not To Die,* appeared in 1987. Gins and Arakawa have exhibited jointly throughout Europe, Japan, and the United States. Their exhibition, *Site of Reversible Destiny,* was on view at the Guggenheim Museum Soho in December 1997 and won the College Art Association's Exhibition of the Year award. Arakawa's large-scale paintings are in the permanent collections of museums throughout the world. Gins's published works include the avant-garde classic, *What the President Will Say or Do!!,* and an innovative art-historical novel, *Helen Keller or Arakawa.*

Branka Arsic teaches critical theory and American literature at the University of Albany. Her book *The Passive Eye* was recently published by Stanford

University Press. She is currently completing a volume on Melville's "Bartleby, The Scrivener" and has begun a project on Henry David Thoreau.

Eduardo Cadava teaches in the English Department at Princeton University. His publications include *Words of Light: Theses on the Photography of History* (1997), *Emerson and the Climates of History* (1997), *Who Comes After the Subject?* (co-editor with Peter Connor, and Jean-Luc Nancy; 1991). He is currently writing a collection of essays on the ethics and politics of mourning entitled *Of Mourning* and a book on music and techniques of reproduction, memorization, and writing entitled *Music on Bones*.

Joan Dayan is Professor of English and Comparative Literature at the University of Pennsylvania. She is the author of *Fables of Mind: An Inquiry into Poe's Fiction* (1987) *Haiti, History, and the Gods* (1995), and numerous articles on North American and Caribbean literature and issues of race. She is currently completing *Held in the Body of the State* and *The Law is a White Dog*, a series of essays on law and spiritual belief.

Deborah Gans and Matthew Jelacic are partners in the firm Gans & Jelacic Architecture and Design. Their architectural, urban and industrial design projects and competitions have been exhibited at RIBA, London, IFA, Paris, the Van Alen Institute, New York City, and Slought Foundation, Philadelphia. In 1999 Gans & Jelacic won an international competition to house refugees in the Balkans hosted by Architecture for Humanity, WarChild, USAID and UNHCR. Deborah Gans is the author of *The Le Corbusier Guide* (1987) and the editor of *The Organic Approach* (2002). Both Gans and Jelacic are Professors in architecture at Pratt Institute in New York.

Thomas Keenan teaches media theory, literature, and human rights at Bard College, where he is Associate Professor of Comparative Literature and directs the Human Rights Project. He is author of *Fables of Responsibility*

(1997), and editor of books on the museum and on the wartime journalism of Paul de Man. His current manuscript is called *Live Feed: Crisis, Intervention, Media,* and is about the news media and contemporary conflicts.

Gregg Lambert teaches at Syracuse University and is author of several books, including *Return of the Baroque: Art, Theory and Culture in the Modern Age* (forthcoming), *The Non-Philosophy of Gilles Deleuze* (2002) and *Report to the Academy* (2001). This chapter is part of a study in-progress on the new philosophy of Right.

Aaron Levy is Executive Director of and a Senior Curator at Slought Foundation, a Philadelphia arts organization and archival resource, also available online (http://slought.org). Since 1999, he has organized over 100 live events and exhibitions on contemporary art and theory. He recently edited *Searching for Romberg* (2001), on artist Osvaldo Romberg, *Untitled (After Cinema)* (2002), on photography after cinema, and, with Jean-Michel Rabaté, *Of the Diagram: The Work of Marjorie Welish* (2003). He curated the exhibition "Cities without Citizens" at the Rosenbach Museum as their 2003 artist-in-residence.

David Lloyd is Professor of English at University of Southern California. He is the author of several books, including *Nationalism and Minor Literature: James Clarence Mangan and the Emergence of Irish Culture Nationalism* (1987), *Anomalous States: Irish Writing and the Post-Colonial Moment* (1993), *Culture and the State,* with Paul Thomas (1997), *The Politics of Culture in the Shadow of Capital,* edited with Lisa Lowe (1997), and *Ireland after History* (2000).

Gayatri Chakravorty Spivak is the Avalon Foundation Professor in the Humanities and presently the director of The Center for Comparative Literature and Society at Columbia University. She is the author of *In Other*

*Worlds: Essays in Cultural Politics* (1988), *The Post-Colonial Critic: Interviews, Strategies, Dialogues* (1990), *Outside in the Teaching Machine* (1993), *A Critique of Postcolonial Reason: Toward a History of the Vanishing Present* (1999) and *Death of a Discipline* (2003). She was the translator of Jacques Derrida's *Of Grammatology* (1976) and of Mahasweta Devi's *Imaginary Maps* (1994) and *Chotti Munda and His Arrow* (2003).

Eyal Weizman and Rafi Segal established their architectural practice in Tel Aviv in 2000 after working together with Zvi Hecker. Their office attempts to integrate architectural projects with research and writing. Amongst their recent works are the re-design of the Ashdod Museum of Art, a set design for "Electra," and the exhibition and publication "A Civilian Occupation" (Verso, 2003). Rafi Segal worked together with Zvi Hecker on the design of the Palmach History Museum in Tel Aviv. Eyal Weizman is developing his "Politics of Verticality" project into a book and a film. His previous books are *Yellow Rhythms* (2000) and *Random Walk* (1998).

**INTRODUCTION**

Eduardo Cadava and Aaron Levy

What is a city? What are the laws or constitutions that make a city a city, that prevent it from becoming something else, even as it inevitably undergoes transformation and change? What would it mean to establish the borders of a city, to define and delimit it in order to confer an identity upon it? How is a city lost, destroyed, abandoned, and then perhaps rebuilt from its ruins, sometimes in other places and in memory of its name and patrimony? What would it mean for a city to remain self-identical to itself, or for it to remain internally consistent? Is this possible, or must a city always remain open to transformation, to the changes that alter and displace it? Must a city remain open, that is, to knowing that it does not yet know what it is or may be? And, if so, what is the relation between this uncertainty, this relation to a future, and the changing, heterogeneous populations within its permeable borders? What is the relation between a city and its inhabitants, between a city and its citizens, or between a city and all the people from which it perhaps withholds its protections? What is citizenship and how is it established or lost, asserted or taken away?

These questions have become more urgent than ever, if not more melancholic or eschatological, since today's city—because of its permeability, because of its relation to the expanding forces of capital, globalization, and information technologies—can no longer be said to name the geographical unity of a habitat, or an insulated network of communication, commerce, sociality, or even politics. But the fact that the city increasingly seems to be an anachronistic feature of the contemporary world does not mean that we have overcome it. If the borders of a city are vacillating, and perhaps less secure than ever before, this does not mean that they are disappearing. In the wording of Etienne Balibar, "less than ever is the contemporary world a 'world without borders.'" Indeed, we have witnessed the proliferation of borders and divisions in recent years—and often within the theater of the bloody conflicts of economic wars, civil wars, ethnic conflicts, wars of culture and religion, and the unleashing of racisms and xenophobias—and this despite the erasure of borders announced by the rhetoric and practices of globalization. This is why this collection of essays takes its point of departure from this series of questions but also from the risk of two propositions, each of which appears impossible in relation to the other, but each of which asks us to think the nature of the city, and especially the nature of its relation both to its citizens and to its non-citizens: 1) there have never been cities without citizens; and 2) there have always only been cities without citizens.

To claim that there have never been cities without citizens is simply to recall that, by definition, cities can exist only if they are inhabited by citizens who, inscribed in a network of affiliations that constitute the very structure of the city, or granted rights such as those of the right to political participation or the right to suffrage or education, can claim that the space in which they live is a city that guarantees these affiliations and rights. This also means that citizenship can exist only where we understand a city to exist—where citizens and foreigners are distinguished in terms of rights and obligations in a given space. To say that there have never been cities without citizens, then, is simply to indicate that there is a relation between the identity of a city and that of its citizens. If cities always have citizens—and this is true even if we know that these citizens have been understood and defined according to several different historical models of citizenship—it is because they announce themselves as principles of articulation between birth, language, culture, nationality, belonging, rights, and citizenship.

To claim that there have always only been cities without citizens, however, is to recognize that any assertion of citizenship can only take place by simultaneously defining the limits and conditions of citizenship—by defining, that is, the non-citizen, the foreigner, the alien, the stranger, the immigrant, the refugee, the criminal, the prisoner, or the outsider—and, similarly, that any delineation of the borders of a city must mark what remains within the city but also what is excluded from it. This means, among so many other things, that there can be no cities or citizens without laws of segregation and exclusion—without borders, barriers, interdictions, displacements, censorships, racisms, and the marginalization and eviction of languages and peoples. In other words, the phrase "cities without citizens" also evokes the violence, the laws of denaturalization and denationalization, the deprivation of civil rights, the strategies of depopulation, forced deportation, enforced emigration, the refusal of the rights of asylum, the murderous persecutions, massacres, colonizations, exterminations, exiles, and pogroms that so often have punctuated and defined the history of cities.

In bringing these two propositions together, the essays in this volume seek to think about the many ways in which cities can be defined, built, settled, developed, and organized, but also how they can be either populated by, or evacuated of, their peoples or citizens. They touch on the figures and forces of citizenship, discipline, settlement, and liquidation that are at the heart of any meditation on the identity of cities but that are also essentially related to the question of what it means to be a citizen, to be human, to have rights, and even to belong to a city, state, or nation. They ask us to think about what it means to live in cities, but perhaps in ways that are not yet, or no longer, defined by citizenship and belonging. They call for a reconceptualization of the relation between cities and citizens—for new experiences of communities, frontiers, and identities, without models, and perhaps even without citizens as we generally have understood them.

Seeking to imagine a democracy that in fact would exist beyond citizenship and citizenry—to imagine cities that, coming without citizens, would open the spaces for new forms of democratic communities—these new communities would involve alliances that go beyond the "political" domain as it has been commonly defined (since this designation usually has been reserved for the citizen in a nation linked to a particular territory), and therefore would define the cities of tomorrow in relation to a democracy that is still yet to come and yet to be imagined. The essays in this collection gesture toward this democracy by asking us to invent the city anew—to invent a city that would be open to the future because it would be open to its own alterity, and because it would enable a sociality that is not determined in advance by the fact of belonging to a community, a state, a nation, or even just a language.

# I. CITIZENS and DISCIPLINE

In 1943, Hannah Arendt published an article titled "We Refugees" in a small English-language Jewish publication, the *Menorah Journal.* At the end of this brief but significant piece of writing, after having polemically sketched the portrait of Mr. Cohn, the assimilated Jew who, after having been 150 percent German, 150 percent Viennese, 150 percent French, must bitterly realize in the end that "on ne parvient pas deux fois," she turns the condition of countryless refugee—a condition she herself was living—upside down in order to present it as the paradigm of a new historical consciousness. The refugees who have lost all rights and who, however, no longer want to be assimilated at all costs in a new national identity, but want instead to contemplate lucidly their condition, receive in exchange for assured unpopularity a priceless advantage: "History is no longer a closed book to them and politics is no longer the privilege of Gentiles. They know that the outlawing of the Jewish people of Europe has been followed closely by the outlawing of most European nations. Refugees driven from country to country represent the vanguard of their peoples."[1]

One ought to reflect on the meaning of this analysis, which after fifty years has lost none of its relevance. It is not only the case that the problem presents itself inside and outside of Europe with just as much urgency as then. It is also the case that, given the by now unstoppable decline of the nation-state and the general corrosion of traditional political-juridical categories, the refugee is perhaps the only thinkable figure for the people of our time and the only category in which one may see today—at least until the process of dissolution of the nation-state and of its sovereignty has achieved full completion—the forms and limits of a coming political community. It is even possible that, if we want to be equal to the absolutely new tasks ahead, we will have to abandon decidedly, without reservation, the fundamental concepts through which we have so far represented the subjects of the political (Man, the Citizen and its rights, but also the sovereign people, the worker, and so forth) and build our political philosophy anew starting from the one and only figure of the refugee.

The first appearance of refugees as a mass phenomenon took place at the end of World War I, when the fall of the Russian, Austro-Hungarian, and Ottoman empires, along with the new order created by the peace treaties, upset profoundly the demographic and territorial constitution of Central Eastern Europe. In a short period, 1.5 million White Russians, seven hundred thousand Armenians, five hundred thousand Bulgarians, a million Greeks, and hundreds of thousands of Germans, Hungarians, and Romanians left their countries. To these moving masses, one needs to add the explosive situation determined by the fact that about 30 percent of the population in the new states created by the peace treaties on the model of the nation-state (Yugoslavia and Czechoslovakia, for example), was constituted by minorities that had to be safeguarded by a series of international treaties—the so-called Minority Treaties—which very often were not enforced. A few years later, the racial laws in Germany and the civil war in Spain dispersed throughout Europe a new and important contingent of refugees.

We are used to distinguishing between refugees and stateless people, but this distinction was not then as simple as it may seem at first

4

glance, nor is it even today. From the beginning, many refugees, who were not technically stateless, preferred to become such rather than return to their country. (This was the case with the Polish and Romanian Jews who were in France or Germany at the end of the war, and today it is the case with those who are politically persecuted or for whom returning to their countries would mean putting their own survival at risk.) On the other hand, Russian, Armenian, and Hungarian refugees were promptly denationalized by the new Turkish and Soviet governments. It is important to note how, starting with World War I, many European states began to pass laws allowing the denaturalization and denationalization of their own citizens: France was first, in 1915, with regard to naturalized citizens of "enemy origin"; in 1922, Belgium followed this example by revoking the naturalization of those citizens who had committed "antinational" acts during the war; in 1926, the Italian Fascist regime passed an analogous law with regard to citizens who had shown themselves "undeserving of Italian citizenship"; in 1933, it was Austria's turn; and so on, until in 1935 the Nuremberg Laws divided German citizens into citizens with full rights and citizens without political rights. Such laws—and the mass statelessness resulting from them—mark a decisive turn in the life of the modern nation-state as well as its definitive emancipation from naïve notions of the citizen and a people.

This is not the place to retrace the history of the various international organizations through which single states, the League of Nations, and later, the United Nations have tried to face the refugee problem, from the Nansen Bureau for the Russian and Armenian refugees (1921) to the High Commission for Refugees from Germany (1936) to the Intergovernmental Committee for Refugees (1938) to the UN's International Refugee Organization (1946) to the present Office of the High Commissioner for Refugees (1951), whose activity, according to its statute, does not have a political character but rather only a "social and humanitarian" one. What is essential is that each and every time refugees no longer represent individual cases but rather a mass phenomenon (as was the case between the two world wars and is now once again), these organizations as well as the single states—all the solemn evocations of the inalienable rights of human beings notwithstanding—have proved to be absolutely incapable not only of solving the problem but also of facing it in an adequate manner. The whole question, therefore, was handed over to humanitarian organizations and to the police.

The reasons for such impotence lie not only in the selfishness and blindness of the bureaucratic apparatuses, but also in the very ambiguity of the fundamental notions regulating the inscription of the *native* (that is, of life) in the juridicial order of the nation-state. Hannah Arendt titled the chapter of her book *Imperialism* that concerns the refugee problem "The Decline of the Nation-State and the End of the Rights of Man."[2]  One should try to take seriously this formulation, which indissolubly links the fate of the Rights of Man with the fate of the modern nation-state in such a way that the waning of the latter necessarily implies the obsolescence of the former.  Here the paradox is that precisely the figure that should have embodied human rights more than any other—namely, the refugee—marked instead the radical crisis of the concept.  The conception of human rights based on the supposed existence of a human being as such, Arendt tells us, proves to be untenable as soon as those who profess it find themselves confronted for the first time with people who have really lost every quality and every specific relation except for the pure fact of being human.[3]  In the system of the nation-state, so-called sacred and inalienable human rights are revealed to be without any protection precisely when it is no longer possible to conceive of them as rights of the citizens of a state.  This is implicit, after all, in the ambiguity of the very title of the 1789 *Déclaration des droits de l'homme et du citoyen,* in which it is unclear whether the two terms are to name two distinct realities or whether they are to form, instead, a hendiadys in which the first term is actually always already contained in the second.

That there is no autonomous space in the political order of the nation-state for something like the pure human in itself is evident at the very least from the fact that, even in the best of cases, the status of refugee has always been considered a temporary condition that ought to lead either to naturalization or to repatriation. A stable statute for the human in itself is inconceivable in the law of the nation-state.

It is time to cease to look at all the declarations of rights from 1789 to the present day as proclamations of eternal metajuridical values aimed at binding the legislator to the respect of such values; it is time, rather, to understand them according to their real function in the modern state. Human rights, in fact, represent first of all the originary figure for the inscription of natural naked life in the political-juridical order of the nation-state. Naked life (the human being), which in antiquity belonged to God and in the classical world was clearly distinct (as zoē) from political life (bios), comes to the forefront in the management of the state and becomes, so to speak, its early foundation. Nation-state means a state that makes nativity or birth [nascita] (that is, naked human life) the foundation of its own sovereignty. This is the meaning (and it is not even a hidden one) of the first three articles of the 1789 Declaration: it is only because this declaration inscribed (in articles 1 and 2) the native element in the heart of any political organization that it can firmly bind (in article 3) the principle of sovereignty to the nation (in conformity with its etymon, native [natío] originally meant simply "birth" [nascita]). The fiction that is implicit here is that birth [nascita] comes into being immediately as nation, so that there may not be any difference between the two moments. Rights, in other words, are attributed to the human being only to the degree to which he or she is the immediately vanishing presupposition (and, in fact, the presupposition that must never come to light as such) of the citizen.

If the refugee represents such a disquieting element in the order of the nation-state, this is so primarily because, by breaking the identity between the human and the citizen and that between nativity and nationality, it brings

7

the originary fiction of sovereignty to crisis. Single exceptions to such a principle, of course, have always existed. What is new in our time is that growing sections of humankind are no longer representable inside the nation-state—and this novelty threatens the very foundations of the latter. Inasmuch as the refugee, an apparently marginal figure, unhinges the old trinity of state-nation-territory, it deserves instead to be regarded as the central figure of our political history. We should not forget that the first camps were built in Europe as spaces for controlling refugees, and that the succession of internment camps—concentration camps—extermination camps represents a perfectly real filiation. One of the few rules the Nazis constantly obeyed throughout the course of the "final solution" was that Jews and Gypsies could be sent to extermination camps only after having been fully denationalized (that is, after they had been stripped of even that second-class citizenship to which they had been relegated after the Nuremberg Laws). When their rights are no longer the rights of the citizen, that is when human beings are truly *sacred*, in the sense that this term used to have in the Roman law of the archaic period: doomed to death.

The concept of refugee must be resolutely separated from the concept of "human rights," and the right of asylum (which in any case is by now in the process of being drastically restricted in the legislation of the European states) must no longer be considered as the conceptual category in which to inscribe the phenomenon of refugees. (One needs only to look at Agnes Heller's recent *Theses on the Right of Asylum* to realize that this cannot but lead today to awkward confusions.) The refugee should be considered for what it is, namely, nothing less than a limit-concept that at once brings a radical crisis to the principles of the nation-state and clears the way for a renewal of categories that can no longer be delayed.

Meanwhile, in fact, the phenomenon of so-called illegal immigration into the countries of the European Union has reached (and shall increasingly reach in the coming years, given the estimated twenty million immigrants from Central European countries) characteristics and proportions such that this reversal of perspective is fully justified. What industrialized countries face today is a permanently resident mass of noncitizens who do not want to be and cannot be either naturalized or repatriated. These noncitizens often have nationalities of origin, but, inasmuch as they prefer not to benefit from their own states' protection, they find themselves, as refugees, in a condition of de facto statelessness. Tomas Hammar has created the neologism of "denizens" for these noncitizen residents, a neologism that has the merit of showing how the concept of "citizen" is no longer adequate for describing the socio-political reality of modern states.[4] On the other hand, the citizens of advanced industrial states (in the United States as well as Europe) demonstrate, through an increasing desertion of the codified instances of political participation, an evident propensity to turn into denizens, into noncitizen permanent residents, so that citizens and denizens—at least in certain social strata—are entering an area of potential indistinction. In a parallel way, xenophobic reactions and defensive mobilizations are on the rise, in conformity with the well-known principle according to which substantial assimilation in the presence of formal differences exacerbates hatred and intolerance.

Before extermination camps are reopened in Europe (something that is already starting to happen), it is necessary that the nation-states find the courage to question the very principle of the inscription of nativity as well as the trinity of state-nation-territory that is founded on that principle. It is not easy to indicate right now the ways in which all this may concretely happen. One of the options taken into consideration for solving the problem of Jerusalem is that it became—simultaneously and without any territorial partition—the capital of two different states. The paradoxical condition of reciprocal extraterritoriality (or, better yet, aterritoriality) that would thus be implied could be generalized as a model of new international relations. Instead of two national states separated by uncertain and threatening boundaries, it might be possible to imagine two political communities insisting on the same region and in a condition of exodus from each other—communities that would articulate each other via a series of reciprocal extraterritorialities in which the guiding concept would no longer be the *ius* (right) of the citizen but rather the *refugium* (refuge) of the singular. In an analogous way, we could conceive of Europe not as an impossible "Europe of the nations," whose catastrophe one can already foresee in the short run, but rather as an aterritorial or extraterritorial space in which all the (citizen and noncitizen) residents of the European states would be in a position of exodus or refuge; the status of European would then mean the being-in-exodus of the citizen (a condition that obviously could also be one of immobility). European space would thus mark an irreducible difference between birth [*nascita*] and nation in which the old concept of people (which, as is well known, is always a minority) could again find a political meaning, thus decidedly opposing itself to the concept of nation (which has so far unduly usurped it).

This space would coincide neither with any of the homogeneous national territories nor with their *topographical* sum, but would rather act on them by articulating and perforating them *topologically* as in the Klein bottle or in the Möbius strip, where exterior and interior in-determine each other. In this new space, European cities would rediscover their ancient vocation of cities of the world by entering into a relation of reciprocal extraterritoriality.

As I write this essay, 425 Palestinians expelled by the state of Israel find themselves in a sort of no-man's land. These men certainly constitute, according to Hannah Arendt's suggestion, "the vanguard of their people." But that is so not necessarily or not merely in the sense that they might form the originary nucleus of a future national state, or in the sense that they might solve the Palestinian question in a way just as insufficient as the way in which Israel has solved the Jewish question. Rather, the no-man's-land in which they are refugees has already started from this very moment to act back onto the territory of the state of Israel by perforating it and altering it in such a way that the image of that snowy mountain has become more

10

internal to it than any other region of Eretz Israel. Only in a world in which the spaces of states have been thus perforated and topologically deformed and in which the citizen has been able to recognize the refugee that he or she is—only in such a world is the political survival of humankind today thinkable.

## The Stranger Today

Who can be defined as a stranger today and from what external boundary, or frontier, does the stranger first arrive?  These questions appear important for us to reconsider, especially when all territorial boundaries have been over-run, have become permeable and changing, and there is neither a distinctly "foreign" place, nor a central location, or *polis* (i.e., *the* Imperial city, *the* Capital).   Along with the obsolescence of an earlier territorial conception of geo-political identity (or the so-called "decline of the nation-state"), this might be classified among the various signs of dispersion that have accompanied the processes of globalization—the multiplication of centers, the permeability and attrition of all borders and territories, and the dizzying loss of orientation between an interior dwelling place, or homeland, and an uninhabited exterior region, or frontier.

It is important to underline that this general disorientation, which is already figured spatially in the metaphor of globalization itself, has had important consequences for the juridical and social determination of the stranger as the one who arrives from a definite place that is "foreign" and "outside." As Émile Benveniste writes, "the stranger is 'one who comes from outside' (Lat. *aduena*) or simply 'one who is beyond the limits of community' (Lat. *peregrinus*) [...]; 'there is no 'stranger' as such; within the diversity of these notions, the stranger is always a particular stranger, as one who originates from a distinct statute."[1] Following Derrida's recent interrogation of the concepts of "boundary" or "limit-horizon" that are implied by the above definition of the stranger's particular appearance, we could say that the stranger is the manifestation of a social, political—perhaps even anthropological—*aporia*. In other words, the stranger is another name for the *aporia* that exists between what Derrida has defined as the insistence of "a universal (although non-natural) structure and a differential (non-natural but cultural) structure."[2]

If it is true, according to Benveniste's definition, that "there is no stranger *as such*" and that every stranger is a case of the particular, then there is no general species (*genus*) from which the stranger originates and the stranger can only appear from the perspective that grasps his or her entire being as the expression of one partial viewpoint. As a result of this "reduction," so to speak, all the other attributes that might define the person or the individual vanish into an abstract image of the stranger as someone who bears only a few superficial traits of resemblance (a name, a language, sexual and racial characteristics, age, etc.). Of course, the stranger is usually determined from the perspective of a subject who is "at home," who dwells within his or her own familiar and customary limits; consequently, the stranger appears as a being who is "outside" these limits, who is out of place, or whose very relation to place is yet unknown and likely to become a subject of interrogation. At the border crossing or checkpoint, I present my passport to the border police in order to declare that I am legally a stranger, that I come from a definite place of origin, that my encroachment into another territory is temporary, and that my estrangement is not volatile or likely to lapse into a permanent state. This is because, first of all, I have presented myself or introduced myself in the sense of *giving myself up*.

I have turned myself in to the authorities at the border for questioning, I already have accepted and recognized the authority of one who questions me with regard to my legal identity and who will determine the rights accorded to this identity, specifically with regard to my right to travel "beyond the limits of my own community."

This moment of identification—one could even say "interpellation," since in this moment the stranger is "*hailed*" and must submit himself or herself to the rule of a Master, or potential Host—is constantly threatened by ambiguity and the possible lapses that overdetermine it as a performative event. For example, recently when returning to the United States, a Nigerian woman and her children who were in front of me in line were questioned for a certain length of time concerning the reason for their entry, the names and addresses of family members in the US, the number of times she has crossed the border in the last year, the address and vocation of the brother that she visited in Los Angeles four months earlier, and why her visit lasted three months; how she paid for travel to the US and, since it was the case that another family member paid for her, who is sponsoring her current trip and what is the source of this money. The woman compliantly answered these questions with an air of familiarity—apparently, she was no stranger to the INS—even though it was obvious that many of the answers to the questions posed to her were already on the computer screen in front of the agent. Nevertheless, it was clear that her rights in this moment were extremely limited; for example, she could not "prefer to remain a stranger," to refuse to answer certain questions, or to claim certain information as private or personal, without subjecting herself to certain peril, including detainment, further interrogation, the possible denial of entry. It would appear, from this routine example, that the law's right to identification (or recognition) was more or less absolute—an absolute right of the Host to identify the stranger as either enemy or guest—while her right to her own identity, including the right to enjoy a certain sovereignty over its attributes, or to offer them freely for the purposes of identification or recognition, is conditional upon the absolute priority granted to the State's right to identify all strangers at its borders.

As another example, while entering Dublin last year, a man in front of me was suddenly detained when it was discovered that he had criminal charges pending in another country. He was denied entry; literally, he was asked to wait outside the gate until officials from Interpol arrived to take him into custody. An armed guard immediately appeared from a room just to the side of the booth to attend to the man and keep him company while the police were en route. He was a Polish laborer who was entering Dublin to undertake some work, but the information concerning his criminal activity in his own country had caught up with him. It was clear that the state had the right to deny his right as a stranger and foreigner—his identity as a criminal had circumvented his rights as a stranger, a visitor, a guest, a temporary worker—and the state was within its right to rescind the rule of hospitality.

From these common examples—I could provide others, including the reports of detainees and certain "other strangers" who are being held indefinitely in prisons in the United States today—it appears that the State has the right, approaching an absolute right, to protect its borders from encroachment by certain kinds of strangers, to identify all who pass through, to determine the hostile or peaceful nature of the temporary guest. Inasmuch as this right appears as unconditional, this right to sovereignty over the integrity of its own territory is not determined by mutual consent or recognition; if it was, then this would be a conditional right, contingent upon the recognition of this right by another subject. As in the case of the Nigerian woman recounted above, the State's right does not flow from her recognition of its authority; it would exist without her consent, which is why she does not have the right to remain a stranger, or to refuse to become subject to its mandate. Of course, as in the second example of the man who was refused entry after being identified as a criminal (in other words, as a potential "enemy"), the state can enforce its right, but this is not the source of its sovereignty, which is to say that the right of territory does not necessarily derive from its force or threat of violence, but, recalling the definition given by Benveniste above, is purely statutory. As Derrida has written concerning this enigmatic tension that is exhibited in both occasions around the question of hospitality: "This collusion between the violence or the force of law (*Gewalt*) on one side, and hospitality on the other, seems to depend, in an absolutely radical way, on hospitality being inscribed in the form of a right."[3]

## The Right to "Universal Hospitality"

In the third definitive article to his treatise on *Perpetual Peace*, Kant argues that the stranger's right to hospitality can be understood as a "universal right." He derives the universal nature of this right from two sources: first, from the law of nature (*ius naturale*), which is the universal right to the preservation of one's own nature, which is to say, one's own life; second, from what could be called the universal right of society (*Gesellschaft*), that is, "a right of temporary sojourn, a right to associate or to visit (*zugessellen*), which all men have."[4] In the Kantian definition, moreover, the right to hospitality can be understood as belonging to the class of rights pertaining to *immunity*. Strangers shall be immune from immediately being treated as an enemy; although "one may refuse to receive him when this can be done without causing his destruction, so long as he peacefully occupies his place, one may not treat him with hostility."[5] Thus, the stranger must not initially be identified as an enemy, nor should the stranger's intention be immediately determined as hostile; such a determination should only come about after the fact, when the stranger violates one of the conditions of hospitality, that of "peacefully occupying his place."

We might wonder, however, what is "universal" in this case, and how this right can be understood over against what appears to be the absolute right of the State? In the article, Kant asserts that universally every stranger has a right to expect hospitality; that is to say, according to Kant's definition, "hospitality means the right of a stranger not to be treated as an enemy when he arrives in the land of another."[6] Of course, this in no way guarantees hospitality, since this right can be violated or simply unacknowledged and the stranger can be just as easily treated with hostility, killed, incarcerated, held hostage, or placed in slavery. As an aside, the United States, post 9/11, can be said to have entered a period in which the principle of universal hospitality has been partially suspended and the State engages in an open violation of every stranger's right to hospitality as this was first defined by Kant. (Again, according to Kant's original definition, "hospitality means the right of a stranger not to be treated as an enemy when he arrives in the land of another.") However, in a period of heightened security, of the tightening of control of boundaries and even a temporary suspension of hospitality to certain foreigners, one might wonder if the right to hospitality can exist in view of the United State's claim that it has the right to suspend the presumption of hospitality, or to treat certain strangers (particularly those whose names indicate Arab origin and descent) as "potential enemies." This question of rights becomes especially acute, moreover, where there is no force of law that can resolve the observance of this right, since there is no universal police who can be present to monitor and, if need be, enforce this right for each and every occasion when a stranger arrives in the land of another. Hospitality is not a law, therefore, and it theoretically can only be said to govern different occasions as an ethical principle in a discourse of rights pertaining to the treatment of strangers. But since *there is no law of hospitality,* there is perhaps a certain ambiguity concerning the different legal and juridical expressions of hospitality as a right. As Derrida writes, "since this right, whether private or familial, can only be exercised and guaranteed by the mediation of a public right or a State right, the perversion [of right itself] is unleashed from the inside."[7]

Returning to the assertion of "the right to society" as one of the underlying principles of hospitality, it is important to notice here that Kant's discussion departs significantly from a traditional discourse of rights.

Although "association" (or society in general) is universally the condition of the discourse of rights—if there were no society, there would be no need for a discourse that stipulates the conditions and the limits of actions that define the social bond—it is also true that "association" is usually not listed as an explicit right, except in the narrower sense of the right to "political association." However, Kant is not speaking here of a right to political association (a right to self-government, or to self-legislation), but rather of a right to "associate" (a right to society) in a more general and even universal sense. That is, he is speaking of the human as an essentially *gregarious* animal, although in a sense not strictly limited to the subject as a political animal, but rather as an animal who "associates" with others in order *to preserve its essential nature.* In the accompanying phrase, "the right to temporary sojourn," moreover, Kant further suggests that the primary motive for "association" is not politics, but rather something more akin to travel, commerce, communication, translation; in short, all forms and manners of "social intercourse." In other words, the universal right of hospitality pertains to the definition of the human as a stranger, and the stranger is always one who travels, who departs from his or her customary or familiar place, who sets out on the open road. But if hospitality is a right that naturally belongs to the stranger who travels, how can the stranger also be defined by Kant as one who "peacefully keeps to his place"? The irony implicit in Kant's definition is the inherent contradiction it contains, since no stranger, *qua* stranger, could ever be said to actually keep to his place. The stranger is, by definition, one who sets out, who departs from his place and arrives at another.

In the *Introduction to Metaphysics* (1953), the German philosopher Martin Heidegger points to the essential definition of the Greek as "a stranger," but also to the Greek *dasein* as involving the process of "becoming a stranger," of estrangement, which is fundamentally bound to the sense of movement. The stranger in movement, or the movement of estrangement, is both the "casting off from" and "casting out of" (*poeisis*) the limits of place (*poria*). Heidegger's commentary in the following passage on this proto-European stranger reveals the essential relation to travel:

> We are taking the strange, the uncanny (*Das Unheimliche*), as
> that which casts us out of the homely, i.e., the customary, the
> familiar, or the secure. The "unhomely" prevents us from making
> ourselves at home and therein it is overpowering. Man is the
> strangest of all, not only because he passes his life amid the
> strange understood in this sense, but because he departs [he sets
> out and travels] from his customary, familiar limits, because he is
> the violent one, who, tending toward the strange in the sense of
> the overpowering, surpasses the limit of the familiar.[8]

From the above passage we might conclude that, in a certain sense, it is a natural state for Man to be in motion, that is, to enter into a state that necessarily entails becoming a stranger. For Kant, however, the implicit aim of the process of estrangement and movement is nothing other than society itself, but society no longer determined by political goals, or by the familial and ethnic kinship; rather, the goal is society itself is determined as visitation, temporary association, communication, and the exchange of hospitality.

At the same time, it is important to emphasize that the universal right to society (*Gesellschaft*) is not entirely a positive state in Kant's account either. It first emerges from the fact that humans cannot disperse themselves across the surface of the globe to avoid each other, and eventually must "finally tolerate the presence of one another."[9] According to this description, the "right to associate" does not practically originate from a positive and gregarious spirit, but rather is something that only gradually develops in Man, begrudgingly, as a spirit of toleration, in other words, *as a spirit of Law*. This is because, left to our own inclinations, we would prefer to be alone, undisturbed or agitated by the irritating presence of others. Implicitly, it is this impulse that functions as the cause of the initial dispersion of individuals and communities in Kant's description of Nature's "grand design," in which each

20

attempts to find, to quote a phrase that is frequently employed by the French philosopher Emmanuel Levinas, "his own place in the sun." Consequently, there is a constant and overriding drive to withdraw from the proximity of others and, one might easily imagine, especially from strangers whose very presence brings an "allergic reaction" on the part of the Ego, since every encounter with a stranger brings with it the inevitable specter of hostility. And yet, because this withdrawal has become practically impossible, when translated onto the confines of the earth's inhabitable surface (basically, the limited number of hospitable regions interspersed by vast wastelands of water, sand, and ice), we inevitably must learn to put up with the presence of others and, according to Kant, even with the most annoying of others, with the presence of strangers to whom we owe a certain debt of hospitality.

It goes without saying that both toleration and hospitality are inherently conditional by their very definition. There is a limit to my hospitality, beyond which I can refuse any further hospitality to the guest who attempts to usurp my place (or, to employ Kant's phrase again, who "doesn't peacefully keep to his place"); likewise, I can only be tolerant of the other's presence up to a certain point, after which I am fully in my rights to refuse my own presence in retaliation, which is to say, to threaten to withdraw from any further society. Both of these conditions, which are common enough to be part of any social relation and could be said to comprise the implicit understanding of the conditions and external limits of the most quotidian of social liaisons, have the possibility of open hostility as their ultimate guarantee. Within these limits, there is society defined as the possibility of hospitality, exchange, communication, generosity; beyond them, there is only the promise of aggression, war, retaliation, and even genocide. Consequently, Kant's use of the word "tolerance" (*Duldsamkeit*) to characterize what could be called the fundamental mood of society (*Gesellschaft*) is extremely appropriate, since toleration (*Duldung*) is merely the "negative" (the absence) of open aggression, or warfare. If Kant seems to designate this as the dominant social spirit, perhaps this is utterly practical, since it perfectly describes the feeling we have toward others we encounter—especially toward others who appear to us as strangers and for whom we have no previous social relationship, except the most abstract relation that defines the spirit of law itself, which only minimally demands of us to be tolerant of the other's right to exist.

What Kant is describing in very subtle terms can be developed in a manner that is not very different from the description of the social relation to another person as a certain "hostage-taking" situation in the writings of Levinas. Like Kant, perhaps to an even more emphatic degree, Levinas describes the personality of the Ego by the natural qualities of solipsism and narcissism, and the interruption of society as an unwelcome intrusion into this state of nature. Therefore, we might even consider the being of the stranger as a *hypostasis* of this intrusive encounter with society, in the sense that every appearance of the stranger is accompanied by a law that demands the subject to be hospitable, to tolerate the irritating presence of another—a law which the solipsistic Ego would naturally understand as one of being hostage to the presence of the stranger. Naturally, such a law cannot but create a degree of resentment—to the stranger, but also to the social ideas of toleration and hospitality. This resentment forms the character of the "social egoism" that marks the inherent limits of any expression of toleration and hospitality.

Recalling the examples offered earlier, we could hypothesize that certain communities, such as the State and its representatives, have incarnated this spirit of resentment and social egoism. This often colors what could be called the fundamental personality of certain groups and associations, even to a degree that certain subjective expressions of this personality are translated to the individual members who identify with the group's overall conservative interests. Why is it, I have often wondered, that the border officials never seem entirely happy to greet me when I visit another country? Why do they respond to my simple request for hospitality with a subtle look of menace in their eyes? Or, returning to my example, why did the US border agent begin yelling at the Nigerian woman, or refuse to smile at her children who were playing at his feet, but seemed quite annoyed at the disturbance they were making, since it distracted him from his interrogation? If this episode seems somewhat "Kafkaesque," perhaps it is because the answer to the above queries can be found in the short parable related to K. at the end of *The Trial*, in which it is said that the Law is neither particularly happy to see you come, nor very sad to see you go. It merely allows you to enter, or gives you permission to depart with an equal amount of indifference. Its affect, therefore, is purely negative, that of tolerating you in principle, but only under certain conditions and never with any display of interest or affection. In this sense, in the eyes of the law, we are all strangers; although this does not necessarily presuppose that all strangers are equal in the eyes of the law, as the above examples implicitly have suggested.

## The Limits of Hospitality: The Homeless and the Refugee as "States of Exception"

One flaw in Kant's definition of the stranger's universal right to hospitality is that it presupposes that every stranger is potentially a host, or that he or she has a commensurable and reciprocal position vis-à-vis the master in his own land. From its origins in the Greek systems of philosophy and civil law (the laws of the *polis*), we might conclude that the concept of the stranger we have been discussing is that of a very particular stranger indeed! The European stranger is essentially a despot (master of the house), and must therefore be capable both of travel and of returning to his own home. In other words, the "universal right of hospitality" is a right that only exists between equals; the host merely recognizes himself in the place of the guest, "respects" his own law, and enjoys his own substance in temporarily "alienating" his own mastery to the guest, who appears in the place of the

Master. The host welcomes the guest, who, in turn, recognizes the host as host, the master as master. It is for this reason, as Derrida argues elsewhere, that the identity of the Master is in some sense completely dependent upon the relation to the guest and the stranger: "it gives the welcoming host the possibility of having access to his own proper place."[10] The concept of right in the right to hospitality, consequently, must be understood specifically in the form of an alienated right—the right of the Master, or host, which has undergone alienation in the place of the Guest. It is this form of alienation that gives all acts of hospitality a certain exchange character, and the German language that Kant employed uniquely offers the resources for distinguishing between alienation defined as "estrangement" (*entfremden*) and alienation defined as "exchange" (*eintauschen*). But this also implies that the stranger is merely an alienated master, and the stranger's right to hospitality, then, only extends to those subjects who can change positions in the reciprocity of the guest/host relationship, or who can temporarily alienate their status as masters in one place in order to enjoy temporary sojourn as guests in another.

If hospitality only pertains to the rights of strangers, and strangers are implicitly defined as displaced masters or hosts who enter into a pact or exchange with other hosts, then how does the right to hospitality extend to those who cannot claim this right? In the case of the particular stranger defined as the refugee, for example, or in the case of the stranger who appears as the homeless citizen within the national borders of the State, the mutual recognition between hosts is not a basis for the claim to hospitality, which is why it often may go unrecognized in their case. In other words, if we have discovered earlier that the right of every stranger to temporary sojourn is based on a more fundamental right, "the right to society," we might notice that, in the exceptional case of these strangers, this right to association remains a source of ambiguity, and this is especially true on those occasions where violence, either natural or man-made, is located as the cause of estrangement. Thus, when the desire for association (or society) is not the motive of the stranger's movement, we might wonder whether there is a right to hospitality, properly speaking? The "refugee," for example, whose very existence petitions a host for refuge, for safety, for protection, is neither a guest nor another host; therefore, the refugee is not a stranger in the sense defined above and, we might expect, has no legal claim to hospitality. There is no pact that the refugee can claim, no exchange of hospitality, but rather a purely dependent and abstract relationship to the host. In this case, it is often only in the name of another master, or a "third" (in the name of justice or of human rights) that intervenes to demand hospitality for the other who cannot claim this right for himself or herself. In other words, it is only in the name of another despot, perhaps even a "universal despot" (Humanity), that the law of hospitality is extended to give temporary sojourn to the stateless and the homeless.

This is the legal character and personality of the claim for "refuge," which is that of a surrogate claim, in the name of another Host. However, because this claim is not made as a pact among equals, a certain ambiguity surrounds it and what is granted is not hospitality, strictly speaking, but merely the minimal recognition of the right to live. Consequently, in the refugee camps that exist under this contract between two Hosts, only a minimal degree of hospitality is guaranteed, barely enough to preserve "the name of humanity," that is, nothing more than to preserve the name of the Host from suffering violence and degradation. As Lacan first argued, acts of charity are not necessarily "altruistic" in nature, but are inevitably invested with a certain narcissistic spirit of self-preservation, most of all, the investment in the proper image of the human body as whole and intact. Consequently, because there is a certain ambiguity that also defines the body as a "host," the care extended to refugees is often limited to the preservation of the body and does not address the particularity of the individuals—unrecognized as a class—or their rights. Although the refugee is also a subject who has suffered the violation of his or her political, legal, and juridical rights, it is primarily to the body that a certain debt of hospitality is paid in the name of the Master-Host. Therefore, the refugee, as a certain limit-example of the stranger, has been reduced to a purely bodily existence, and exists only to the degree that the violence suffered by the body causes the host to suffer through sympathy, to feed, clothe, and nourish the body of the refugee defined as an unwelcome and temporary guest.

## The Perversion (of Hospitality) Begins at Home

Earlier on, I cited a passage by Derrida in which he locates the degradation of the stranger's right to hospitality at the interior of the private and familial space of intimacy. According to Derrida, all perversion begins at home. But perversion of what exactly? Or rather, how is the stranger's right to hospitality perverted by the formations of interest and power (and desire) that flow from these intimate and familial spaces? These spaces have traditionally been defined according to the exclusive sense of the Master (of the host and despot), in which the stranger has no place. In the sphere of the family, the stranger is first recognized as absolutely strange or foreign, or as not belonging and, therefore, as having no place from which to appeal in the name of rights. Recalling a familiar scene from a play by Brecht in which a stranger suddenly enters the kitchen of a family dwelling, prompting the shock and fear on the part of the members of the family and the father's violent response, every incursion of the stranger into the home is perceived as an act of violence, and thus, the stranger is immediately greeted there as an enemy. If there is no stranger in the sphere of the home, then we might conclude that there is no hospitality either, and no possibility of any discourse of rights, unless this is first introduced or mediated by some public law or civic right also accorded to members of the familial bond, as in the right to immunity from violence in laws prohibiting child and spousal abuse. We might even phrase this in a more extreme sense by saying that the stranger has no relation to those spaces defined predominately by intimacy or familial belonging, and this is confirmed by the subjective mood that characterizes our relation to strangers as distinctly lacking these qualities.[11]  Hence, the subjective and emotional qualities that define our relation to strangers are bereft of any attributes of intimacy; in fact, they are characterized by the opposite affects—by a coolness of detachment, a certain indifference or lack of interest with regard to the person of the stranger, even by a certain sense of hostility or enmity toward the stranger's presence.  These emotional qualities that so naturally characterize our relation to strangers are not arbitrary, but originate from the statutes that determine the stranger's "place in society" at the boundary of the association (or "pact") of the so-called natural bond—of kinship, blood (or race), intimate or private ties of affection and desire.

One can see why Derrida would determine these intimate spheres as the origin of the potential perversion of the rights accorded to strangers, since first of all the stranger has no place there, but is constitutionally defined as being outside or beyond these pacts (of kinship, blood or race, linguistic community, including the quasi-contractual bonds of friendship and sexual intimacy).  Consequently, as Derrida writes, "there is no foreigner *(xenos)* before or outside the *xenia*, this pact or exchange with a group, or more precisely, this line of descent."[12]  In other words, recalling the definition given by Benveniste above, if there is no stranger that does not originate from a distinct statute or law, then the specific statute in question is the one that first constitutes the "pact" or "exchange" between members of a group, but particularly the exchange and lawful transmission of identity and territory through a line of descent.  The family member, or the one whose identity is constituted by the pact of the Father's name, can enter the home without first asking permission, since this is already a stipulated term of the "association"; however, the stranger cannot, since he or she approaches from "outside" the pact (or *xenia*) and has no right to claim the provisions of this original social bond.  From our analysis, therefore, it seems that the stranger's right to hospitality is immanently pervertible from the fact that this very right can only be defined in relation to the law of the Host. As Derrida writes:

> To suppose that one could have a perfectly stabilized concept of hospitality, something I do not believe, is the moment when it is already in the process of being perverted. The passage from pure hospitality to right and to politics is one of perversion, inasmuch as the condition [of perversion] is already implicit in this passage and, as a consequence, so is the call to a certain perfectability [of hospitality], to the necessity of ameliorating without end, indefinitely, its determinations, conditions, legislative definitions whether familial, local, national, or international....Hospitality is, thus, immediately pervertible and perfectible at once: there is no ideal hospitality, but only statutes that are always already in the process of being perverted and of being ameliorated, even though such amelioration carries with itself the seeds of all future perversions.[13]

## The Future of Hospitality, or the Idea of a Hospitable Future

Finally, let us return once more to the Kantian notion of "universal hospitality" in order to raise again the question concerning the origin of the stranger's right to hospitality and how this can be understood over against the group's right to assign the terms (or statutes) that determine the very identity of the stranger "*as if from the inside.*" As Kant argues, the stranger's right to lay claim to the surface of the earth stems from an original state in which "no one had more right than another to a particular part of the earth."[14] As the earth became more peopled and territories were established, particular rights were recognized by treaty and by colonization. However, according to Kant, it is the design of the great artist, nature (*natura daedala rerum*), to populate the entire globe and war becomes an instrument to distribute populations equally across its surface, even to the most uninhabitable and desolate regions of the earth (deserts, oceans). Here, Kant resorts to a speculative myth concerning an original and even primordial time when no one enjoyed the right to lay claim to any part of the earth, since everyone possessed the surface of the earth equally. Thus the stranger's right to demand hospitality—also the right to associate through travel and visitation, a right which "all men have"—has its origin in the "common possession of the surface of the earth."[15]

In its most obvious sense, this original state can be defined temporally, referring to a time before the invention of "territory," before the families and clans lay claim to homes and tribal plots, or principalities and nations emerged to claim certain whole portions of the earth's surface, which they determined to solely possess and to enjoy exclusive rights to as their own native soil. Nevertheless, Kant also asserts that this original determination continues to define the "uninhabitable parts of the earth," such as the seas and deserts (and today, one could also add the air to Kant's list of vast wastelands between communities). Thus, the common possession of the earth also extends to define these spaces which no one can exclusively possess, but which are defined as spaces of pure communication or translation. Because these spaces cannot be inhabited, the notion of "territory" cannot be applied to them; moreover, because they are invested by mutual interests to protect these spaces, they are defined primarily by international laws that stipulate their possession, universally, as the open spaces that lie between and outside the boundaries of the Home. Moreover, the laws that define the guest/host relationship would not extend to these spaces either, since there are no Masters, consequently no Hosts, and everyone is equally a stranger in these uninhabitable regions of the earth. It is precisely here, as Kant argues, where there is neither guest nor host, master nor stranger, *xenos* nor *xenia* (foreigner nor native), that the idea "of a law world citizenship is no high-flown or exaggerated notion [...] but rather a supplement to the unwritten law of the civil and international law, indispensable for the maintenance of the public human rights and hence also of perpetual peace."[16]

The unwritten law that Kant speaks of serves as the basis for the stranger's right to hospitality: the right to association (or society) and to communication (linguistically, but also through travel). The precedence—even *transcendence*—of this unwritten law can easily be demonstrated by the fact that, despite its absolute claim to sovereignty over its own borders and the right to enforce this claim by threats of violence or power, or by the constant vigilance of its border police, all borders nevertheless remain indefinitely open to communication with what lies outside, to the inevitable intercourse with strangers and foreigners (even before these are determined as "guests" or "enemies"). Here, we might pause to reflect that one of the underlying principles of globalization has been the sheer increase in communications of all kinds, particularly the rapid and almost instantaneous forms of intercourse such as the television, faxes, the internet, cellular and satellite transmissions). These forms of communication can also be defined as pure spaces of communication and translation between communities governed by pacts and, thus, as subject to international and civil laws that pertain to spaces outside the rules of exchange that determine the host/guest relationship. It has almost become a cliché to say that globalization has been marked by the quantitative increase of space, but what is important to underscore is the growing frequency of the encounters where there is neither guest nor Master, encounters which exist outside or even before the question of hospitality, since they take place outside the laws that continue to define the boundaries of the territory, even though they often occur inside the very limits of the proper domain, native soil, or home.

We might see this phenomenon as the materialization of Kant's thesis concerning the unwritten law of association, that is, the new forms of society that are emerging as a result of the communication between particular strangers, for whom the statutes concerning pact and hospitality are still in the process of being written. In response to this situation, of course, the State has adopted what could be considered a nostalgic and

30

reactive assertion of its sovereignty over territorial borders that have been outmoded and overrun by these new forms of communication and *the future possibilities of society*, and by the reassertion of war as an archaic principle of state-power, which might be viewed as a "fundamentalist" claim in the current geo-political context. (The problem of fundamentalism cannot only be relegated to religious and cultural forces that resist modernization, but it can also be found in certain extreme factions of ideologies that define the modern State's own resistance to the weakening of territorial sovereignty.) Today we could regard the position of the United States, specifically its claim to "guard and to closely monitor the integrity of all its borders" as stipulated in "The Patriot Act," as not only unfeasible in the current global context—as not only an open violation of civil and international laws and of public human rights, and the stranger's right to society and hospitality, in particular—but as an offense against the ideas of world citizenship and perpetual peace, if not, as Kant would say, against the very idea of Reason itself.

At the dawn of the civil war in what would become known as the "former Yugoslavia," at the dawn of a war that would efface people and cities, their histories, stories, and languages, but also in the dawn of his own exile, the photographer Vladimir Radojicic produced a portfolio of sixteen photographs entitled "Looking for/at Identity." Each of the photographs in the portfolio is of his face, but of his face in a disappearance; his face is there only a trace of a face, a face caught in the process of its own vanishing, its own becoming faceless and impersonal. It is already a face without the skin, which is the archive of a face that archivizes its wrinkles, its expressions, gestures, sadnesses and joys, childhood and adulthood, life and death. The face—or what once was a face—is now only a bloody trace, but a trace that itself vanishes, the red blood gone pale orange on its way to the whiteness of non-existence. As if in the process of preparation for exile, in the process of leaving his language and the past embedded in that language, the photographer waves goodbye to his identity through photographs that have to capture the impossible: the face in the gap between identities and ID papers, in the abyss that separates departing from arriving, in the gulf between destinations. The photographs of the faceless face that has abandoned itself and gone into exile from itself are thus the photographs of a process that another Yugoslav artist, Marina Abramovic, formulated as a dialectic without dialectic: "more and more of less and less." But more of less is not simply "more of a loss." More of less is the process whereby a face is compressed into a black hole of muteness that cannot say or witness its own disappearance, its own loss of itself. In the "more of less," the loss becomes endless.

Once in exile, in 1992, in his New York studio, the faceless photographer continued his work on identity, but this time, since he himself had already lost his face, he sought to catch the identity of the faces of others in the moment of their disappearance. That is how *The Aliens* started. *The Aliens* was a work-in-progress, a never ending series of black-and-white Polaroid portraits of Yugoslav expatriates, labeled with ID number, name, occupation, and departure date. In her review of the New York exhibition "Remember Yugoslavia," where *The Aliens* was first exhibited in 1993, Beth Gersh wrote: "At the time of a death in Yugoslavia photographs are published in the newspaper with the obituary and placed on the gravestone. To express a collective 'death' or loss of a cultural and political identity, Vladimir Radojicic has lined up [at that time] seventy-two black and white photographs from his on-going project *The Aliens*. Here, former Yugoslavian citizens who are living outside their homeland appear in 'mug shots': stripped to their waists, standing straight and frontally with the vacant eyes of prisoners or hostages who have been emotionally emptied. The death of Yugoslavia has spilled over into becoming a death in themselves." The death of Yugoslavia was, therefore, by the same token, the death of the identity of all those subjects who identified themselves as Yugoslavs.

But if those subjects were thus left bereft of their identity, bereft of themselves, are they dead or alive? If identity is the condition of possibility for mourning, how then can those who do not have identity mourn? If identity is the condition of possibility for memory, how can those who have lost their identity memorialize anything, what kind of temporality constitutes

Vladimir Radojicic, *Looking For/ At Identity*, no. 4

their strange, non-subjective lives, what is the past of the life that does not belong to any identity? Or, to put it differently, by what life do those who lost themselves live, can they bear witness to that loss even though they themselves are no more, is it possible that a witness can witness his or her death while dead? And finally, is it by chance that all such questions are most pregnantly addressed in the medium of photography?

### Looking for/at Identity, or Policemen, Artists, and Photographers

AT—Reports about the early reception of the relationship between photography and identity differ somewhat. Benjamin reminds us that in the early morning of the life of photography artists were the ones who expressed misgivings regarding its artistic value, believing that, being defined by an apparatus, photography was nothing other than a purely technical reproduction of what was photographed. As Benjamin puts it: "Artists on the other hand begin to debate its artistic value. Photography leads to the annihilation of the great profession of the portrait miniaturist... The technical reason lies in the long exposure time, which demanded utmost concentration by the subject being portrayed."[1] In other words, photography was thus conceived by certain artists as an "absolute" reproduction of identity, its freezing in its eternal truth. It is therefore understandable that, in his effort to explain what it is that photography does, Oliver Wendell Holmes referred to Democritus and his theory of *eidolas*. Democritus "believed and thought that all bodies were continually throwing off certain images like themselves, which subtle emanations, striking on our bodily organs, gave rise to emanation."[2] Democritus' fantasy that we see the face of the other only thanks to the physical, material separation of the surface film or layer of its face, which then travels through the medium of light to the eyes of the spectator, was rooted in the idea that it is possible to double the other, and to see its face in its "reality," in its absolute truth. But, says Holmes, after the event of photography one may say that the idea of appropriating the truth of the face of the other is no longer just an ancient dream of the Laughing Philosopher, for photography is the realization of his dream: "This is just what the Daguerreotype has done. It has fixed the most fleeting of our illusions, that which the apostle and the philosopher and the poet have alike used as the type of instability and unreality. The photograph has completed the triumph, by making a sheet of paper reflect images like a mirror and hold them as a picture."[3] Photography is similar to the mirror insofar as it is an apparatus of identification, but in contrast to the mirror, which is incapable of fixing the image so that it perishes instantly when its source is withdrawn, and thus introduces a fundamental instability into identity, the photograph is an absolute triumph of identification—it holds the picture, it captures it. It makes possible what was impossible for God and demons, for apostles and philosophers alike: to capture identity in its inflexible, unchangeable, substantial truth. Needless to say, the logic of every police inspector for whom identity lies neither in the signature nor in the name but in the photo ID is rooted in Holmes' Victorian presupposition that photography captures identity in its unchangeability and that therefore to look at the photograph is to look at identity (the identity of its referent).

FOR—Foucault's understanding of the relationship between identity and photography in its early days provides a somewhat different perspective. Thanks to photography, he says, the 19th century witnessed "a new frenzy for images...with all the new powers acquired there came a new freedom of transposition, displacement, and transformation, of resemblance and dissimulation, of reproduction, duplication and trickery of effect... Photographers made pseudo-paintings...There emerged a vast field of play where technicians and amateurs, artists and illusionists, *unworried about identity*, took pleasure in disporting themselves."[4] Photography, in other words, brought about the possibility of various plays with identity, plays that found their pleasure precisely in the distortion and destruction of every oneness, in the frenzy of multiplicity that went all the way to the dissolving of the real in the imaginary so that the unstable imaginary overwhelmed any stability of the referent. Photography introduced the possibility of multiple identities that, for their part, subverted the identity of the photograph itself, until finally photography became another name for the false image: "In those days images traveled the world under false identities. To them there was nothing more hateful than to remain captive, self-identical in *one* painting, *one* photograph, *one* engraving, under the aegis of *one* author. No medium, no language, no stable syntax could contain them."[5] In a word, the new power of photography lay precisely in its undermining of the identity of its referent through the undermining of its own identity; photography enabled the mixture of identities thanks to its power to mix itself with other images and thus to be "mistaken for another" image. Photography was the art of non-capturing, an anti-disciplinary art of the multiplication of identities.

This anti-disciplinarian effect had much to do with the "countless amateur photographers: photomontage; drawings in Indian ink over the contours and shadows of a photograph...developing the photograph on a silk fabric...photos on lamp-shades or lamp-glass, on porcelain; photogenic drawings in the manner of Fox Talbot or Bayard; photo-paintings, photo-miniatures, photo-engravings, photo-ceramics."[6]  To put it simply, photography in the hands of amateurs became a paradise for the endless multiplication of *bootleg identities*.  According to Foucault, the reactionary emergence of 19th century realism in art was caused by the artists' incapacity to bear this falsification of identities.  The realists confronted all the smugglers involved in the games of plagiarizing identity with their demand for fidelity to things themselves: "The emergence of realism cannot be separated from the great surge and flurry of multiple and similar images.  A certain penetrating and austere relation to the real [was] suddenly demanded by the art of the nineteenth century..."[7]  The artists themselves now assumed the disciplinary role of fixing identities.  They wanted to know how things really looked.  They imposed a demand of identification on the amateurs, those looters of images.  And so, "the party games are over.  All the ancillary photographic techniques the amateurs had mastered and which enabled them to run their illegal imports have been taken over by technicians, laboratories and businessmen.  The former now 'take' a photo, the latter 'deliver' it; there is no longer anyone to 'liberate' the image.  The photographic professionals have fallen back on the austerity of an 'art' whose internal rules forbid the crime of plagiarism."[8]

That the party is over means no more fooling around with identification and identity.  That is why for Foucault the political question par excellence becomes: how to throw the party again?  How to escape the disciplinary force of both the realists and policemen?  The possibility of reverting to an escape from identity, image, signifier and its syntax is, however, nothing other than the possibility of reverting to madness.  For that reason Foucault formulated his political question by asking precisely how we might recover a madness, this insolent freedom. Or, differently, how we might recover the possibility of the unheard-of migrations of images of identity, how we might recover the "absolute" migrations that migrate from the paths of all migrations into the outsideness of the image, of representation, of identification, into an exile in which all that occurs is the unrepresentable becoming-imperceptible of an identity. So that every looking at an image, at a photograph, would instead be a joyful search, an endless looking for an identity that has migrated irrevocably into a play of "the fragile pattern without a line," without a trace.

IN BETWEEN FOR AND AT—But what happens when instead of being the effect of playful migrations that aim at an insolent freedom, an identity is *forced* into migration? What happens when instead of there being a frenzy of resistance to the political representations of identity, identity is itself crushed by the "freedom" of the political, by war? What happens when identity collides with a "naked" experience that comes about in a "pointlike fashion," breaking it without leaving any background as a source for recovery? The stroke [*coup*] of this unbearable moment is what leaves neither the possibility of fixing an identity, the possibility of its (self) recognition, nor the possibility of escaping it through the endless process of joyful migrations. Instead, identity is frozen in its own death, in between looking at and looking for.

The series of photographs *Looking for/at Identity* is produced in this abyssal space. In the wake of the Yugoslav civil wars, in 1991, and in order not to be forced to fight in those wars, in order, therefore, not to be forced to participate in the murdering of a linguistic, cultural, and historical identity that is his identity, a photographer is about to leave his country, everything that is homelike (or unhomelike) to him; he is forced to leave himself behind himself and thus to murder his identity. Caught in this strange temporality where what is about to happen is already happening, caught in the ruse of the war that forces him to kill his identity in order to escape the war on his identity, a photographer tries to capture or "fix" the moment of this temporal madness, the moment of the black stroke that places him between two murders, between one murder of his identity and another. Or: in order to betray the force of the political that demands representation, that requires the visibility of every face so that they can all be identified and called to kill, mobilized to massacre the faces of others in the name of identity, in the name of the face of the murderer, a photographer gives up his face. His ethical gesture could therefore be summed up in the following way: in order to be able to look at the faces of the others (who are going to be exposed to defacement), he has to give up his own face. My own defacement should precede the defacement of the other. What this series of "Identification" photographs seeks to catch is precisely this insane moment of giving up one's own identity. The photographs attempt to fix the unfixable, to see the abyss between two deaths or two lives, in any case the abyss between two identities. They thus aim at the impossible: to capture the abyss not in order for a face to recognize itself by looking at itself but in order to stop the endless, unbearable falling, in order finally to find the place where one shatters into pieces. And all that he "gets" or catches is the lost face, the negative of the face.

But what is the negative of the face? It is situated between negation and affirmation of the face. It is not the reverse of the face, the mirror image of its truth or the black hole that swallows it. It is not the ghostly presence of an absent face that already has migrated into different identities, leaving us with its deceptive appearance. Neither is it a simple affirmation of the face for, paradoxically, it conceals its forms while letting them be visible. What is exposed in Radojicic's photographs is thus the paradox of the face that is not a face. This is the mode of existence of the negative of the face: it is the face that is not, it is the visibility of the effacement of the face in the moment of its effacement. It is therefore the presence of the impossible: of a face that no longer belongs to the archive. But what remains when the face-archive is removed by a stroke that

40

precisely forces one to give up one's own face? What remains is what always remains after a massacre: a red spot, the pool of blood. The whole archive of the face has sunk into the absoluteness of this bloody "now." And this bloody effacement of the face says only this much: that nothing can come to rescue it, that nothing will come to restore it. Instead of a restoration there is only the pure presence of blood, of a non-archival, inexperienced life, a liquid texture without a text, without a language, a naked life not covered by skin, a life reduced to its pure innocence in the way that life always is in the moment of death, which is the moment before death. Instead of a rescued identity there is a vast wound, but a wound that already belongs to no one, for it is not the wound on the face, it is the face crushed into the wound that will never find its being, that will never find repose in the shelter of skin or mask.

But, curiously enough, there, in the midst of that bloody spot, eyes appear, staring. How are we to interpret these eyes sinking in blood? In his analysis of the phenomenology of testimony, Giorgio Agamben points to the fact that "testimony appears as the process that involves at least two subjects": the one whose identity has been crushed (the one who did not survive), and the one who was present at the death of the other but did not die in the place of the other. This is why, paradoxically, he was not present at that death, and can witness only what he did not witness by allowing the other, the one who died, to speak through him. He desubjectivizes himself, and thus becomes the survival of the other who did not survive. The testimony that "appears as the process that involves at least two subjects" thus turns out to be the process that involves two subjects who are not subjects. Testimony to the desubjectivation of the victim is thus a labor of the desubjectivation of the witness: "Testimony takes place where the speechless one makes the speaking one speak and where the one who speaks bears the impossibility of speaking in his own speech, such that the silent and the speaking...enter into a zone of indistinction...This can also be expressed by saying that the subject of testimony is the one who bears witness to a desubjectivation."[9]   This means that a witness always witnesses a desubjectivation of the other. That is why testimony needs at least two subjects.

This series of "Identification" photographs, however, attempts the impossible: to produce the witness who would testify to his own non-surviving. They precisely show or testify to that horrifying moment in which the dead one bears witness to its own death, when the silence of ruined identity, the muteness of its blood, is survived by its own eyes, its own tongue or nose or ears, in any case by its own senses capable of feeling its own body or face becoming an unformed red spot that can look at its own vanishing, that can smell its own death and hear its own dying cries. At first glance this is the paradox of testimony that Maurice Blanchot summed up in the formula: the instant of my death. The instant that is at the same time the instant of my death and the instant of my testimony about my death, which is to say the instant in which life is at the same time dead and alive: "the feeling of lightness that I would not know how to translate: freed from life? the infinite opening up?  Neither happiness, nor unhappiness.  Nor the absence of fear and perhaps already the step beyond."[10]  This impossible "structure" of the "instant of my death" is made possible precisely by taking a "step beyond," which, for Blanchot, is the step into outsideness, into the space of the neuter, into a dying/living that does not belong to anybody, which is outside any subjectivized death or life. As Blanchot writes: "The Neuter, the gentle prohibition against dying, there where, from threshold to threshold, eye without gaze, silence carries us into the proximity of the distant. Word still to be spoken beyond the living and the dead, testifying for the absence of attestation."[11]  In other words, this testimony, because it takes place beyond the living and the dead, already introduces a split between the eyes and the gaze, requiring eyes without the gaze, a tongue without language. For Blanchot, testimony about one's own death can occur only in a space without language and without the gaze, which is why, according to Derrida's reading of Blanchot, nobody can witness for the witness who has made the step beyond. For him, Blanchot's thesis that the only testimony possible in the space of the neuter is testimony about the absence of attestation therefore "resonates in what is perhaps a contrasting echo with the 'no one/testifies for the/ witness' [Niemand/zeught fur den/Zeugen] of Celan."[12]

This witnessing of which there is no witness, or this testimony to the absence of attestation is the effect of the vertiginous temporality of a testimony that takes place in "the instant of my death." For "to testify is always on the one hand to do it present—the witness must be present at the stand himself...And yet, on the other hand, this condition of possibility is destroyed by the testimony itself. Ocular, auditory, tactile, any sensory perception of the witness must be an experience. As such, a constituting synthesis entails time and thus does not limit itself to the instant."[13] In other words, it is not that the time of the synthesis of experience fails to limit itself to the instant; rather, there occurs a temporality of the instant itself: the instant (of my death) is split within an instant, as it were. The eyes are separated from the gaze, the tongue from language. Thus, not only does Agamben's phenomenology of testimony presuppose at least two subjects and the temporality of their desubjectivation, but the structure of Blanchot's testimony that takes place in the instant also produces the temporality of the instant, a temporality required by the time of the translation of a silent perception into a speaking voice, of a personal death into a neuter dying, or of the attestation of death into a testimony to the absence of attestation.

The series of "Identification" photographs—and precisely thanks to the very medium of photography—therefore enables a different phenomenology of witnessing: it enables the instant of my death and the instant of my witnessing of my death to appear within the same instant. The photographs bear witness to a different temporality of witnessing, a temporality in which the past is contemporaneous with its present. In his short essays (essayistic snapshots) on photography, portraits, self-doubling, self-mirroring, and déjà-vu images, Ernst Bloch refers to this capacity of photography to join together, within the same present, the instant that had broken into two, as the possibility of forming a "frightful picture." What is a "frightful picture"? It is a picture of the "one" (of the one life, one event, one gaze, one identity) that "breaks apart into two completely different sections" which are then reunited by the snapshot.[14] Everything here depends on the "reunion." The snapshot does not negate the split; reunion is not the annihilation of the traces of the split. Rather, it refers to the temporality of the photographic "click," to the power of the snapshot to make the temporality of two instants appear within an instant, an instant that Eduardo Cadava has called "the *almost-no-time* of the camera's click."[15] The snapshot shoots the temporality of different temporalities so that a "deadly second" that splits the instant can be "removed from time and affixed on a photographic plate,"[16] thus producing the phenomenon of different temporalities taking place within one second. The eyes seen in these photographs—and witnessing their own death—are therefore not eyes without a gaze. On the contrary, what we get here are the eyes and the gaze, the testimony of the eternal (because removed from time) presence of the attestation of death, the witness eternally witnessing its own death and to its own death, the subject eternally present at its own desubjectivation: the eternal witness. And we get that witness' eternal testimony of the falling of the "for" (the absence of identity) and "at" (the fixation of identity) into a zone of indistinction, or into an impossible sentence: "I am not."


## Aliens or Snapshots From the Outside

HOUSE—When one is thus caught between life and death, where does one go? What trace does this "in between" leave? Who are those who are not? They are those who do not live and who therefore cannot die. Or, to put it differently, they are those who are able not to be able to live, who are capable of inhuman existence, of an alien form of life. For this "can cannot" is precisely what is captured in the series of black-and-white polaroids called

44

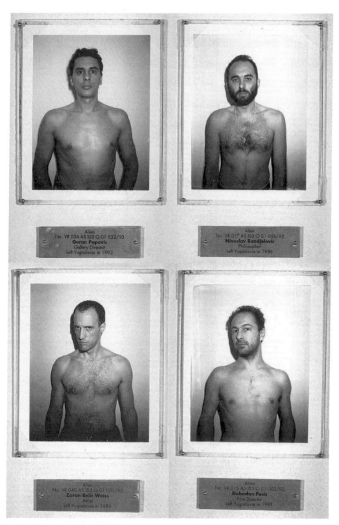

Vladimir Radojicic, *Aliens*

*The Aliens.* Thus the first question is: why are they called "aliens," to which the first, "easy" answer could be: because they were forced by the war to leave their country, their home, and their language, and have gone into what is called "exile." But what does it mean to "be in exile"? What is exile?

Granted, being in exile is the fundamental experience of subjectivity. Nothing other is at stake in Freud's philosophy of identity: what is homelike [*heimlich*] is always already inhabited by what is unhomelike [*unheimlich*]. To be in one's own home is precisely never to be in it, always to be expelled outside it; to live inside (the home) is to live outside. The subject always leaves itself, desubjectivizes itself or mediates itself by what negates it. This mediation or this exteriority is precisely what triggers the lever of subjectivation and is therefore what enables it. This is to say that the subject is the subject not in spite of the fact that it is alien to itself but thanks to it; it is the subject because it exits itself, because it is always already in exile: the subject is the subject only insofar as it is homeless. But this homelessness, this exile produces an exile different from that of the exile. I am saying this in order to avoid the cynicism that would reduce the experience of those whose cities, houses, homes, and cultures were destroyed in a war to the neurotic dialectic of subjectivation. But, by saying that one should try to avoid the reduction of one experience of exile to another, I also am saying that there is a structural difference between the two. In one case, it is a question of exile as the overcoming of identity into a new identity that keeps within itself or shelters within itself the "former," sublated identity. In the other case, it is a question of a total interruption of identity. Interruption means: what constituted an identity is not sublated but gone, vanished so that there is nothing left that could assume another identity, so that what is left is only the pure outsideness of an impersonal life. That outsideness is exile. In other words, exile is the unbearable space in between in which there is nobody who could assume what has to be assumed in order for a new identity to be born. The photographs of the "Aliens" are the photographs of those who inhabit such an exile, photographs of interrupted ones. Photographs of those who have left the house with its homely uncanniness, of those who have left the archive and so become those who cannot be archivized.

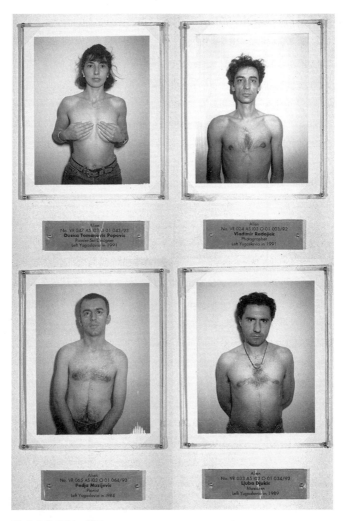

Vladimir Radojicic, *Aliens*

Again, it is not by chance that this departure from the archive finds its most uncanny expression in the medium of photography. For photography is precisely the perversion of the archive, the point at which the

47

archive makes the step beyond. According to Derrida's determination of the archive, if every archive requires a certain outside ("there is no archive without consignation in an external place which assures the possibility of memorization, of repetition, of reproduction...No archive without outside"[17]) it is in order to enable the archivized "to shelter itself and sheltered to conceal itself." This concealment in the shelter of the archive, however, is not to be understood as an operation immanent to the archive, which will then shelter the identity of the subject, but, on the contrary, the very process of subjectivation should be understood as the operation of the archive (concealment through exposure): the subject is the subject only insofar as it can keep something of itself for itself and thus maintain access to itself. The photographs of hundreds of people taken at the moment when they have already left one home but still have not found another thus becomes the series of photographs of people arrested there, in the photographs. They did not exist "before" the photographs were taken (since their identity died without being archivized), and they do not exist after it, since whatever exists "after" can only be called the future, which is what does not exist. These people thus do not have a house other than the house of the photograph: the photograph is their house arrest, which is to say the archive. But this archive does not shelter or conceal anything. It is the archive that archivizes the very moment of the disruption of the archive. It is an archive without walls, an archive that exposes them in the visibility of their nakedness, in a nakedness without secrets, and thus an archive that does not shelter anything: an archive without the archive. Or the subject without itself. If these photographs are photographs of "aliens," it is because they capture and make visible "what we all fear the most, the fog that lacks a center... complete externalization." What we see when we look at these photographs is the violent gesture of the reduction of subjectivity to its nakedness, a succession of naked bodies that do not belong to a subject anymore. We are witnessing faces without secrets. We are witnessing exile.

SHAME—Or else: we are witnessing flight in suspense, neither subjects nor objects. That is where the disturbing paradox of these photographs lies: what is photographed is not the subject any more but it is not yet the object. The photographs are taken at the moment when the photographed subjects are violently exposed to their desubjectivation while still preserving traces of their subjectivity. The fact that this process is captured in the medium of photography once more asserts its importance. For there is no photography without exposition of the photographed, without its subjection to objectivation. Or, according to Barthes' formulation: "The Photograph (the one I intend) represents that very subtle moment when, to tell the truth, I am neither subject nor object but a subject who feels he is becoming an object: I then experience a micro-version of death (of parenthesis)."[18] One should register here Barthes' insistence on the intended exposition. The desubjectivation to which the subject is exposed in the photograph is intended by the subject so that precisely the presence of intention in desubjectivation enables the subject to preserve itself in this process of losing itself: "Now, once I feel myself observed by the lens, everything changes: I constitute myself in the process of "posing," I instantaneously make another body for myself. I transform myself in advance into an image. This transformation is an *active* one."[19] In other words, the transformation of the subject into the object is its own activity of becoming the object and this activity is what preserves its subjectivity, what enables it to find another body for itself, to double itself or to transform itself "in advance." The time of exposure is thus the time in which the subject "reassumes itself" as object.

However, in this series of photographs, the "logic" of exposure is different. Here, there was no "intention" to be exposed. Instead, those posing are violently subjected to the eyes of the camera (to the eyes of the other). Violently means that there was no time for them to save themselves, no time in which their activity could give them a different body and thus preserve them. They are, instead, overwhelmed by a loss of intention, by a passivity that reduces them to the helpless life of their naked body. The photographs are taken in that very moment: when naked life makes one last, hopeless gesture to fold itself into itself in order to hide its nakedness with its nakedness: women thus try to cover their breasts with their naked hands. As if the unprotected body is trying to cut itself in two and to veil itself by itself in order to hide its shameful nakedness. We are therefore looking at hundreds of photographs of shame.

In his effort to reinforce Levinas' thesis according to which what is shameful is "our intimacy, that is, our presence to ourselves," Agamben determines that intimacy as "what is most intimate in us (for example our own physiological life). Here the 'I' is thus overcome by its own passivity, its ownmost sensibility; yet this expropriation and desubjectification is also an extreme and irreducible presence of the 'I' to itself. It is as if our consciousness collapsed and, seeking to flee in all directions, were simultaneously summoned by an irrefutable order to be present at its own defacement, at the expropriation of what is most its own. In shame, the subject thus has no other content than its own desubjectification; it becomes witness to its own disorder, its own oblivion as a subject. This double movement, which is both subjectification and desubjectification, is shame."[20] Shame would thus originate from the subject's own exposure to its passivity, to its own disorder or inability to act. Shame would therefore be the last order that subject gives to itself when witnessing its disorder, an order to witness its losing itself. Shame would mean that the subject is ashamed of losing itself. But the fact that the subject is ashamed of its own defacement becomes precisely its "innermost" feeling, so that shame, as witnessing of defacement, becomes the origin of the restoration of the subject's face. Shame is thus the last resort of the subject. The subject who is ashamed subjectivizes its own desubjectivation precisely through shame, so that it can look at its face again. "I" can look myself in the face because I have experienced the shame of losing my face. Common parlance and common sense are quite aware of this dialectic. The expression "shame on you"

Vladimir Radojicic, *Aliens*

addressed to the other presupposes that, through the feeling of shame, one would resume one's own subjectivity and, thanks to the shame, be able to look oneself in the face. *The Aliens* are thus unintentionally exposed to their own defacement and the "click" of the camera catches the moment of their own presence at their own disorder. But a disorder caused by what? A defacement imposed by what?

By asking these questions I address another aspect of Agamben's analysis of shame. Namely: is shame always caused by one's own defacement? Is the subject always ashamed only of the disorder of its physiological life? Of what are those who flee in shame from their own country during the war ashamed? My provisional answer to this question could be formulated in the following way: their abandoning of the home (their leaving the country in the wake of the war or during the war), together with the shame that they feel and that haunts them, is itself the effect of the twofold negation of shame. On the one hand, there are thousands of others (in Croatia, in Bosnia) who have been effaced without even being exposed to the witnessing of their own disappearance, without even being exposed to shame, having been simply and brutally murdered (in an instant that was not split in itself by the temporal dialectic of the instant). On the other hand there are "warriors" waging the war in the name of their own national identity and committing the crimes of murdering others, but who do not feel desubjectivized by their own crimes. On the one hand, there is thus a barbarous annihilation of the shame of the other; on the other hand, the absence of shame on the face of a murderer. *The Aliens*, the exiles or shameful ones, are thus caught in this double absence of shame, and their shame follows a logic different from that described by Agamben. They are not overwhelmed by losing themselves, they do not face any kind of physiological disorder, and they are not oblivious as subjects. On the contrary, they actively assume their own desubjectivation, their own de-identification in response to the murderers and in responsibility to the victims. They desubjectivize themselves actively in order to assume upon themselves the shame of the shameless murderers so that there is finally some shame caused by the murderous acts of warriors, so that the effacement of the others does not come to pass without shame. By giving up their own identity and assuming shame as the only content of their "subjects," they, by the same token, announce their unwillingness to identify themselves any more by means of the "cultural" and "national" identity of a nation that effaces the faces of others. Thus their response to the warriors, criminals or war criminals becomes an act of resistance to the identity in the name of which war crimes are executed. This is why in these photographs they are all lined up as prisoners, as prisoners of war in front of the platoon of soldiers who are about to kill them as traitors, or simply as others.

But their active desubjectivation, their active looking for shame, as it were, is also their act of "responsibility" towards the effaced others. How does one respond to the effacement of the other, how does one respond to the face that has neither eyes, gaze, nor language, and that therefore asks for nothing? How does one hear, and with what kind of auditory apparatus, this absence of the call? How does one understand, feel or experience the fact that this unbearable muteness calls for a response? The answer to that call is not only mourning (even though it is always mourning). For even though mourning gives to the effaced other a (spectral) life, even though mourning thus gives the life of the mourner to the mourned one, mourning nevertheless enables the mourner to stay alive, it subjectivizes him/her, it keeps the gaze in their eyes, it gives them a (mournful) face. This is why the radical response to the effacement of the other has to be an "impossible mourning." A mourning, that is, which would keep the other alive through the defacement, effacement, or self-negation of the mourner. Hence it is only by their own defacement, only by reaching the very "origin" of their shame (of the shame of the other as their own shame), only by being so overwhelmed by shame, that these faces—that is their hope—are able, faceless, to look at the effaced face of the other. Their own defacement, their own witnessing of their own defacement aims here not at self-reappropriation through shame. On the contrary, their only hope is that there will be no end to their shame, in the same way in which there is no end to the death of the already killed other. Only by being endlessly ashamed could they—that is what they feel— respond to the mute call of the victim. That is why these photographs are configured like an endless succession of graves, to which are attached little metal plaques with their names, as if these were precisely the tombstones of those who are vanishing in shame.

But the uncanny effect of the photographs lies in the fact that they represent at the same time graves *and* life in resistance, defacement *and* shame, that they have caught their subjects in between total defacement and shame, death and life. Or, in other words, that they are photographs of exiles. For exile is precisely that: death and resistance, muteness and panic, effacement and rebellion. Shame. The heart of every exile is shame. In exile shame comes home, and finds itself, at home.

Gayatri Chakravorty Spivak

Alice Attie showed me her photographs of Harlem. The images haunted me and interpellated me as a New Yorker. A month before this, twenty-one photographs at the base of the eleventh century Brihadiswara temple in Thanjavur, taken in 1858 by a Captain in the British Army, had beckoned. What was that interpellation? I have not come to grips with that one yet, but it launched me for a while on the question of photographs and evidence of identity. Harlem moved on to a big map.

In Dublin I could juxtapose the Harlem images with allochthonic Europe. What is it to be a Dubliner? Romanian, Somali, Algerian, Bosnian Dubliners? What is it to be a hi-tech Asian Dubliner, recipient of the 40% of official work permits? Diversity is class-differentiated. How does the anti-immigration platform—"Return Ireland to the Irish"—relate to the ferocious dominant-sector culturalism that is reconstituting Harlem today? A class-argument subsumed under this culturalism, pronouncing received anti-globalization or pro-working class pieties, will nicely displace the question. This became part of my argument.

In Brazil's Bahia, I learned what the *movimento negro* owed to African America in the United States.[1]

In Hong Kong in 2001, I saw that the word "identity," attached to the name of a place such as Hong Kong, indicated yet another species of collectivity: postcolonial. Between Great Britain and China, the Hong Kong cultural worker staged a loss of identity. If the quick sketch of Dublin foregrounds the class-division in diversity, the staging of Hong Kong makes visible the fault-lines within what is called "decolonization."[2]

This is "Map," by the Taiwanese artist Tsong Pu.

In 1996, the artist thought of this work as marking a contradiction between "lucid Chinese names and maps, and [the] ambiguous concept[s] of China and [its] names," questioning precise identities, as set down by names and maps.[3] He was, perhaps, inserting Hong Kong, via repatriation, into the confusion of the question of two Chinas, of one country two systems. 1997 was the official repatriation, the promise of a release. The artist could be conceptualizing this as a frozen series of bilateralities—no more than two chairs, a small rectangular table, rather emphatically not round. Hong Kong and the PRC, Hong Kong and Britain, UK and PRC: bilateralities. The rough concrete block, commemorating the promised release, in fact imprisons the two unequal partners. (Only one chair back has something like headphones attached.)　Rough concrete blocks weigh down bodies that must drown without trace. The chairs are empty, no bodies warm them, they cannot be used. The figure "1997" is engraved on one side of the block and embossed on the other. To what concept might this refer? To the strength of the piercing of that date into the history of the city-state as it displaces itself? To the fact of piercing out, but not through? The power of conceptual art is that, as the visual pushes toward the verbal, questions like these cannot be definitively answered.

Culture as the site of explanations is always shifting. The cultural worker's conceptualization of identity becomes part of the historical record that restrains the speed of that run. It feeds the souls of those in charge of cultural explanations, who visit museums and exhibitions. The British critic Raymond Williams would call this restraining effect the "residual" pulling back the cultural process.

I spent five months in Hong Kong. I never saw anyone looking at "Map." Culture had run away elsewhere.

This is a dynamic mark of identity, sharing in the instantaneous timing of virtual reality. The "Ethernet" band can be put away tomorrow, but is always available round the corner. Conceptuality moves on a clear path here—from the slow cultural confines of postcoloniality as repatriation into the quick fix of the culture of global finance. What is the relationship between the innocence and charm of these young people and the occlusion of class interests?

Who sends the collective messages of identity? Who receives them? It is surely clear that the artist Tsong Pu may not have been the real sender of the many messages that his piece can project. And of course I, a female Indian academic teaching English in the United States for over two-thirds of her life, may not be its felicitous receiver.

I want to keep the question of the sender and the receiver in mind as I move myself from Port Shelter, China, to Harlem, U.S.A. Who sends, and who receives, when messages assuming collectivities are inscribed? What are identities in mega-cities like Hong Kong and New York where floating populations rise and fall?

Harlem is a famous place, "a famous neighborhood rich in culture," says PBS. If the intellectual and the artist stage Hong Kong as emptied of cultural identity, the general dominant in New York is now interested in pronouncing Harlem as metonymic of African-America in general.

In 1658 Peter Stuyvesant, Dutch governor of New Netherland, established the settlement of Nieuw Haarlem, named after Haarlem in the Netherlands. Throughout the eighteenth century, Harlem was "an isolated, poor, rural village."[4] In the nineteenth century, it became a fashionable residential district. Following the panic of 1893, property owners rented to Blacks, and by World War I much of Harlem was firmly established as a black residential and commercial area, although race and class crosshatching was considerable.[5] From then till the 1990s, Harlem has been the scene of fierce deprivation and fierce energy. The chief artery of black Harlem is 125th Street. Columbia University, a major property owner in the area, spreads unevenly up to the edge of 125th. Since the 1990s, Harlem has been the focus of major economic "development," and the property ownership graph is changing. Part of the "development" package seems to be an invocation of a seamless community and culture marking the neighborhood, on left and right, finally working in the same interest, the American dream. The US thinks of itself as "global" or "local" interchangeably. At this point, nothing in the USA, including Harlem, is merely counter-global.

This essay is not part of the voluminous social history of Harlem, now coming forth to code development as freedom in the name of culture. I have not the skill. Robin Kelley's Introduction to Alice Attie's *Harlem on the Verge* integrates the photographs into that particular stream.[6] I only raise questions. That is my connection to Aaron Levy's *Cities Without Citizens.*[7] Like Levy, I question archivization, which attempts not only to restrain, but also to arrest the speed of the vanishing present, alive and dying. I question the evidentiary power of photography. The question changes, of course. Here in the Upper West Side of New York, the question becomes: In the face of class-divided racial diversity, who fetishizes culture and community? The only negative gesture that I have ever received from a black person in New York has been from a near-comatose drunken brother in the 96th Street subway station who told me to "take my green card and go home." That is not culture turned racism, but a recognition of the class-division in so-called diversity. At the end of the day, my critical position (though, as he noticed, not my class position or my class-interest) is the same as his.

DuBois describes the African American at the end of the last century as "two souls...in one dark body, whose dogged strength alone keeps it from being torn asunder."[8] In the development and gentrified "integration" of Harlem today, the hyphen between these two souls (African and American, African-American) is being negotiated. Therefore Alice Attie and I attempt *teleopoiesis*, a reaching toward the distant other by the patient power of the imagination, a curious kind of identity-politics, where one crosses identity, as a result of migration or exile.[9] Keats tries it with the Grecian Urn, Joyce with the *Odyssey* and the Wandering Jew. We beg the question of collectivity, on behalf of our discontinuous pasts, her mother in

59

Damascus, I in India, as New Yorkers. If the ghost dance accesses something like a "past" and grafts it to the "perhaps" of the future anterior, *teleopoiesis* wishes to touch a past that is historically not "one's own" (assuming that such a curious fiction has anything more than a calculative verifiability, for patricians of various kinds). We must ask, again and again, how many are *we*? who are *they*? as Harlem disappears into a present that demands a cultural essence. These are the questions of collectivity, asked as culture runs on. We work in the hope of a resonance with unknown philosophers of the future, friends in advance.

The *Encyclopedia Britannica* says "Harlem as a neighborhood has no fixed boundaries." Of course the Encyclopedia means this in the narrow sense. For Alice Attie, a photographer with a Euro-US father and a mother from Damascus, and for me, Resident Alien of Indian origin, these words have come to have a broader meaning. It has prompted us to ask: what it is to be a New Yorker? We are New Yorkers, Alice and I. Our collaboration is somewhat peculiar in that I emphasize our differences rather than our similarities. In the summer of 2000, I said, "Alice, you're not to mind the things I say about you. One thing is for sure. The photos are brilliant." She came up to me from behind, gave me a hug and kissed me on my neck. You decide if these words are a record of betrayal.

"For the past thirty years," Alice wrote in her field notes, "I have lived on 105th Street and West End Avenue, a fifteen minute walk from the heart of Harlem in New York City. Only recently, in April of 2000, did I venture into this forbidden territory and experience a community of warmth, generosity, openness and beauty. The dispelling of some deeply embedded stereotypes has been a small part of the extraordinary experience I have had walking the streets and conversing with the residents of Harlem."[10]

I have lived in the United States for forty-two years and in Manhattan for twelve. I went to Harlem the first week of arrival, because my post office is in Harlem. Someone in the office warned me that it might be dangerous. In the middle of the day! I have been comfortable in Harlem since that first day, perhaps because Harlem gives me the feel of, although it does not resemble, certain sections of Kolkata. But write about Harlem? Identitarianism scares me. That is my identity investment in this. It is in the interest of the catharsis of that fear that I have tried this experiment and asked: how do we memorialize the event? As "culture" runs on, how do we catch its vanishing track, its trace? How does it affect me as a New Yorker? Has the dominant made it impossible to touch the fragility of that edge?

*Eine differente Beziehung.*[11] This is a Hegelian phrase, which describes the cutting edge of the vanishing present. The present as event is a differencing relationship. I could add a modest rider to that. By choosing the word *Beziehung* rather than *Verhältnis* for relationship, Hegel was unmooring the present from definitive structural truth-claims, for he invariably uses the latter word to indicate the structurally correct placement of an item of history or subject. I must repeat my question: how does one figure the edge of the differencing as "past" as something we call the "present" unrolls?

I myself have been making the argument for some time now that, on the ethical register, *pre*-capitalist cultural formations should not be regarded in an evolutionist way, with capital as the telos.[12] I have suggested that culturally inscribed dominant mindsets that are *defective* for capitalism should be nurtured for grafting into our dominant. This is a task for which all preparation can only be remote and indirect. It does, however, operate a baseline critique of the social Darwinism implicit in all our ideas of "development" in the economic sense and "hospitality" in the narrow sense. I am a New Yorker. As Harlem is being "developed" into mainstream Manhattan, how do we catch the cultural inscription of de-lexicalized cultural collectivities?

(To lexicalize is to separate a linguistic item from its appropriate grammatical system into the conventions of another grammar. Thus a new economic and cultural lexicalization, as in the development of Harlem, demands a de-lexicalization as well.) Identitarianism is a denial of the imagination. The imagination is our inbuilt instrument of othering, of thinking things that are not in the here and now, of wanting to become others. I was delighted to see, in a recent issue of the Sunday *New York Times* devoted to the problem of race, that Erroll McDonald, a Caribbean-American editor at Pantheon Books, thinks that "at the heart of reading is an open engagement with another, often across centuries and cultural moments."[13] In the academy, the myth of identity goes something like this: the dominant self has an identity, and the subordinate other has an identity. Mirror images, the self othering the other, indefinitely. I call this, in academic vocabulary, an abyssal specular alterity.[14] In order to look for the outlines of a subject that is not a mirror-image of the dominant we have to acknowledge, as does Erroll McDonald, that any object of investigation—even the basis of a collective identity that we want to appropriate—is other than the investigator. We must investigate and imaginatively constitute our "own" unclaimed history with the same *teleopoietic* delicacy that we strive for in the case of the apparently distant. The most proximate *is* the most distant, as you will see if you try to grab it exactly, in words, or, better yet to make someone else grab it. If we ignore this, we take as demonstrated the grounds of an alternative identity— that which we set out to establish. This may be useful for combative politics but not so for the re-invention of our discipline.[15] Yet the combat cannot be forgotten.

I asked Attie to give me pictures that had inscriptions, no live figures. The humanism of human faces, especially in a time of mandatory culturalism, guarantees evidentiary memories, allows us to identify the everyday with the voice of recorded and organized public protest. "Of a necessity the vast majority of [the Negroes in Harlem] are ordinary, hard-working people, who spend their time in just about the same way that other ordinary, hard-working people do."[16] These inscriptions, each assuming a collectivity, are a bit exorbitant to both public protest and the mundane round. The inscriptions are now mostly gone. New building has replaced them. Already when they were photographed, there was no longer sender or receiver for these collectivities, in a sense that is different from the way this may be true of all messages, although the messages could still be read. This is the eerie moment of de-lexicalization, congealing into a "past," even as I speak. Inscriptions are lexicalized into the textuality of the listener, and it is the unexpected that instructs us. Therefore I asked for shots that inscribe collectivities and mark the moment of change.

We are both parts of the text—"New Yorker" is a collective term. How many are we? We are residents of Morningside Heights. How much of us is Harlem? How is *synoikismos* possible?[17]

This is on the wall of a landmark warehouse on 123d Street. Today, knowing that the building is standing skeletal and gutted, after passing through consideration by Columbia, Robert De Niro and a community-group that would have turned it into a cultural center, it seems more interesting that the message was on a warehouse. My fellow-critic is still the Brother in the subway station. No amount of pious diversity talk will bridge the constant subalternization that manages the crisis of upward class-mobility masquerading as the politics of classlessness. Who is this Black Man and to what would he have awakened? Who wrote on the warehouse wall? Was it a felicitous writing surface? Questions that have now disappeared.

I come from an inscribed city, Kolkata, whose inscriptions are in the mode of disappearance as the state of West Bengal moves into economic restructuring. The inscriptions of Kolkata, in Bengali, are never read by international commentary, left and right.[18] As I write, I have a vision of writing a companion piece for my hometown. How will it relate to the early imperial photographs, imprints taken by egg-white smoothed on waxed paper, of the temple inscriptions that set me to read photographs? Questions that must be asked before the Kolkata street inscriptions disappear.

I am not suggesting that there is any kind of located meaning to this inscribed collectivity as the movement is taking place. That too is a hard lesson to learn. On the other side is the convenience of facts. Attie and I have resolutely kept to rumors, with the same boring "authenticity" as all poorly edited oral history. Selected facts confound the ordinary with the resistant, thus fashioning identitarianism and culturalism. Our sources do not comment on the inscriptions, but rather on the built space. The gutted warehouse is an architectural moment in the spectrum between spatial practice (here inscription) and ruin (not allowed by developers), as the disappearing movement is taking place, the differentiating moment as the present becomes past, indefinitely.

Let us create a pattern. Here is "Wake k people," on an old Harlem storefront, which grandly and inadvertently provides an allegory of reading "MOVING." Discontinuous inscriptions, the old economy a space for inscribing, both under erasure, both gone, united in Harlem's current seamless culturalism. You can tell the lost word is "Black" simply by that "k," "up" is assumed, "male female, young old," once tied to my allegory of reading, is at the time of photography, anchorless. Indeed, what Harlem has and others use is now covered over. The object is not just lost by the covering over. It is the lost object in the future of the new Harlem.

Let us read this as an effective allegory of the anonymity. No one is sure as to who has asked whom to keep out of this lot. Here there is no built space yet to distract the inhabitants' attention. The inscription commands reading, yet is meaningless. It is now gone. The small rubble-strewn empty lot surrounded by barbed wire has been flattened. No one knows what will come up there. We could know if we made it a new political science (I am on the editorial board of a journal of that name) research project, with predictable results. I am keeping the convenient conclusions at bay, they can have the predictable pluses and minuses depending on the investigators, but the inhabitants are not there.

This is a store front on 116<sup>th</sup> Street, which has been filled with concrete.  The current inhabitants of the tenement above are relative newcomers, Haitians, who are suspended between the history of the store and the imminent future.  The small notice is in French because it acknowledges this floating present.  For the English speaking, a more austere notice: "NO/sitting/standing/loitering.  Thank you.  Owner."  The amiable Haitians, in suit and tie of a Wednesday evening, may have put this up.  I didn't ask.  One thing is sure.  The only name scribbled on the soft concrete—"Allen"—is not the signatory of the message, and not only because of the absent patronymic.  The archaeologist would undo the implausible text: Owner Allen.

An allegory again?  I am a reader of words, not a drawer of foregone conclusions from images read as if evidentiary.  Therefore inscriptions.

Then we come to "I still don't believe my man is gone." This is a memorial on which Robin Kelley comments movingly.[19] Here a felicitous public space of mourning/inscription is moving into that anonymous public space that memorializes the differantiating present as it disappears. Neither Robin nor I will know "Buster." This is in excess of the general structure without structure where all mourning, seeking to establish traffic with a transcendental intuition, is definitively unmoored. There is no guarantee that Buster is still at 1972 7th Avenue. We have not looked for him.

An essay such as this one can have no ending. We are commenting on culture on the run, the vanishing present. But there is a closure for the historical record, the "residual" restraint that I mentioned in my

opening. The Lenox Lounge will remain—a different urban text will sediment meaning as it lexicalizes the lounge into the historical record. The insistent culturalism of "Harlem Song" at the Apollo Theater and the various television programs is the ideological face of that lexicalization. It will appropriate the Harlem Renaissance and the New Negro.[20] Indeed it can appropriate the theme of loss in a golden nostalgia. In a show at the Museum of the City of New York, there are some images devoted to Harlem–and they belong to that genre.[21] That too is how architecture inhabits the spectrum between spatial practice and ruins. By scholarly hindsight a collectivity will be assumed or assigned to have intended this bit of built space. That will be a structural truth-claim. The anonymous, provisional, ghostly collectivities inscribed in and by these photographs, the edge of changeful culture caught on camera, will be de-lexicalized. This is an aporia of history, forever monumentalizing the stutter in the classic identity-claim "I am (not) one of us." Memory has a "posterior anteriority"—an I was there after the fact—to which the historically established so-called cultural memory can only aspire.[22] "Living" memory sustains us because it privatizes verifiability, effectively cancelling the question. The incessant production of cultural memory aspires to the public sphere by a species of subreption, the word Kant uses to designate the attribution to nature of a sublimity which actually belongs to our "respect for our own determination."[23] It is a word that, in Ecclesiastical Law, means the "suppression of truth to obtain indulgence." By using this word for the built-in or constitutive character of the production of cultural memory I draw a structural parallel with Kant's use of the word and have no intention to tie it to Kant's argument about nature and the moral will. The problem, at any rate, is not so much truth and falsity as public verifiability of culture by history.

To situate the lexicalization of the Lenox Lounge, I will recall once again a moment in W. E. B. DuBois's *Souls of Black Folk*—the outsider's hospitable entrance into Afro-Am.

*The Souls of Black Folk* is the prototype of the best vision of metropolitan Cultural Studies. At the head of each of its chapters, DuBois takes a line of an African spiritual and writes it in European musical notation. There we have the desire to convert the performative into performance—an active cultural idiom lexicalized into the encyclopedia or the museum—that is at the core of it. This is how the Lenox Lounge will enter the historical record—in a New World notation.

The DuBois of the last phase moved to a different place. Disaffected with the United States, the Pan-African DuBois became a citizen of Ghana in Africa. We situate the traces of the other, ghostlier demarcations of collectivity caught in Attie's photos with the obstinate remnants of DuBois's cherished *Encyclopedia Africana*, moldering in anonymity, disappeared in its refusal to disappear, in a locked room in Ghana; as the official encyclopedia of Africa is placed on the Internet. What we offer here is related to that refusal to disappear. DuBois's call for a state where "the crankiest, humblest and poorest...people are the...key to *consent of the governed*," seeking to redress Marx's regret at the end of "The Eighteenth Brumaire of Louis Bonaparte," that the lumpenproletariat could not "represent themselves," is now being claimed by the moral entrepreneurs of the international civil society who would represent the world's minorities without a democratic mandate.[24]

What is it for DuBois, the African-American who made that hyphenation possible, to become American-African? Hong Kong, British until day before yesterday, asks this question in terms of Asia and the United States, as Asian-American intellectuals come back after re-patriation. For Dublin, Irish America is the next parish, whereas Little Bosnia is elsewhere.[25] These are movements in different directions. We must place Harlem in the world, if we want to claim anti-globalism.

What are the remains of the event as *différance*? What is the responsibility of the memorializing collectivity? What mark will the old imprecise ghostly "singularity"—the scattered "Harlem" of these inscriptions—leave on film as the historical archives define it for scholarly use in a present that will cut itself off from it? A handful of photographs, deducing a collectivity from the ghost's track. These questions lead to different conclusions if you remember that politics is gendered.

The inscribed collectivities in the photographs are hardly ever women, and of course, never queer. This can be read in many ways. I have made the argument in another context that specific women's access to activism, not necessarily feminist activism, is socially produced in ways rather different from the male mainstream. I will not reproduce that argument here. I will repeat that, especially in the case of developmental activism, collectivity is constantly subsumed under the prevailing religion of individualism and competition, and this is true even of women. The activist may *speak of* collectivities, even *work for* groups of people, but it is the individuals who enter History. Thus the *New York Times* and the well-known liberal left journal *The Nation* have picked up the cases of Dorothy Vaughan,

whose old Harlem Reconstruction Project is going to be taken over by the gourmet supermarket Citarella, and Una Mulzac, who founded Liberation Bookstore in 1967, and has been threatened with eviction.[26]

They may not be immediately lexicalizable, like the Lenox Lounge, for which we go to Toni Morrison, Hortense Spillers, bell hooks, Queen Latifa, Maya Angelou. But they are, as it were, convertible to the format of the lexicon. We do not have their photographs, because they do not belong to the anonymous unclaimable delexicalized collectivities. We are not privileging de-lexicalization or anonymity; we are memorializing the moment before obliteration. It is in that caution that I now turn to a couple of images of "representative" Harlem women, unconnected to the inscriptions of collectivities.

The lesson that I have learned over the last decades is that, unless there is infinite patience, not just in one of us but in all of us to learn to learn from below, we cannot stand for their collectivity, if anyone ever can, when freedom from oppression turns around, one hopes, to the freedom to be responsible. Thus, to that impossible "if only..." I add another statement from Djebar: "If only I could cathect [*investir*] that single spectator body that remains, encircle it more and more tightly in order to forget the defeat!"[27] This is where developing the possibility of "being silent together," perhaps,

becomes our task. This task is unverifiable and the desire to claim it on the part of the one above who wants to be downwardly mobile is strong.

Because "woman" remains a special case, there are human figures here—as if in a rebus. Their distance from the inscription of collectivities is part of a "thing-presentation" rather than a "word-presentation," to analogize somewhat irresponsibly from Freud to signify a position behind access to collective verbality.[28]

Here now are prosthetic inscriptions of female collectivity, shoes, hats, buttocks, heads.

There was a gap in the window of "Coco Shoes" and in "Virgo Beauty Salon Restaurant" through which one could glimpse the inside. Today this kind of combination and merger has been institutionalized on another level of capital abstraction. But here there is no attempt at coherence. To the outsider today the storefronts mark a doubling that seems humorous, naïve, perhaps witty. Was it always thus?

Now "Corvette," one of the original large businesses in Harlem. Driving down 125th Street toward Triborough Bridge, Alice saw this blazing storefront as she was growing up. At the time of picture-taking, there were rumors, what would come in its place? HMV, OLD Navy, Modell's, Starbucks, SONY? Corvette is gone now and in its place is Duane Reade.

And here is one of Attie's shot of the future, this one a palimpsest of old Harlem revamped ("THE UNITED CHURCH OF PRAYER FOR ALL PEOPLE") and held reversed in the new globo-America:

The power to displace the new lexicalization, perhaps?  But I am not speaking of individuals.  I am talking about the disappearance of disenfranchised or disabled collectivities as we develop.  I am talking about everyday social Darwinism, not only the survival of the fittest, but also, if one thinks of the patter of the developers, "the burden of the fittest."  Remember the innocence of the bearers of "Ethernet?"  Through an indoctrination into a relentless culturalism in the dominant, these kids will get the charge of the New Empire, not the bereft instrumentality of the hi-tech Hong Kongers.

As it was, this picture took its domestic place with the international critique of my interlocutor in the subway station. "I *had* a dream, it is for you to fulfill it," Martin Luther King weeps. Now, the tears painted over, the mural shines with fresh color between a new Lane Bryant and the old "Kiss." A bit of a Lenox Lounge here, although not quite so royal.

In 1939-41, "a few dozen [anonymous male] photographers fanned out to every corner of every borough [of metropolitan New York] to shoot virtually every building then standing."[29] The purpose here is not to memorialize, but to construct a database for tax purposes. I have seen fourteen of these.

### A Lost City, Frozen in Time

Collections of the Municipal Archives of the City of New York

189 Second Avenue, Manhattan

"If only I could cathect that single spectator body that remains, encircle it more and more tightly in order to forget the defeat!"

Could those anonymous male photographers have imagined a situation in New York City when, more than sixty years later, this wish would be expressed, by way of an Algerian sister, by a female East Indian New Yorker? That is the force of the "perhaps," the undecidability of the future upon which we stake our political planning. Nothing may come of it. But nothing will survive without this effort. Love feeds research. It is a love that can claim nothing.

Was there a failure of love in that silent independent short film of Orchard Street in the Lower East Side of New York City, made by Ken Jacobs in 1956, nine years before Lyndon Johnson relaxed the quota system in US immigration law? Because I am somewhat critical of the film, I felt hesitant about asking Mr. Jacobs to let me include clips, although I believe that he is no more caught in his time than we are in ours. White male independent filmmakers like him were attempting to distinguish themselves from Hollywood. Before the age of political correctness, the film betrays certain stereotypes, which give legitimacy to identity politics. The beautiful young

East Asian woman, dressed in what could be sex-work clothes, sashays across the screen. The white child on a tricycle moves out of the screen at speed. A pair of African-American legs in baggy trousers sweeps refuse up and down the screen, the only repeated shot in this short film. You wouldn't have guessed that Malcolm X was active in the City at this time. To be a New Yorker is also to keep the neighborhoods separate.

I will close with the permissible narrative of what disappears as development happens. "What is an endangered species?," asked the wall

text of Cynthia Mailman's exhibition in the Staten Island Institute of Arts and Sciences. "Simply put," the text continued,

> it is any organism whose population has declined to the point of possible extinction. During the past 400 years the human species has played an important role in the extinction of certain species. The most celebrated extinctions in recent times involve birds. The passenger pigeon, which once occurred in flocks numbering in the millions, the Carolina parakeet, great auk and Labrador duck all succumbed to the pressures of either over-hunting or habitat destruction, all within a relatively short period of time...[W]e have to rely on the artist's renderings of the fringed gentian [warns the text], chokecherry and blue marsh violet since all have disappeared from the Staten Island landscape.[30]

The intent to memorialize can be signified by way of the frames, in the style of medieval illuminated manuscripts. And, because nature is presumed to be without history in this time frame, a species here can presumably come back as the same from the verge of extinction.

"This magnificent raptor," runs the wall text, "was once on the verge of extinction due to thinning of its eggshells caused by pesticidal spraying. A ban on the use of DDT in the 1970s, coupled with Federal protection, paved the way for a successful comeback. In the 1990s it was removed from the endangered species list."

This romantic conviction ("no hungry generations tread thee down") is dubious at best. "Biologically, the gene pool is badly impoverished; ecologically, its relation to the environment is radically altered. Are the herds of bison raised in national parks 'the same' as the herds the Indians hunted?"[31] But it is certain that there can be no hope of a successful comeback as a repetition of the same for inscribed collectivities, forever vanishing. A seamless culturalism cannot be as effective as Federal protection and a ban on DDT.

At the Staten Island Institute, this head (next page) is part of the permanent collection. The curator, Ed Johnson, writes as follows:

> The story of its finding is perhaps best told by George F. Kunz, who presented the head at a meeting of the Natural Science Association of Staten Island on May 10, 1884... *"The features are too well cut for a common off-hand piece of work by a stonemaker: the style is not Egyptian or Eastern; rendering it unlikely that it is a part of an antiquity thrown away by some sailor; it is rather Mexican, and still more resembles Aztec work. This leads to the inference that it is possibly of Indian origin..."*

Johnson also comments on the name "Lenape" given to the Indian head: "a term derived from the Unami language, meaning 'common,' 'ordinary' or 'real' people." *For convenience*, used to describe the Indians who lived on Staten Island and New Jersey in late prehistoric and early historic times.[32] It is indeed convenient to have one serviceable name; as in

the case of Yoruba, collectively naming, for convenience, the de-lexicalized collectivities of Òyó, Ègbá, Ègbádò, Ijèsà, Ijèbú, Ekítí, Nàgò into a single colonial name.[33]

    Where does originary hybridity begin? What, indeed, is it to be a New Yorker? We must push back on the trace of race in identity rather than insist on exclusive culture in order to ask that question. This is not to forget that the other side oppresses in the name of race, but its opposite: not to legitimize it by reversal.

The naming of the "Lenape" loosens us from location, as does the convenience of "Yoruba." Music mixes it up, jazz is hybrid at the origin.

The "originary" is a move—like the clutch disengaging to get a stick-shift car moving. The originary is precisely not an origin. Thus the most recent arrival engages that originary move as well. Alice and I are caught in it. In the fierceness of divisive identitarianism and/or benign diversitarianism, how many such New Yorkers are we? What are the implications of the corporate promotion of culture as a tax shelter in today's Harlem? New York is also the foremost financial center in the United States, perhaps in the world. Was there ever a felicitous sender and receiver of those inscriptions that Alice photographed?

But it is the negotiability of senders and receivers that allows *teleopoiesis*, touching the distant other with imaginative effort. The question of negotiability, like all necessary impossibilities, must be forever begged, assumed as possible before proof. Space is caught in it, as is the calculus of the political, the economic, and everything that writes our time. I ask you to negotiate between the rock of social history and the hard place of a seamless culture, to honor what we cannot ever grasp.

*"And I will set my face against you."* In Leviticus the face of God ordains retribution for turning away from the law. Besides the burnt offerings of bullocks, sheep, goats, and turtle-doves, there is the central sacrifice of the Day of Atonement: the goat set apart for Azazel. In the days of the Temple, the High Priest went before two goats, alike and equal. Two lots made of gold were thrown together into a casket from which he drew one lot as sacrifice on the altar for the *"name Most High, and one for the rocky steep,"* released into the wilderness to Azazel. The priest cried aloud, putting both hands on the goat: *"A sin-offering unto the Lord."* Then he sent this goat with a scarlet fillet around its jowls and the congregation's sins on its head out beyond the city's gates and into the desert, *"sending it away into the wilderness, into a barren region,* or according to Rashi, to *"a land which is cut off."*

Rituals of exclusion, whether banishment from the realm in Tudor England or expulsion through law of attainder, or persons imprisoned for life in eighteenth-century New York who suffered strict *"civil death,"* have created the as yet improperly apprehended person in law. This marking of perishables, consumed by use, says something unique about the sober *intelligence of ritual. Extending the notion of ritual to the exercise of law, I will venture what we might call a legal ritual, although this would be a form of law from which religion could not be divorced. I believe that rituals of law have their ground and impetus in a rather tortured idea of the sacred, which commanded in this seventeenth-century North American colony a very old, very colonial way of understanding crime and punishment.*

*Not a Pauline substitution of the law of the heart for the written law, but an elaborate return to Mosaic law in documents as varied as Nathaniel Ward's Body of Liberties (1641) or John Cotton's Code—An Abstract of Laws and Government (1655), written for but never adopted in the Massachusetts colony. The transformation of the old law in the new Canaan left its traces on later jurisprudence and would account for the severe rules of laws and codes of penance in this corner of the New World. The meaning of sin and redemption are inflected by an idiom of servility. The change marks a shift in jurisprudence, in the extent of punishment, and the line drawn between things and persons.*

*St. Paul—and I realize that there is some risk in turning to his epistles in the current debasement of belief by our head of state, something akin to Papa Doc's perversion of the substance of Haitian vodou in service of domination—St Paul knew that to serve in the spirit, to carry the law in the heart, meant that worms and pollution could no longer be sent away on the backs of animals or burned up in flames on the altar. Instead, filth became the gist of the identity of sufferers in Christ. Evil is not sweet in the mouth. But the calamity and affliction, the dead weight of matter borne, laid the ground for a new life of spirit. "We have become like the rubbish of the world, the dregs of all things, to this very day" (I. Cor. 4:13). Rubbish—what Kenneth Burke once famously called "fecal matter," the cultivation of waste product as backdrop to civil community—remains crucial to the tracking of law.*

## Security

After the September 11th attacks, George W. Bush Jr. elevated the identity of law and morality to a guiding principle. We witness with increasing amazement the ongoing disintegration of formal law and the subordination of the judiciary to the orders of the Washington central authorities. The new "Anti-Terrorism Act," known as "The Patriot Act" (with a subhead that reads "Uniting and Strengthening America by Providing Appropriate Tools Required to Intercept and Obstruct Terrorism"), carries to an extreme the rules for containment already elaborated in Bill Clinton's 1996 "Anti-Terrorism Bill." The Patriot Act purports to change well-established federal criminal constitutional law. In April 2003, Congressional Republicans maneuvered to make permanent the sweeping antiterrorism powers granted to federal law enforcement agents. The targets are the weak, the socially oppressed, and the racially suspect.

To the extent that "probable cause" and "due process" protections of the Constitution are repealed in the wake of the "war on terrorism," the directive is illegal by any post-Magna Carta standard. Legal boundaries are being equated with the legitimacy of the government's goals. This is one of the reasons why every announcement of imminent attack by the Office of Homeland Security translates into a system of rule by emergency decree. Need I point out the way this persecution of those detained on something called a "terror classification" echoes the situation-oriented, highly arbitrary structure of Nazi law? Evidence for the legality of political action in a particular case loses significance in relation to a general presumption of legality. What is decisive is the status the person possesses in society: their "innate character," the "nature of their personality," or "general disposition" largely replace objective characteristics, making the uncertain boundaries between the legal and illegal still more indeterminate.

Under the anti-terrorist law of "The Patriot Act," a person can be indefinitely detained *tout court* for an immigration-related violation if he or she is "certified" as a terrorist. This certification requires the minimal "reasonable grounds to believe" standard. Since September 11th, over two thousand Arab and Muslim men have been apprehended, for visa infractions that before would rarely result in prolonged detention. Or they have been detained in haphazard ways, for example, at traffic stops or through tips from suspicious neighbors. Though no indictments or charges have been lodged against them, they are detained by the INS in "preventive detention" without any chance to contact their family or attorneys. A rather crude form of social protection, what Ashcroft calls "national security," becomes the main content of a criminal law whose functions are being sacrificed to a drive toward greatly expanding its sphere of application, even to the point of extending criminal jurisdiction over foreigners in foreign countries.

How should we speak about the multiple forms of unfreedom, the archaic vessels for new terrors that we confront today? I am reminded of Carl Schmitt's critique of the operations of liberal and parliamentary democracy in *The Concept of the Political,* written right before his conversion to Hitlerism in 1933: "When a state fights its political enemy in the name of humanity, it is not a war for the sake of humanity, but a war wherein a particular state seeks to usurp a universal concept against its military opponent....To confiscate the word humanity, to invoke and monopolize such a term probably has certain incalculable effects, such as denying the enemy the quality of being human and declaring him to be an outlaw of humanity; and a war can thereby be driven to the most extreme inhumanity." Schmitt's examination of the highly political uses of the nonpolitical term "humanity" is especially useful in the current climate of terminologies that condemn juristically and morally those named "terrorists," those who inhabit the ever-widening "axis of evil." "Operation Enduring Freedom" and the guarantee of "Infinite Justice," whatever the cost, demonstrate how the formal language of beneficence and grace masks rapacious economic power. Such a use of words will, according to Schmitt, "turn into a crusade and into the last war of humanity."

Can we explain the extremism of current practices of punishment in the United States, anomalous in the rest of the so-called "civilized" world—even before September 11th—not only through a colonial legal history that in singular ways disabled the slave while inventing the legal person, but also through the extremely legalistic nature of the American system in general? Polity as social contract, citizens first and foremost as rights-holders, rights claims gone wild: in this context, the supra-legal negation of civil existence remains to be deciphered.

The national emergency proclaimed May 27, 1941, has never been terminated. Indeed, a state of war still exists. Thus, the authority upon which the Attorney General acted remains in force. A German-born woman married an American war veteran, Kurt W. Knauff, with the approval of his Commanding General. Knauff had served honorably during World War II. His wife, who had left Germany when Hitler took power, went to Czechoslovakia and then to England as a refugee. In England she served with the Royal Air Force and later worked with the War Department of the United States in Germany. On August 14, 1948, she tried to enter the United States to be naturalized under the War Brides Act. The Attorney General excluded her without a hearing , since she was "excludable" on the basis of information of a confidential nature. Neither she nor the court would ever know the reason for her exclusion. Temporarily detained at Ellis Island, two months later, the Assistant Commissioner of Immigration and Naturalization recommended that she be permanently excluded without a hearing, since her admission would "be prejudicial to the United States."

To test the right of the Attorney General to exclude her without notice of charges, without evidence of guilt, and without a hearing, she began habeas corpus proceedings in the Southern district of New York. The district court dismissed the writ, and the court of appeals affirmed. Then, in a 4-3 decision in United States ex Rel. Knauff v. Shaughnessy (January 16, 1950), the Supreme Court held that the Attorney General's decision was not reviewable by the courts. She did not, in Minton's words, "stand the test of security." The conjuring of *status*, the admission of aliens set forth not as a right but a privilege, the inherent power of exclusion, and the retroactive operation of regulations appeals to us as a true symptom of madness, but a madness that never really goes away, that lies dormant, and, waiting to return, to enact a redemption which has no object.

*Old legal strivings read as a time of grace, for some spoke words sufficient to recant wrong done.* Justices Felix Frankfurter, Robert Jackson, and Hugo Black dissented, writing that in such Acts of Congress "'The letter killeth.'" What they call "a process of elaborate implication" is, in their words, "ruthless." In repeating again "The letter killeth," they answer the Government's justification of an apparently arbitrary detention as a security requirement with a contextual and institutional warning:

> Security is like liberty in that many are the crimes committed in its name. The menace to the security of this country, be it great as it may, from this girl's admission is as nothing compared to the menace to free institutions inherent in procedures of this pattern. In the name of security the police state justifies its arbitrary oppressions on evidence that is secret, because security might be prejudiced if it were brought to light in hearings. The plea that evidence of guilt must be secret is abhorrent to free men, because it provides a cloak for the malevolent, the misinformed, the meddlesome, and the corrupt to play the role of informer undetected and uncorrected.

Following the Supreme Court decision, Congress took action on Knauff's behalf, convening hearings on her case. She remained in detention in Ellis Island for two and a half years before the Attorney General, under congressional pressure and in the face of substantial adverse publicity, ordered the INS to reopen proceedings and give her the benefit of a full exclusion hearing. At the hearing, the government's so-called confidential information was revealed. The evidence was, in the words of the Board of Immigration Appeals, "uncorroborated hearsay." A former scorned lover of Knauff's American husband had provided the evidence against Ellen Knauff.

Derived from Magna Charta, the writ of habeas corpus guaranteed that individuals could not be imprisoned or restrained in their liberty without due process of law. William Blackstone argued in his 1769 *Commentaries on the Laws of England* that execution and confiscation of property without accusation or trial signaled a despotism so extreme as to herald "the alarm of tyranny throughout the whole kingdom." Yet he foresaw that these practices were not as serious an attack on personal liberty as secret forms of imprisonment. The "confinement of the person, by secretly hurrying him to gaol, where his sufferings are unknown or forgotten," because it is "less public" and "less striking" is "a more dangerous engine of arbitrary government." Immigration law, however, often operated outside the norms of constitutional reasoning. The right to exclude, detain, or relocate "enemy aliens" in time of war, as the Alien Enemies Act of 1798 authorized, remained under varying guises part of the standing order of a United States bent on prohibiting foreign incursion.

For twenty-five years, the provisions of the McCarran-Walter Act of 1952, which excluded and deported communists, anarchists, and "subversive organizations," were upheld by the Supreme Court. On September 1, 1954, the Social Security Act was amended to terminate benefits payable to an alien deported for past membership in the Communist Party. In the case of *Flemming v. Nestor* (1960), the Supreme Court retroactively forfeited Ephram Nestor's social security payments, after he was deported in 1956 for having been a member of the Communist Party from 1933 to 1939. Though he had been a resident alien in the United States for forty-three years, having immigrated from Bulgaria in 1913, the majority opinion, written by Justice John Marshall Harlan, extended the forfeiture power of Congress, making him ineligible as a deportee to receive benefits.

In his dissent Justice Black condemned the 1954 Act as a bill of attainder. "Attaint" or "attainder" for treason, a word meaning to strike or hit, through a false derivation in taint, found its gist in "corruption of blood." Attainder had traveled from medieval England across the Atlantic to the colonies. Though abolished in the US Constitution, it was reclaimed as tradition and precedent in order to ensure the ban that could be recycled for new rounds of exclusion. "It is a congressional enactment aimed at an easily ascertainable group," Black argued; it is certainly punishment in any normal sense of the word to take away from any person the benefits of an insurance system into which he and his employer have paid their moneys for almost two decades; and it does all this without a trial according to due process of law." Justice William Douglass focused his dissent on a speech by Irving Brant, later published as "Congressional Investigations and Bills of Attainder": "By smiting a man day after day with slanderous words, by taking away his opportunity to earn a living, you can drain the blood from his veins without even scratching his skin....Today's bill of attainder is broader than the classic form, and not so tall and sharp. There is mental in place of physical torture, and confiscation of tomorrow's bread and butter instead of yesterday's land and gold."

The transmutation of legally-induced forfeiture, deprivation, and suspension of civil and political rights has accounted for much of the history of the United States. These rituals of cutting off have made the fact of inclusion a sign of privilege. Even Thomas Jefferson's enlightened precepts were nourished by rather dark convictions. The blessings of things democratic necessitated a vile reasonableness. As late as the 1820s, he sought solutions to the presence of African Americans in the United States that ranged from sending them to fit "receptacles" in Haiti to the deportation of newborns in order to keep the nation pure. But if punishment without trial and detentions or expulsions without due process existed before the exclusions mandated after September 11th, what, then, is distinct about the current administration's security measures? In the perpetually shifting imperatives of what is heralded as "eternal war," ever-larger groups of persons can be named and claimed as "threats." Against the backdrop of war without end, the historic exclusion of aliens confronts the passion for retribution demanded by an "infinite justice." One of the forms that retribution takes is the literal disappearance of persons held in secret on the basis of secret evidence. What are the demands of the infinite? What makes it so spacious, so huge and boundless? Its justice is not meted out to individuals, to persons accused of criminal acts. Its broad sweep calculates what is innumerable; and its generality subsumes all kinds of individuals who fit the criminal type, whose nature qualifies them as dangerous or degenerate. These continuously evolving and aggressive measures that claim to protect national security operate both inside and outside this country. They arbitrarily take hold of all kinds of newly identified "aliens," making indistinct the old divide between "legal" and "illegal," as various euphemisms mask the rubric of punishment.


## Blood

Instead of "servile law," I might assume the place of rights and disabilities as "enthralled ground," ground in thrall to the "dominants" with the "servients" bound under a thralldom. Enthralled ground. The ground that is a dead zone, a juridical no-man's land, where region, or what is regional can be everywhere. The persons currently deprived of rights, most importantly through labeling, through words in time that sustain the idea of the wicked or unfit, carry the idea of region with them. They make up a world that has no political boundaries, and where even geographical boundaries are dislodged from their proper places. How can I describe the place that becomes synonymous with the incapacitation of the person? In untangling a philosophy of personhood in the rules of law, we ought to understand how two apparently distinct discourses—expulsion and dehumanization—are joined, or, more precisely, operate along a continuum.

*The haunt of Guantanamo Bay where the spirits of persons lie dead.* The military gazette website, in its brief history called "The Least Worst Place," explains how in 1991 the naval base's mission expanded as "some 34,000 Haitian refugees passed through Gauntanamo." The naval base received the Navy Unit Commendation and Joint Meritorious Unit Award for its effort. We might recall a different history. In November 1991, approximately 310 Haitian men, women, and children were imprisoned on the grounds of the U.S. Naval Base at Guantanamo. Fenced in and guarded by Marines armed with machine guns, they lived in tin-roofed huts and used rarely cleaned portable toilets. Surrounded by vermin and rats, they were subject to disciplinary action and pre-dawn raids. For over a year and a half, from 1991 to 1992, following the charge of George Bush Sr., the United States government retained the use of Camp Bulkeley.

These Haitians were prisoners in the world's first and only detention camp for refugees with HIV. Not only were boatloads of refugees redefined as "economic" not "political" refugees, but they were also called "migrant contaminants." Identified as carriers of bad blood, these "aliens" were categorized as a "high-risk" group that threatened an unsuspecting populace. The locale for stigma established Guantanamo as a new receptacle for the incapacitated. Judge Johnson's opinion in *Haitian Centers Council v. Sale* (1993), described conditions at the camp:

> They live in camps surrounded by razor barbed wire. They tie plastic garbage bags to the sides of the building to keep the rain out. They sleep on cots and hang sheets to create some semblance of privacy. They are guarded by the military and are not permitted to leave the camp, except under military escort. The Haitian detainees have been subjected to predawn military sweeps as they sleep by as many as 400 soldiers dressed in full riot gear. They are confined like prisoners and are subject to detention in the brig without a hearing for camp rule infractions.

The forced repatriations of 1991-92, the arguments heard by the Supreme Court in March 1992 concerning the Haitians detained at Guantanamo, and their forced removals in 1994, just months before the return of Jean-Bertrand Aristide to Haiti in what became known as "Operation Sea Signal," were not the first nor would they be the last interdictions of Haitian refugees by the United States Coast Guard.

*New rules of law prevail without promise of recantation or prospect of voice.* After September 11th, the current Bush administration announced their decision to subject all non-Cuban asylum seekers arriving in the United States by sea to mandatory detention and expedited removal proceedings. On October 29, 2002, 230 Haitian refugees, arriving by boat in Miami, leapt into Biscayne Bay and tried to make it to shore. They were quickly detained by the Miami police and INS officials. As Dina Paul Parks, the Executive Director of the National Coalition for Haitian Rights (NCHR) argued in words that now read as if a fable of exclusion: "History has repeatedly shown how Haitians remain the only ethnic group who continue to be treated unlawfully once in the hands of U.S. authorities." In April 2003, Attorney General John Ashcroft ruled that *any* illegal immigrant who has not threatened national security but fits into "a security threat category" can be indefinitely detained rather than released on bond. In this bizarre logic, to seek asylum is to commit a crime. David Joseph, one of the hundreds of Haitians who sought asylum, had won the right to be released on bail while he awaited a decision on his claim. Overruling an appellate panel of immigration judges, Ashcroft, under the sign of the Department of Homeland Security, argued that even though Joseph posed no security threat, his individual qualities or circumstances no longer mattered. He had become the first sacrifice to what Ashcroft invoked as the threat of "unlawful and dangerous mass migrations by sea."

*"Navy Service personnel to Wear the Gimbel Glove While Processing Afghani Prisoners....A latex glove will protect the wearer from any contact he or she may sustain with a prisoner's blood or other bodily fluids."*

As we mark the 100th Anniversary of Guantanamo—it was acquired in 1903 as a coaling station—Guantanamo has become the hold for the so-called unlawful belligerents from the Afghanistan war. Within a maze of chain-link fences, razor wire and guard towers, metal cages baked in the tropical heat and inmates inhabited what was described in the early months of its existence in *The Guardian* as a "densely packed zoo." These cages at Guantanamo have now been replaced with a penal colony designed to hold up to 2,000 prisoners indefinitely.

How do these images of incarceration tell a history of punishment and retribution in the United States? What is the standard for treatment of prisoners taken in the current "war against terrorism"? Spokespersons for the military have stressed that "the prisoners are being properly fed, watered, and housed." What does it mean to satisfy these minimal needs? In a penal system now extended not only to those called "terrorists" or "aliens," but also to the dispossessed and dishonored, terms such as "minimal civilized measure of life's necessities" or "the basic necessities of human life" imply something unique about those caught in the grip of legal procedures. Is there a local legal history to the current detention of those denied prisoner-of-war status, those held indefinitely without being told why they are detained, without hearings or any charges being filed against them? Beyond the jurisdiction of U.S. law, the government can hold them as long as it wishes without judicial review or access to due process.

*Punishment, and the legal assurance that it be reasonably sustained, depends on the selective forfeiture of remembrance.* In presenting the motives and results of "servile law," I suggest that U.S. prison law itself, while resting on the ideals of fairness and due process which is heralded as the core of our belief system, has, during the years of the Rhenquist court, eroded the meaning of "due process," as it has gutted the possibility of proving "cruel and unusual punishment" in the courts. During the past twenty years, the Supreme Court has limited not only the rights of prisoners, but redefined these entities in law. That redefinition—the creation

98

of a new class of condemned—has introduced a mobile, endlessly adaptable strategy of domination and control. Administering exceptional punishment as if natural and usual provides the template for what is happening "off-shore" in Guantanamo Bay. The tendency, now rampant throughout US prisons, to use solitary confinement as the preferred discipline for any infraction of prison rules is extended into technologies of sensory deprivation that effectively create a portable form of confinement. In transport, prisoners sent from Afghanistan to Guantanamo are shackled by the hands and limbs, made to wear ear cuffs, blindfolded by blacked-out goggles and hooded. The new techniques of sensory deprivation, once fixed on the body of the suspected terrorist, shrink the space of isolation into a second skin.

## No right to have rights

The words of Marine Brigader General Michael R. Lehner, who runs the detention operation at Guantanamo Bay, prod us to reconsider the nature of legal inquiry. "There is no torture, no whips, no bright lights, no drugging....We are a nation of laws" (*Washington* Post, 2/3/02). In the past decade, prison administrators within the newly engineered "lawful prison," have devised forms of torture—for example, prolonged and indefinite isolation or the use of electro-shock weapons—while the Supreme Court has turned extraordinary practices—disciplinary sanctions, renamed "administrative segregation" that obviates the need for "due process" in the call for "security"—into nothing more than what are deemed the "ordinary incidents" of prison life. Trying to counter the judicial activism on behalf of prisoners in the late 1960s and early 1970s, cases as diverse as *Rhodes v. Chapman* (1921) and *Wilson v. Seiter* (1991) laid the ground for new regulations that ignored earlier claims of cruel and unusual punishment in the lower courts.

How might I deepen my argument that the model for what seems to be the unprecedented evasion of due process and of limits to detention were already preceded by a series of definitional sleights of hand from the late seventies to early nineties in the U.S. Supreme Court? The real change accomplished by the Rehnquist Court is the transformation of the idea of the *person restrained by law*. The rules of law create a philosophy of personhood, a metaphysics that goes beyond the mere logic of punishment, as first redefined by Richard Posner in the chilling *Franzen v. Duckworth* (1985), where prisoners in transport were burned alive due to shackles and locked doors, and then readopted by Scalia in *Wilson v. Seiter*. Both Posner and Scalia define punishment according to its 18th-century meaning—"an act intended to chastize or deter." They thus remove from the arena of judgment anything that happens after the judge's sentence—whether that be deprivations within or accidents outside the prison.

*Not that I question that the dead shall be raised with bodies.* Once you create the category of the *stigmatized*, even as a fiction, the legal embodiment remains: not only as fragments of words sustained through time as precedent, but the bodies of those made visible again in the flesh by these fictions of law. These shades of a type of body, whether wrapped up in the chrysalis of confinement or reduced through the rules of constitutional minima to a specific kind of human, remain so powerful, or rather so markedly indigestible, that opposing terms such as "deficient" and "normal" can be joined, their distinctions blurred as the intact person turns into the senseless icon of the human.

Speaking broadly, I suggest that in legal documents and under legal forms the social arrangements of times remote and present are made visible to us. The black codes, penal sanctions, the juridical no-man's land of illegal immigration and deportation, as well as wide-ranging territorial redefinition and administrative enforcement form the skeleton of the body politic. But we cannot be too scornful of bones, even if they're dry bones. We must know their anatomy, for in the legal structures, once held in the mind and repeated over time as precedent, lie the enhancing of *status* that makes and unmakes persons. In the range of comparative disabilities, it could be argued that legal constructions should not be given such free play. Can a statute with the purpose of punishment be changed from *penal law* if it imposes some other legitimate purpose besides punishment? What if something that sounds like penal law, once announced to be a congressional exercise of the war power, becomes non-penal, as if a new label has just been pasted on it?

In the case of a citizen denaturalized because of criminal desertion, the substance of the sanction, the rendering stateless, remains. In *Trop v. Dulles,* the 1957 case that decided loss of citizenship due to court-martial for a one-day desertion during wartime was cruel and unusual punishment, Chief Justice Warren gave for the first time a psychological component to what had long been delimited in eighth amendment decisions as corporeal harm. In 1944 a private in the United States Army, serving in French Morocco, escaped from a stockade at Casablanca, where he had been confined for a previous breach of discipline. In Warren's words:

> There may be involved no physical mistreatment, no primitive torture. There is instead the total destruction of the individual's status in organized society. It is a form of punishment more primitive than torture, for it destroys for the individual the political existence that was centuries in the development. The punishment strips the citizen of his status in the national and international community. While any one country may accord him some rights, and presumably as long as he remained in this country, he would enjoy the limited rights of an alien, no country need do so because he is stateless...his enjoyment of even the limited rights of an alien might be subject to termination at any time by reason of deportation. In short, the expatriate has lost the right to have rights.

The undoing of citizenship has a long history in the United States, whether in creating slaves as persons in law, criminals as dead to the law, or that unique and perpetual recreation of the rightless entity. The hard-won definition of citizenship in the Fourteenth Amendment (1868) would be undone in five years. The *Slaughter-House Cases* (1873) gave the legal presence of chattel a proximate space of enclosure in *the double offering of cows and slaves* in a new region of servitude. And in the *Civil Rights Cases* (1883), the region of legal rights were redefined as social rights. What if, and I must urge this possibility, statute or case law were as important as social custom or belief in upholding the racial line, in effecting strategies of exclusion? What if rituals of law, and the legal fictions ordained by these practices, restructured categories of identity, thereby reinventing a taxonomy from the point of view of disavowal and lack? Finally, what if, no matter the humanitarian claims, within the legal language of "evolving standards of human decency," blood sticks to the new rules?

## Accursed things

What is the standard for treatment of prisoners taken in the current "war against terrorism"? In spring 2003, the Bush administration refused to sign the treaty establishing an International Criminal Court. Unwilling to be held to an international standard for treatment of prisoners, the United States has in turn refused to recognize the prisoner of war claims for humane treatment of the current 690 prisoners from 43 countries detained in Camp Delta at Guantanamo. By renaming the detainees "enemy combatants," "unlawful combatants," or "battlefield detainees," the US can elude the provisions of the Geneva Convention, demanding that prisoners be treated humanely, that they cannot be closely confined, that they be protected against violence, cruel treatment, and torture, and that neither mental nor physical torture may be applied in order to gather information. By not labeling the detainees as "prisoners of war," they may be tried in a military tribunal, as a result of an emergency executive order signed by President Bush in November 2002. The Department of Defense will have the power to write the rules of the tribunal, as well as to choose members of the panel.

For over a year now, the transport to and detention in the newly built units at Guantanamo continues. The pentagon has agreed to push through the release of one hundred or more prisoners, who have, in the words of one official, "no intelligence value," sought by the allies, including Britain, Russia, Pakistan, and Spain. At least eight detainees at the naval base tried to hang themselves in just three weeks this past winter, bringing to a total at least 19 suicide attempts, including one detainee who has tried to kill himself twice, since the detentions began. In these regions of stripping bare, where bodies, once bound and desensitized, are placed in solitary cells without being told the reason for the transport or the detention, without access to lawyers or permission to contact families, how do we describe how much of the person is civilly alive and how much civilly dead?

These creatures of law are not quite spectral, since their materiality is crucial for the continued power of the *state of exception or the realm of exclusion* to work its effects on the minds of the as yet included. For the non-descripts deprived of freedom in what Britain's appeal judges have labeled a "legal black hole," they bear the instability of literal region with them. They make up a world that has no political boundaries, and where even geographical boundaries do not necessarily separate state from state or nation from nation, giving, I might add, a new, foundational meaning to Walcott's cryptic line in "Schooner Flight": "either I'm nobody or a nation."

Schmitt's *Der Nomos der Erde* (1950) describes the lines drawn to divide and distribute the earth with the discovery of the New World. At this "line" Europe ended and the "New World" began. "European public law ended....Beyond the line was an 'overseas' zone in which, for want of any legal limits to war, only the law of the stronger applied." In these places, spheres "outside the law and open to the use of force," the distinctions between dominions and non-dominions kept alive what Schmitt identified as a specifically English sense "for specific spatial orders." His identification of what he calls "the relation between order and location—the spatial context of law" is crucial to our understanding just how what we know as a "normal legal order" can be suspended. The new Republican Empire is, as numerous maps demonstrate, intensely spatial. Within the designated zones free of law, within this context, "everything required by the situation is permitted." Whether in unnamed detention centers in the United States, in the camps at Guantanamo, or offshore at Bagram air base, the headquarters of U.S. forces in Afghanistan or at the military base on Diego Garcia, an Indian Ocean island the US leases from Britain, the non-place becomes synonymous with, and merges into the non-person. Guantanamo is outside of legal jurisdiction, as decided by U.S. District Judge Colleen Kollar-Kotelly, when she dismissed the case *Al Odah, Khaled A.F. v. United States* in July, 2002, because the naval base is "nothing remotely akin to a territory of the United States."

     *Unlike a traditional electric cattle prod, which causes localized pain, stun weapons are designed to temporarily incapacitate a person.* "Torture warrants," "stress and duress," these words for techniques of interrogation take us back in time to the fantastic response of the United States to the UN Treaty on Torture, which followed the United Nations Convention Against Torture in May 2000. Having been the focus of the UN mandate against contemporary cruel and unusual practices of punishment, the United States refused to accept Article 16 of the mandate, which prohibits, and these are the terms: "cruel, inhuman, or degrading treatment." The prohibition must be binding, according to the United States, "only insofar as the term 'cruel, inhuman or degrading treatment or punishment' means and is, therefore, limited to the phraseology of 'cruel and unusual punishment'" prohibited by the Constitution. According to Amnesty International's *Briefing for the UN Committee Against Torture* (May 2000), the reservation to Article 16 "has far-reaching implications and can apply to any US laws or practices which may breach international standards for humane treatment but are allowed under the US Constitution, for example, prolonged isolation or the use of electro-shock weapons."

In retaining the elusive phraseology of what reads almost as an afterthought—"Excessive bail shall not be required, nor excessive fines imposed, or cruel and unusual punishments inflicted"— the U.S. continues to redefine what is harsh, brutal, or degrading as customary, expected, or deserved. As the only provision of the Bill of Rights that is applicable in its own terms to prisoners, the Eighth Amendment proffers a limit on the state's power to punish. The importance of this negative guaranty expands in the prison context. But during the past twenty years, the Supreme Court has narrowed, or to be more precise, gutted the application of the Eighth Amendment, raising the threshold of suffering necessary to trigger a violation. In refusing to recognize prisoners' claims based on intangible marks of suffering such as "degeneration," "degradation," "imposed dependency" or "cultivated debilitation," to cite from the 1977 New Hampshire case *Laaman v. Helgemoe*, the Supreme Court has instead reconstituted the prisoner not only as incapable of rehabilitation, but as so much material exposed to institutional degradation.

The *Prisoner's Litigation Reform Act*, signed into law on April 26, 1996, dramatically curtails prisoner litigation into the next century. Designed to limit what was said to be a massive increase in "frivolous" inmate litigation, the PLRA permits preliminary injunctive relief related to prison conditions, but it erects substantial hurdles that must be negotiated before such relief can be given. In order to get an injunction, a plaintiff must prove that every plaintiff or member of the proposed class has suffered actual, physical injury, thus prohibiting damages for mental injury. The prisoner must prove that the request for relief is narrowly focused, extends no further than necessary to correct the injury, and is the least intrusive means necessary to correct or prevent the harm. As an inmate wrote to me recently, "Only prisoners are excluded from relief or damages stemming from mental pain and suffering (as if such pains are rightfully reserved for us alone)."

*The noxal surrender of the slave or ox, even lifeless chattels, must be handed over to the king, for God's sake, to appease the wrathful dead.* Now that the negative personhood of the prisoner has been more extremely extended to those suspected of terrorism, a new language of kinship has been invented. Some of these new prisoners are delivered—or "rendered" in official parlance to the foreign intelligence services of US allies who have been accused of practicing torture, notably Egypt, Jordan, or Morocco. In defense of the practice, officials explain that they're sent to these countries not because of their tough interrogation methods, but because of their cultural affinity with the captives.

What this culture of intimacy amounts to has not been divulged. But the choice of the words "rendered" or "rendered up" in this second transport are crucial to our understanding the work of expiation that I referred to in the goat rendered to Azazel in Leviticus. The ritual, we must remember, is not a *sacrifice*, but *a going away*. A being *sent away for some kind of death in a land which is cut off, or "precipitous."* What is the design of the juridical no-man's land that has been created when war loosens the link between human being and citizen? What is being redeemed when *rendered suspects*—another often used name that describes the sending of detainees to and from varying places for security and intelligence?

If we try to measure redemption, we will always return to the sound of coins: the payment of a debt, the satisfaction of what is owed, the purchasing back of something that has been lost. These men—and I have heard of no cases of women detainees—in redeeming by payment, which is to say, by substitution give us a sense of the nature of this war that is not like war, the war that has no end in sight. In the crossing of religious and legal, terminological questions become highly political. The state department describes those transported for further questioning as "rendered transports." In scrutinizing this more closely, however, it may be seen that the word "rendered" is highly charged. It has the effect of suggesting sacrifice for a greater good. To render. A payment from a tenant to a feudal lord, from a servient to a dominant. To give what is due or owed. To give in return or retribution. To surrender or relinquish. But to render also means to reduce, convert, or melt down.

## The lawful prison

390,690 cubic feet of concrete. 2,295,000 cubic feet of earth moved. 22,000,000 pounds of gravel. 2,363,138 pounds of reinforcing steel used in foundation and walls. 1,408,000 pounds of security steel used in cell door bars security system. 254,000 masonry blocks placed on site. 1,100 security keys . For three years, from 1996-1998, I had unusual, and still not fully understood access to Special Management Unit II in Florence, Arizona,

the high-tech, state-of-the-art prison, the most restrictive super-maximum security prison in the United States, even harsher than the well-known "Pelican Bay." In SMU II, those called "the worst of the worst" are bound in thrall to the most draconian rules in the history of the contemporary prison. This locale—a model for other "special housing" or "special treatment" units in the United States—was built for those inmates called "strategic threat groups" (meaning gangs), or "special needs groups" (meaning psychologically disabled) or "assaultive" (meaning never divulged).

The process by which such words are specified, by which their technical meaning is determined, remains a curious and illogical process. Segregation decisions, in these cases, are based upon the mere "status" of gang affiliation, not evidence of an actual infraction of prison rules. In other words, something assumed to be "criminal will" is not based on "criminal action." The labels, demarcating those identified as threats to "the safe, secure and efficient operations of [prison] institutions," carry with them the unwholesome possibility that solitary confinement can extend indefinitely, that 23-hour lockdown status cannot be judged a constitutional violation, and, finally, that the absence of training programs, vocational training, education, personal property, and even human contact, are nothing but the expected elements of confinement when administrative security is the primary goal. Special Management Unit II in Florence, Arizona is singular among these control units in that it also includes in its walls those on death row.

The isolation is unremitting. Cell doors, unit doors, and shower doors are operated remotely from a control center. Physical contact is limited to being touched through a security door by a correctional officer while being placed in restraints or having restraints removed. Verbal communication occurs through intercom systems. Television, water, and lights are manipulated by remote control. Inmates have described life in the massive, windowless supermax as akin to "living in a tomb," "circling in space," or "being freeze dried." As federal Judge Thelton Henderson wrote in *Madrid v. Gomez* (1995), the class action suit against Pelican Bay,

prolonged supermax confinement "may press the outer bounds of what most humans can psychologically tolerate." The degrading strictures of confinement, the psychological torture, and excessive force ask us to reassess the meaning of "cruel and unusual" punishment, and to ask: Has the current attention to the death penalty allowed us to forget the gradual dissolution of mind in solitary confinement, the long process of executing the person?

What happens when the materials of thought are removed, when memory only is left and nothing comes through the portals of the senses? Writing on "Our Ideas and their Origin" in his *Essay on Human Understanding*, Locke answers the question. He asks us to imagine a foetus in the womb as if nothing more than a vegetable, but as time passes, perception and thought come together to move the senses. And with that movement out from a place "where the eyes have no light, and the ears so shut up are not very susceptible of sounds," the mind jostled by the senses, awakens, and "thinks more, the more it has matter to think on." In the chilling logic of solitary, we follow the execution of thinking matter. Since there are no outward objects to impinge on the senses, the mind has nothing to think about. Within the bounds of this vacancy, the mind empties itself of thought, or in Locke's superb compound of senses and ideas, where there is no sensation, there are no ideas. After the wrecking of the furniture of the mind, the relic of incapacitation remains. Nothing more than an icon of memory, or in Locke's words, a "tomb of dead ideas."

*"I have been validated as a member of the Aryan Brotherhood, after three previous hearings that cleared me of gang activity. My validation is based on nothing I did. Instead, it is based on the simple fact that other inmates possessed my name after I have been a jail house lawyer, approved legal assistant and representative—educated by the Arizona Department of Corrections for over ten years....Due process has been violated in every manner possible. The most frequent claims are denial of witnesses and denial of access to alleged evidence...I was denied all my witnesses and denied the opportunity to see any evidence by the blanket reasoning of 'confidential.'"*

With these words Mark Koch sought legal representation for his alleged identification as a "Security Threat Group" member. In the precedent-setting decision *Koch v. Lewis* (August 30, 2001), Judge James B.

Moran ruled that Mark Koch's five-and-a-half years in SMU II, with no end in sight, gave rise to a protected liberty interest under the "atypical and significant" clause of *Sandin v. Conner*. Arguing that the deprivation was extreme in both degree and duration, Moran adopted the Sandin test of "atypical and significant hardship in relation to the ordinary incidents of prison life." Koch was locked in his cell 165 out of 168 weekly hours. His three weekly hours out of his cell were spent in shackles. He got only eight minutes to shower and shave. For the three hours a week out of his cell, Koch walked twenty feet down the hall in one direction for a shower and ten feet down the hall to an empty exercise room, a high-walled cage with mesh screening overhead. When Koch appeared in district court in Phoenix, he had not seen the horizon or the night sky for more than five years.

Considering the severe "conditions" of Koch's "confinement" and the "duration of the deprivation at issue," the court found that Koch's solitary confinement violated his right to due process under the 14th Amendment, because there was no evidence that Koch had committed any overt act to warrant such action. The label of "Aryan Brotherhood" was not sufficient. As Judge Moran explained in the middle of the trial: "We are not talking about punishment for misconduct; we are talking about incarceration because of status and subsequent indefinite confinement in SMU." He questioned what the Department of Corrections called "a basic and irrebuttable presumption" that "status=risk": "We are not unmindful of the danger posed by prison gangs, but we do not agree with the defendant's conclusion that indefinite segregation in SMU II based on status alone passes constitutional muster." In other words, according to Moran, Koch "cannot constitutionally be held indefinitely in virtual isolation because of his status and not because of any overt conduct."

What had Koch done to be validated as a member of the Aryan Brotherhood STG or Security Threat Group? What allowed him to receive little notice or details of the charges against him? How could he be placed in a situation where his status and the concomitant level five institutional risk score effectively foreclosed any possibility of parole? Moran noted that Koch's "legal practice has been remarkable." The most disciplined group of prisoners remains jail-house lawyers. Over a period of twenty years, Koch had helped other prisoners in understanding their convictions and filing suits. According to his testimony, retaliation led to spurious attacks on his person and his property, and to numerous transfers—not in themselves violating due process rights, since according to *Meachum v. Fano* (1976), officials have the discretion to transfer inmates for "whatever reason or for no reason at all." Such discretion is loaded with arbitrary power.

Because of Koch's assumed gang involvement, the only way out of SMU II was to debrief. But how could he debrief if, as he continued to argue, he was not a gang member? Falsely accused, he would be condemned to serve out his time indefinitely because he knew of nothing to tell, and could not, therefore, effectively debrief. Since de-briefers are targeted for execution by gang members, Koch would have been sent to another restrictive segregated facility, SMU I. Anyone suspected of gang affiliation is thus, whether he debriefs or not, condemned to what amounts to solitary confinement for the rest of his life. As Moran noted, only in Arizona are gang members held in these facilities without prospect of returning to the general population, without any chance for re-classification for good behavior. "Its restrictions upon the return of inactive gang members, Moran wrote, "is apparently unique....A policy preference is not without constitutional limitations. It would certainly ease the burdens of a correctional system if all prisoners were executed or perpetually chained to a wall, but no one, we believe, would suggest that such a system would pass constitutional muster."

According to lead counsel in Koch's civil rights litigation, Dan Pochoda, the reliance on substantive not procedural due process was absolutely necessary, for, in his words, "you can have all the procedures in the world to prove that *x* is true, but if there is no connection between *x* being true and the actions taken in connection with that assumption, you've got a

substantive due process violation. It's as if the officials had said, 'If he's got red hair, then we're going to put him in SMU. If $x$ leads to $y$, then there's got to be some rational connection between $x$ and $y$. Otherwise, it's absolutely arbitrary." In other words, there is no rational, reasonable, demonstrable connection between Koch being a member of the Aryan Brotherhood and being put in lockdown in SMU. Pochoda explained, "A finding of imminent danger based on gang membership alone is an abstraction without foundation."

"Is this not a servitude?" We are dealing with the kind of *stigma* summoned in Taney's infamous decision in *Dred Scott v. Sanford (1856)*. No matter where Scott finds himself, his skin, and the history of conversion marked by that sign of degradation, condemns him never to be free of the status that consigns him to be a slave in the eyes of the law. Although Taney's ruling against African-American citizenship was reversed soon enough—first by the Civil Rights Act of 1866 and then more conclusively by the Fourteenth Amendment, which passed Congress the same year and was ratified in 1868—Radical Reconstruction failed in the federal Supreme Court through a series of decisions from the 1870s to the end of the century. As I've been suggesting, *the badge of servitude* has remained, especially for prisoners caught perpetually in the exception of the Thirteenth Amendment, which abolished slavery *except* in the case of convicted criminals.

The disparaging and unequal enactments of those suspected of involvement in an STG designation assails the rights to liberty, the fundamental privileges and immunities of citizens that remain even in the restrictions of prison, even those entailed by criminal conviction. The imaginative re-coloring of certain groups in order more easily to remove them from legal protection is accomplished by the call of status. Again, the judicatory fact that matters is not what the person has done, but *what he is like*.

The due process clause of the Fourteenth Amendment, adopted in 1868 reads: "nor shall any State deprive any person of life, liberty, or property, without due process of law." The facially clear meaning is that a state has to use sufficiently fair and just legal procedures whenever it is lawfully going to take away a person's life, freedom, or possessions. In the prison context, any transfer or treatment for disciplinary proceedings generally finds certain procedures necessary to satisfy the minimum requirements of procedural due process: advance written notice of the alleged violation, a written statement of evidence, and the ability to call witnesses. Under the vague contours of "substantive due process," however, the Supreme Court developed a broader interpretation of the clause, one that protects basic substantive rights, as well as the right to process. Substantive due process holds that the due process clauses of the Fifth and Fourteenth Amendments guarantee not only that appropriate and just procedures (or "processes") be used whenever the government or the State is punishing a person or otherwise taking away a person's life, freedom, or property, but that a person cannot be so deprived without appropriate justification, regardless of the procedures used to do the taking.

## Bullets and handshakes

War is never a humanitarian enterprise. Beneath a cloud of black smoke from oil fires, the sound of shelling and machine gun fire, the forces for "good" gave candy to children in Nasiriya, shook hands with children on a street in Najaf on the road to Baghdad. The State Department's public diplomacy web site included a gallery of photos that showed soldiers dousing oil fires and bandaging wounds but never firing weapons. Khaled Abdelkariem, a Washington-based correspondent for the Middle East News Agency emphasized the ruses of charity: "The Arabs or Muslims are not 4-year-old kids who don't know what's happened around them....The feed-and-kill policy—throwing bombs in Baghdad and throwing food at the people—is not winning hearts and minds." The word "freedom" has acquired new meaning since the fall of Baghdad. As Rumsfeld put it, after the destruction of the National Museum of Iraq, perhaps the greatest cultural disaster in recent Middle Eastern history: "There is untidiness...And it's untidy. And freedom's untidy." And so persists the disposal of bodies, docile and disciplined or enraged and liberated. In this taxonomy tooled during and after variously named wars, the unnamed objects of solicitude or retribution remain, the recipients of ever new trials of definition.

After 9/11, coverage of the increasing numbers of persons removed from the general prison population to the new indeterminate solitary confinement ceased. Instead, through the media's absorption in the faces of terrorism, this tactical and local penal law turned outward, shaped into war measures used to rid oneself of the ever-multiplying bodies of "terrorists." As Deputy Assistant Attorney-General John Yoo explained when questioned about the U.S. Southern Command at Guantanamo. "What the administration is trying to do is to create a new legal regime…It's not a legal matter. This is a matter of security. It's a matter of war."

There is something oracular in the ordeal of punishment meted out to the suspected enemies of our "enduring freedom." What is the logic of testing, when the apparent betrayal of an individual's guilt is not as important as the sign or the label itself? The category of the Security Threat Group in prison has been expanded to those named "unlawful combatants" in the off-shore compound at Guantanamo or "suspicious aliens" on the mainland. In all these cases, the judgment precedes the proof. The indefinite "war on terrorism," as the indefinite detention of prisoners at Camp Delta, or the indefinite isolation of inmates confined in special management units, relegates ever-increasing numbers of "suspects" to the protracted limbo of life-in-death. What we now confront is nothing less than a regressive regionalism, marking a new kind of terror that acts as if impelled by some preternatural pressure from no particular state, from no particular nation. Through new operations of law, old structural modes or topographies have become containers for those deemed, as early as Clinton's first Anti-Terrorism Bill, "criminal aliens." It is as if the category created in the compound of "criminal" and "alien" has granted reasonableness to a critical *deraison*.

* This essay, part of the "Due Process" section of *Held in the Body of the State* (forthcoming, Princeton UP), is a result of sustained conversations with Susan Stewart and our writing on Guantanamo Bay. Excerpts were presented at seminars and workshops at Columbia, Cornell, NYU, and Irvine. I thank Saidiya Hartman, Stephen Best, Cheryl Harris, and members of the Sawyer Seminar, UCHRI (April 28, 2003), for pressing me to know what is at stake in the turn to the unspeakable.

# II. LIQUIDATION and SETTLEMENT

They got indeed what they could hardly give, a time-honoured conception of humanity in ruins, and perhaps even an inkling of the terms in which our condition is to be thought again.

—Samuel Beckett, "The Capital of the Ruins"

What constitutes the charm of our country, apart of course from its scant population, and this without help of the meanest contraceptive, is that all is derelict....Elysium of the roofless.

—Samuel Beckett, "First Love"[1]

The story still circulates in Ireland that, on his presidential visit to the country, Ronald Reagan asked to be brought to the family home of his grandfather, who was believed to have emigrated from Co. Tipperary at the time of the Great Famine of the 1840s. The presidential calvacade arrived in tiny Ballyporeen, not so much even a village as a "townland" [*baile*], the vestige of an old form of Irish landholding which preserved into the nineteenth century forms of the commons wherein small strips of land were regularly redistributed among the inhabitants. As was wryly pointed out at the time, Ballyporeen itself is Irish for "townland of small potatoes," and the president's place of origin could scarcely have appeared more humble. With due solemnity Reagan was led to a strip of bogland and shown a small mound that was all that remained of his grandfather's dwelling. Typically, the Irish peasant's home had been a single roomed hut built almost certainly of mud or turf and roofed with reeds or sods. In the course of time, after the departure or death of its destitute and derelict inhabitants, the dwelling would decay back into the bogland from which it had risen, leaving only a slight ridge or hump to mark its passing. Such, it seems, was the fate of Reagan's family home.

What is striking about this anecdote is not perhaps the comical picture of the president's disappointment at not finding there one of those stone thatched cottages that are the staple of tourist brochures, or the satiric or edifying image of power humbled by the sight of its origins in the common muck. It is, rather, the peculiar plausibility with which, in Ireland, local lore might well have retained the memory of what this insignificant bump in the landscape might have been and the names of those who had lived there. One may suspect the possibility that Reagan was being had, if only for reasons of state, in order that the desire of this returning emigrant, representative of his kind, be satisfied. Yet the aesthetic probability of the gesture is nonetheless underwritten by the knowledge that such local memory might indeed persist. While canonical narratives rapidly work to recuperate such an event into a moral history of immigrant success in the promised land of the new world, transforming it into a symbolic moment in a universal history, what lingers is that ineradicable trace, in the land as in local memory, of what has passed away. The trace of the passing is what does not pass on even in its gradual decay.

The Irish landscape is seeded with ruins, multifarious remnants of the disappeared: the contours of ring forts and the angular thrust of the dolmen; the stubs of round towers and shattered castles or abbeys; the

122

burnt-out shells of great houses and coast-guard barracks. One could even say that it is a landscape peculiarly composed of ruins, where even the grey stone walls that mark the legal fictions of use and ownership, imposing themselves on the older commons, have the appearance of decayed structures. These latter are, in fact, no less the marks and traces of historical violence than are the broken forts and towers whose materials they seem to echo. A landscape of ruins, if not in ruins, the country is intensely readable, littered with runic letters:

> Apart from the more or less datable remains of church and rath, castle and cairn, the land is covered with the marks of man's toil. The history of rural Ireland could be read out of doors, had we the skill, from the scrawlings made by men in the field boundaries of successive periods. In them the unlettered countryman wrote his runes on the land.[2]

It is in these most vestigial of ruins—primitive marks and traces of the "unlettered," which seem to occupy the very threshold at which human artifact passes into nature and nature into the artifice of human readings, that we might equally apprehend the lapsing of those very categories that sustain the archaeological and historicist interpretation of landscape and its ruins. For the historicist—whether by profession archaeologist, anthropologist, folklorist or plain historian—ruins mark the foregone stages of a passage from the savage's primitive embeddedness in nature to the full emergence of human rationality expressed in the orderly organization of the land for production or in the complexity of advanced civic relations. Their at times barely perceptible jutting into the present is no more than the sign of an unequivocal pastness, of a being on the very vanishing point of historical time, lodged in an inertness in relation to the present and, by the same token, one with the inertia of a landscape defined by its subordination to human ends. Ireland, indeed, has long been viewed from such a perspective as one immense ruin, a belated survival in the present of archaic social and cultural formations that have elsewhere been surpassed:

> The importance of Ireland is that, thanks to the "time-lag," it has rendered to Anthropology the unique, inestimable, indispensable service of carrying a primitive European *Precivilization* down into late historic times and there holding it up for our observation and instruction.[3]

Held in suspension as a mere object for contemplation, this "Precivilization" is a harmless and passive archaism that puts up no resistance to the modernity that is its fate in the double sense of destination and nemesis. Accordingly, ruins that are the evacuated remnants of human activity dissolve back into natural forms in a landscape that is everywhere reduced to human domination and surveillance. As the actual and active presence of human agents is replaced by their inert residues, the historical narrative converges here with a tourist aesthetic that dissolves the violence of the past into the quasi-natural contours of a now pacified, picturesque landscape. The softened contours of masonry reduced to rubble, overgrown by vegetation and devoid of distinct military or cultic function, blend with those of the land itself to erase the memory of conflict.

The picturesque aesthetic of such a rendering of ruins has its counterpart in the image of the land evacuated of inhabitants that recurs with remarkable consistency in an Irish imaginary that is expressly linked to a reconciling historicism. In an aesthetic contemplation of that land—as if it were mere natural landscape rather than a terrain deeply formed by human labor and conflict—historically based antagonisms are laid in abeyance. The irony of such fantasies is not simply that, in seeking to erase the history of conquest and expropriation in which states, polities, and economies are founded, to dissolve it, so to speak, into the landscape, they in fact merely repeat a longstanding settler colonial myth. This attempt to erase history also seeks, though with less evident violence than that of the state apparatus itself, to erase the refractory populations that continually remind us of what cannot be assimilated or reconciled to the state. In such moments, utopian longing reveals its roots in murderous desires. The insistence of the removal of the human figure from the landscape is indicative of a premature redemptiveness that would transform the actual "fallen" world of antagonistic difference and domination into an image of reconciliation, but can only do so by way of a symbolic eviction of unwanted human presences. The fetishism of the "cleared" landscape is the correlative of those declarations of *terra nullius* that are everywhere the alibi of settler colonialism.

The relationship between the land and the human figure is telling. Evacuated of human figures, the land becomes the most effective of symbols, an expanse unmarked by boundaries that nonetheless prefigures a reconciled social totality. Yet, at the same time, it marks the anxious failure of a symbolist discourse that is the aesthetic counterpart of historicism with which, formally and epochally, it has deep relations. Both the romantic tradition of symbolism and the notion of universal history "in which historicism culminates"[4] emerge toward the end of the eighteenth century around a related set of concerns with the development and unification of the human figure. It is no accident that this figure, which is the object of universal history, is also defined as the ultimate symbol, embodying and reconciling particularity and universality, matter and spirit, temporality and eternity. "This is," as Walter Benjamin puts it, "the voice of the will to symbolic totality venerated by humanism in the human figure."[5] The evacuation of the human figure and the positing of unmarked land as the primordial symbol of unity—which is a process which recurs with virtually neurotic consistency in colonial discourses—wins its victory over unreconciled historicity at the expense of betraying its incapacity to accommodate either the difference of humans or the inscription of those differences on the worked and divided landscape.

This recoding of the always-preoccupied land as a *terra nullius* performs an aesthetic naturalization of the catastrophic process of clearance

125

and depopulation that overtook Ireland from the mid-nineteenth century down even to the late twentieth century. Not only starvation but evictions that sought literally to clear the land of what was seen as a redundant population effected this reduction. Between 1845 and 1851, in the course of the Famine, the Irish population fell from around 8.5 million to around 5 million. Perhaps a million and a half people died in the Famine itself, while another two million emigrated to England, the United States, and to Britain's settler colonies. The flow of emigration continued for more than 130 years, with the result that the Irish population remained static at around four million until at least the late 1980s. Such bare and familiar statistics, together with the increasingly conventional appreciation of Ireland as a land of "scant population," natural emptiness, and pastoral wildness, belie the historical violence that underlies them. Neither the subsistence crisis that became the Famine nor the continuing outflow of emigration can be understood apart from the concomitant processes of enclosure, rationalization of capitalist agriculture, and eviction that were prescribed by the linked governmental discourses of political economy and anthropology.[6] The economic and administrative modernization of Ireland was undertaken across this period, and even throughout the post-colonial reaction of the nationalist state, in order to make up post-haste the "time-lag" that Irish cultural difference from Britain had come to represent. From the moment of the Famine itself, when Charles Trevelyan, the treasury secretary in charge of famine relief, declared in 1847 that the crisis had been providential, making way for the emergence of capitalist farming and the proletarianization of the rural poor as wage labor, the reduction of "surplus population" was programmatic. The transformation aimed at the eradication both of the population and of the modes of life and labor that sustained them. The tiny small holdings on which peasant families survived, the "scattered means of production" as Marx describes them in *Capital*, retained certain forms of common ownership and economic reciprocity that were profoundly recalcitrant to capitalist development and had to be destroyed to allow for the concentration of land

and the extraction of surplus value to take place.[7]  Identifying the depopulation of Ireland as continuous with the violence of enclosure and consolidation that had, if at a slower pace, undergirded the processes of primitive accumulation in Britain, Marx recognized the savage relentlessness of this colonial desire to empty the country of its population:

> The fact is that, as the Irish population diminishes, the Irish rent-rolls swell; that depopulation benefits the landlords, therefore also benefits the soil, and , therefore, the people, that mere accessory of the soil. He [Lord Dufferin] declares, therefore, that Ireland is still over-populated and the stream of emigration still flows too lazily.  To be perfectly happy, Ireland must be rid of at least one-third of a million of laboring men...And as l'appétit vient en mangeant, Rentroll's eyes will soon discover that Ireland, with 3 1/2 millions, is still always miserable, and miserable because she is over-populated.  Therefore her depopulation must go yet further, that thus she may fulfill her true destiny, that of an English sheep-walk and cattle-pasture.[8]

The relentlessness of Ireland's deliberate depopulation is an effect of the subjectless logic of capital, and there is no doubt that Marx's sardonic account of primitive accumulation and its motives in Ireland converges in this respect at least with historicism's narrative of modernity: the iron rationality of development, historical and economic, takes on the aspect of a determination without alternatives.  Domination of nature and of the human becomes, as Adorno and Horkheimer suggested, a form of fate as terrible and inevitable as its archaic personification.  Reason devolves into myth as human agency succumbs to impersonal forces.[9]  The idyll of historicism that transforms ruins into picturesque landscape, like the idyllic myths of Marx's bourgeois economists, belies the violence that is its necessary condition. *Et in Arcadia ego*: the ruin is the mythic equivalent of a submission to the fatality of history, a submission that is no doubt the interested celebration by the victor's representatives of the destruction upon which they rise.

Ruins, indeed, have the structure of myth, though not always in the same sense or with the same valence. And they are subject to the paradox of myth. Detached from a given moment of the past, they float free into relation with the present, fragments of an archaic past that continue to work in and on the present. The meaning of a ruin is thus not exhausted by whatever archaeology assigns to it a cause, a function, a date in the recorded time of historicism. Indeed, such an archaeology, as a science of origins, would miss, in its exact reason, the penumbral meanings that accumulate around the ruin that has been incorporated in the landscape, even as it peels back the layers and accretions of contingent time to lay bare the ruin in the purity and abstraction of its pastness. Similarly, the historicist mentality regards the mythic as archaic, as the recurrence of mental processes and attitudes that should have been developed out of culture by reason, and whose recurrence is the power of a baleful return of the past. Such thinking disavows the relationality of the ruin in the present, the form of its living on in the present, with the present. The ruin is that part of a past that lives on to find its place and meaning in a relation with the present, as myth is that element of the meanings of the past that find significance still in the present, if only, though not solely or always, by representing the dimension of loss.

Myth in this sense is not defined by its content, but by its temporal structure. That is, where Adorno and Horkheimer emphasize the anthropomorphic tendency that defines myth for them as against the abstraction of reason, I would stress, against that still historicist division of the mythic (as past and as a relation to the past) from the enlightened, precisely what historicism itself distrusts as myth, its appearance as the rhythmic return of the past in an uneasy haunting of progress by the ghosts of its unfinished business.[10] It is the persistence and insistence of the archaic that reason should have eradicated, exhibiting the tenacity of irrational attachments and the violence of primordial drives.  The putatively archetypal content of the mythic is less significant, however readily invoked, than its unruly capacity to return.  In this, of course, the mythic shares the characteristics of the unconscious to which, on a social and an individual level, it is generally assimilated.  In a certain sense, the content of both is subordinated to the rhythmic opening and closing that allows elements of a past that have been subject to traumatic repression to surface.  It is damaged societies, as it is damaged individuals, that are thought to be driven by the unconscious forces that myth articulates.  Insofar as historicism itself participates in the rationalization that represses the past and reduces its multiple forms to a single, serial narrative, it must perforce envisage the mythic as pathological.  Where myth was, historical time must come, to lay the past to rest and to cure its violence with reason and progress.  The therapeutic drive of historicism, which relates the universal narrative of civility, is thus peculiarly repressive, seeking less to release the past in the unruliness of its ever-present possibilities than to discipline it.

It is in such terms that Ashis Nandy theorizes the relation between myth and history after Gandhi.  Far from representing an entrapment in a primitive and atavistic past, myth performs the constant reinscription of the possibilities contained in a past that is grasped as perpetually present and insistently unclosed.  As against western historicism, with its determinate and singular unfolding of time as progress, myth allows for a continual recurrence of and to the past as a repertoire of redeemable possibilities:

> In Gandhi, the specific orientation to myth became a more general orientation to public consciousness.  Public consciousness was not seen as a casual product of history but as related to history non-causally through memories and anti-memories.  If for the West the present was a special case of an unfolding history, for Gandhi as representative of traditional India

history was a special case of an all-embracing permanent present, waiting to be interpreted and reinterpreted....The idea of "determination" could apply to the present or to the future, as the notorious Indian concept of fatalism implies; in the past there are always open choices....Gandhi implicitly assumed that history of *itihasa* was one-way traffic, a set of myths about past time or the *atit*, built up as independent variables which limit human options and pre-empt human futures. Myths, on the other hand, allow one access to the processes which constitute history at the level of the here-and-now. Consciously acknowledged as the core of culture, they widen instead of restrict human choices. They allow one to remember in an anticipatory fashion and to concentrate on undoing aspects of the present rather than avenging the past.[11]

Myth continues to be active in relation to the present; indeed, it only appears at all in relation to the present. It is not the representative of dark psychic forces by virtue of whose necessary internment civility and rationality can dominate, forces through which the furies of the past return with violent effect, but rather the return of the *present* to its pasts.

Nandy's account of myth suggests that we need to displace the historicist prejudice that what returns from the past is always the not-yet-civilized force that precedes reason and civility, rather than the memory and the potentiality of that which was with violence arrested and put down. The singular and fatal course of history truncates as it proceeds the possible unfoldings of innumerable cultural and social formations, each one of which at some point opened out onto alternative potentials. To say this is not, as in some versions of the appeal to myth, to seek to superordinate any given past as a state that was already utopic, adequate to human desires, but to acknowledge that each cultural formation and moment envisages its own potential for transformation in its own materially available terms. Every culture imagines its own possible transfiguration in ways that cannot be

130

contained by a single historical narrative or canonical path to development. In Adorno and Horkheimer's terms, enlightenment's singular imagination of the transfiguration of human conditions follows the track of a progressive emancipation from nature and from the mythic mentality that is, for enlightenment, the correlative of subordination to the terror of nature. The ecology of enlightenment pits the emancipated human subject against nature, separation from nature being the condition of the latter's domination by human reason and its techniques. Myth, insofar as or wherever it survives, represents the trace of the domination of humans by nature—a domination which, one might say, becomes increasingly internalized as *psychic*: at once the terror of superstition and the terror produced when forces relegated to the unconscious are unleashed in violence. The proper figures for the rational domination of the earth are the systematic enclosure of the land—its rationalization by measure and productive use—and the containment of the wilderness. The rational demarcation of the earth, the division of the humanly appropriated from unworked mere nature, is the condition for the exploitation of its potentials, whereas the mythic mentality fails to establish adequate boundaries between human and nature. And those who, partly human, adhere to myth become, being partly nature, proper objects of domination as the unemancipated remnants of an archaic world.

The state, as the regulative instrument of domination, is the ultimate antagonist of myth. In Ireland, for well over a century, the colonial state sought to extirpate what was at once an alternative ecology and an alternative mentality, alternative forms whose transgressiveness from the perspective of modernity was vividly figured in the glaring absence of proper boundaries. Not only did the rundale system, as a survival of ancient rights of commons, refuse and resist permanent and rationalized boundaries, knowing neither walls nor established hedges, but it also sustained social formations in the *clachan* that defied the norms of property and propriety. The houses themselves appeared as if scarcely emerged from the material of the earth itself and abutted one another in ways that seemed irrational and disorderly, "as though the houses...had fallen 'in a shower from the sky'":

> As a visitor during the famine years wrote: "The villages in which the greater portion of the people [of Western Ireland] reside... consist of collections of hovels...grouped without regularity, formed of clay, or loose stone with green sods stuffed into the interstices."[12]

Miserable as Irish conditions may have appeared to outside observers, the adherence of the people to the forms of life they sustained was, by almost all accounts, tenacious and passionate. Precisely the material conditions that were regarded as irrational and as scarcely emerged from nature sustained not only an alternative ecology apparently unconcerned with extending domination over nature, but also a social ecology that has been characterized by the colloquial term "throughotherness."[13] The word describes both the spatial arrangement of land distribution and of dwellings in close contiguity with one another and the social relations that accompanied them: the mingling of work and pleasure in the rituals of shared labor, the collective culture of story-telling, and the music and dance that the close proximity of unwalled dwellings permitted. Only the catastrophic devastation of the Famine could have so drastically abolished such a culture. What went down in that disaster was not mere "surplus population," that abstraction of a political economy dedicated to transforming the peasantry into units of proletarian waged labor, but a concrete mode of life that stood in sharp antagonism to capitalist modernization.

Perhaps fittingly, then, the ruins that are the traces of that violently curtailed way of life are not the monumental forms of tower and fortress that still in places dominate the landscape, but scarcely more than ridges intersecting the pattern of more recently walled fields, merging with the contours of the surrounding land as discretely as formerly they emerged from it. In the very ambiguity of the threshold they mark between human artifice and natural form, they memorialize the alternative ecology of a non-capitalist mode of life. Nothing utopian in itself, the product of centuries of dispossession and difficult survival, that mode of life looked towards another transfiguration than its violent reduction in the long and continuing process of primitive accumulation. The ruins that encrypt the unexhausted potentiality of a damaged form of life, as in places they literally encrypt the corpses of the famine dead on which cottages were collapsed as mass graves, speak as myth speaks to the indeterminate relation of the past to the present, to the pained and painful defiance of domination that accompanies survival in the no less damaged forms of the present. The relation of the ruin to the past, in the very dereliction that refuses to be subdued in an historicist picturesque but resonates with the continuing ruination of the present, is one in which lament and possibility are constellated, in which natural decay and human memory redeem and efface by turns.

That the ruin might embody the passage between lament and possibility, representing not the fixity of the past as past but the very opening of the past with the present by way of their mutual and unclosed damage, is a principle at work in the contemporary Irish artist Alanna O'Kelly's haunting visual "keen" or lament for the Famine and the dispossessed, "No Colouring Can Deepen the Darkness of Truth."[14] The work consists of slowly metamorphosing images and sounds, some human, some natural, that merge with and emerge from one another cyclically, threaded through by images of swirling, flowing water. Juxtaposed with and echoing the forms of a woman's breast expressing a cloud-like milk into the water that surrounds it is the mound of the Teampall Dumhac Mhor, the great sand chapel, an ancient church built on a pile of stone on the Mayo shore, that centuries later became the site of a mass famine grave that was eventually washed away by the storms and tides in 1993. [fig. 1] The formal echo of these merging images composes a constellation of cryptic histories and recurrences in

Alanna O'Kelly, *Teampall Dumhach Mhór*, photograph (fig. 1, top), and video still (fig. 2, below), from *No Colouring Can Deepen the Darkness of Truth*, from the series *"The Country Blooms...A Garden and a Grave."* 1992-1995

which human images and shifting natural forms dissolve one another's boundaries just as, on the soundtrack, the human keening voice flows in and out of the sound of a whale's song. The installation composes a lament for the dispossessed that is at the same time a recuperative refusal of the rationale that justified their displacement by modernity. Simultaneously, the boundaries between human and natural objects and between apparently irretrievable pasts and the living on that is their survival dissolve and fade. In the midst of the series of gradual, almost painful metamorphoses that compose the video work, an image emerges that looks at first like an aerial picture of furrows in dark clay, only to reveal itself as that of fingers caked in thick mud, presumably as a consequence of long laboring in the earth. [fig. 2] The fingers seem at once organic, resembling first furrows or scaly, dark roots, and painfully, compassionately human in their vulnerability and dereliction. The human body, in its life and its labor, becomes itself the ruin that embodies simultaneously a pained lament for the losses that compose the past and the mythic image of an alternative possibility opened by the refusal to hold apart mourning and transfiguration. Across the work as a whole, the rhythmic process of metamorphosis, through which each of the images, human and material, flows in slow motion into the next, suggests the potentiality of a relation of the human subject to its past and to the natural world that defies an ecology of domination. The lament for the Famine dead refuses any elegiac adjustment to the violence of history, insisting rather on the ethical, no less than political, demand for a commemoration of past loss that refuses here and now the forms of domination that shape the ruins of the present.

Eduardo Cadava

My recall is nearly perfect, time has faded nothing. I recall the very first kidnap. I've lived through the passage, died on the passage, lain in the unmarked, shallow graves of the millions who fertilized the Amerikan soil with their corpses; cotton and corn growing out of my chest, "unto the third and fourth generation," the tenth, the hundredth.

—George Jackson, *Soledad Brother* (1970)[1]

How is it that the dead speak? How is it that the dispossessed can tell their stories? How is it that the past survives in the present and informs the future, silently, but without pacifying or silencing a single torment, or a single torture? What can memory be when it seeks to remember the trauma of captivity, loss, and displacement? What makes someone choose death over living? In what way does death leave behind a decomposing trace that, turning into earth at the time of death, gives meaning to the memory, the violence, the wounds, the protests, the cries of anger or suffering, the several death sentences on which a nation—America, for example—has been founded?

How can an event that takes place only in its passage, only in its decomposition, leave something behind that, guarding a trace of itself, inaugurates, and even composes, a history—in this instance, a history of dispossession and diaspora, a history without which the history of America could never be written? The very moment there is death, the very moment slavery exists, the very moment populations are removed and exterminated, wealth and rights are distributed unequally, acts of discrimination are committed in the name of democracy and freedom, America finds itself in mourning, and what it mourns is America itself.

This mourning begins, Jackson suggests, with "the very first kidnap." Identifying himself with the millions lost in the passage and the fifteen million and more captured and enslaved in the Americas—we should not forget that he is in prison as he writes, that he is, as he puts it, living a kind of death, as if he were in the hold of a ship—Jackson transforms the space of his captivity into a space haunted by the ghosts of a broken and painful past. Remembering the wounds of history, the violent displacements effected by the transatlantic crossing of black captives and reinforced by the ensuing processes of exploitation and enslavement, he bears witness to a consciousness of dissociation that, acting as a mode of testimony and memory, registers the violence of the historical processes he describes.[2] The stakes of the past are experienced in terms of death and mourning. Jackson's act of memory endlessly reenacts this condition of loss and displacement—"'unto the third and fourth generation,' the tenth, the hundredth"—not in order to overcome captivity or facilitate survival, but to reenact the story of slavery, to embody the death and mourning that makes America America. Without the recognition of this loss, he seems to suggest, we could never respond to the historical caesura introduced by slavery. What is at stake here is a body that bears the traces of what it undergoes, the trace of its decomposition but also its loss of citizenship and rights, its transformation into commodities and capital, and its inscription within an exploitative economic system of international dimensions.

What is at stake is also a mode of language that would remain faithful to the traces and history of this body, that would give body, make tangible, what it wishes us to understand. This strategy can be read in the way in which Jackson enacts his sense of dispossession and displacement by dispersing his voice across several voices, by sundering the singularity of the historical moment in which he is writing. The voice he stages—the voice of the "I" who has "nearly perfect" recall, but also the "I" who has "lived through the passage, died in the passage, lain in the unmarked, shallow graves of the millions who fertilized the Amerikan soil with their corpses"— belongs simultaneously to the past, the present, and the future. It is the voice of a living ghost, or, more precisely, the living voice of several ghosts. The movement of the passage reinforces this ghostly survival of the past in the present and future since, as is so often the case in black diasporic writing, everything in it proceeds by citation—and not only when it cites a fragment of the biblical refrain—"unto the third and fourth generation"—that appears repeatedly in the five books of Moses. Nevertheless, by alluding to the story of Exodus, Jackson evokes the biblical story most central to the lives of his dispossessed and enslaved brethren. The appropriation of the Exodus story became a means for African Americans to articulate their sense of historical identity as a people. Identifying the story of the bondage and slavery of the Israelites with their own servitude, they drew from the story the hope that they, too, would be delivered to freedom.

This helps explain why, if Jackson evokes the centrality of the Exodus story within the history of enslavement and violence to which he refers, he does so not only to direct us to a significant, neuralgic point in the shared history and social memory of black religious discourse—a history and memory that belong to his inheritance—but also, in particular, to remind us that the refrain he cites belongs to the curse that God declares he will impose on *the guilty*—who will not be cleared of their transgressions and sins and who will have the "iniquity of the fathers" visited "upon the children and the children's children, unto the third and fourth generation." Jackson's use of the refrain therefore points, from his perspective, to the irony of God's curse: that the sins of *the guilty*—the sins of the slaveholders, for example, and not the sins for which he has been *declared* "guilty"—are visited on the damned of the earth. In other words, Jackson suggests that the suffering and death experienced by the violated bodies and minds of dispossessed populations is visited upon them by men and not God, by the greed and lust of men and not the jealousy or anger of God, by racist and capitalist policies and not heavenly dictates. If these oppressed minority populations are "chosen," it is not by God, but rather, as in this case, by an America that seeks to flourish over the fertilizer that these minorities will have become, over the death and mourning that defines their experience.

If we can take Jackson's passage as evidence of what would be required for us to speak in the name of freedom—there is little doubt that the passage belongs to his efforts throughout his prison letters to define the nature and conditions of freedom—what it tells us is that, in order to speak in the name of freedom, in the name of justice, we must speak of the past we inherit and for which we remain answerable, we must speak of ghosts, of generations of ghosts—of those who are not presently living, whether they are already dead or not yet born.[3] We must speak of the victims of political, nationalist, racist, colonialist and capitalist violence, or of any of the other forms of oppression and extermination that we still today have not overcome. We must engage in a politics of memory that is also a politics of the future. This memory and this future, in order to be just, in order to be worthy of their names, would emerge from a respect for the dead, and perhaps especially for the living dead. Together, this memory and this future would name an obligation: remember the dead, keep the memory of the dead alive, think your relation to a past that, never behind you, haunts you, tells you for what you are answerable.

Why begin this way? For at least three reasons. While these memories from a singular moment in our history may seem discreet, distant, even gnomic, many paths cross there, the relations among an entire network

140

of motifs: slavery, destiny, fate, violence, racism, colonialism, subjectivity, memory, history, rights, language, death, mourning, and so forth—all of which raise fundamental questions about who we are in relation to what we call "America." If this beginning imposes itself, then, it is not in order to begin an analysis of a singular political writer—here the Black Panther Field Marshall and founder of the People's Army, George Jackson—but rather to begin to expose something essential to our history that goes beyond his particularity, that gives us to our history. Jackson's assassination in San Quentin Prison on August 21, 1971 sealed the fame he already had achieved with the publication of *Soledad Brother* one year earlier and ensured that this hero of the movement against black oppression and American imperialism would become a canonical figure for various movements of resistance, for the often violent struggles for freedom and justice both inside and outside America—resistances and struggles that, as Jackson well knew, belong to the long history of efforts to actualize equality, to realize, that is, the promise of the right to representation for everyone, the promise of an America that to this day still does not exist—which is why it must always be mourned. It is toward this experience of mourning that Jackson's writings are oriented. If, as Jean Genet wrote in 1986, the Panthers were "haunted by the idea of death,"[4] Jackson argues that this hauntedness delineates the contours and conditions of ethical and political gestures that, organized around extended acts of mourning, can be joined to moments of affirmation, even if such affirmation is linked to a critical insistence on death and mourning.

Second, in order to begin to evoke and lay out the terms of what the work of Emerson compels us to think, especially as it engages the world of which his work is such an important articulation—a world which bore witness to vast capitalist development, to the rise of various secondary institutions (such as schools, asylums, factories, and plantations), rapid urbanization and industrialization, a growing inequality in the distribution of wealth, and several modes of displacement and extermination—a world in which debates over the nature of war, revolution, race, slavery, liberty, democracy, and representation were of crucial importance in America's effort to invent its national and cultural identity. Emerson's engagement with the changing historical and political relations of this world, with a process of transformation wherein his language works to change further the shifting domains of history and politics, and wherein the traces of the historical and the political are inscribed within the movement of his language, remains, I think, a model for us, not only for thinking the relation between political gestures and the language without which they would never take place but also for responding to the demand that we become answerable for our future by, among so many other things, confronting the ways in which the past lives on in the present. Emerson's turn toward the past, his turn toward the loss, death, and mourning that characterize our experience, becomes the condition for his conviction—a conviction I believe he shares with Jackson— that, in transforming the language he inherits, he can perhaps change much more than language, he can perhaps work to transform the relations within which we live, he can perhaps, in spite of the impossibility of ever securing freedom and justice, delineate the experience of freedom and justice as a *praxis* of thought that begins from the presupposition that we are always, in advance, related to others. I emphasize this last point because, as we will see, a call to rethink the concepts of freedom and justice traverses his work. We might even say that Emerson's works are nothing but the very trial of these two concepts.

Third, in order to respond to a passage, to the dictates of a passage that is haunted both by the memory of the dispossessed over whose deaths America grows and expands and by its relation to the entirety of the history that is encrypted within the passage from Jackson with which I began. The passage can be found in Emerson's essay, "Fate," an essay that, although not published until 1860, had its beginnings in the months immediately following the passing of the Fugitive Slave Law in 1850, and in the context of heated debates over the question of slavery and the slave trade, the admission of territories into the union with or without slaves, the unfolding of the ideas of manifest destiny and racial difference, the removal and extermination of the native population, the expansion of the American empire into the Pacific and the Caribbean, and emancipation and secession. As such, "Fate" is perhaps Emerson's most profound and searching engagement of the idea of manifest destiny in terms of questions of race, his most moving effort to provide a kind of secret genealogy of what makes racism and slavery possible. Perhaps Emerson's principle statement about the conditions and possibilities of human freedom and justice, the essay seeks to convey to us the reasons why, already in antebellum America, three or four generations before Jackson's publication of his prison letters in 1970, everything is haunted by death, oriented around death, and especially around the death encrypted within the American landscape. Indeed, in the closing lines of the passage to which I refer, Emerson tells us that "the German and Irish millions, like the Negro, have a great deal of guano in their destiny. They are ferried over the Atlantic, and carted over America, to ditch and to drudge, to make corn cheap, and then to lie down prematurely to make a spot of green grass on the prairie."[5] Once these few lines are contextualized within the historical moment in which they were written, and within the essay to which they belong—both of which refer to the violent history of American colonization and imperialism—they put before us the violence, the inequality, the economic oppression and colonialist and racist exclusions that affected—and continue to affect—so many human beings in the history of not only America but of the earth. Emerson here reminds us that instead of celebrating the ideals of liberal democracy and of the capitalist market in an affirmation of America's expansionist desires, we should never neglect this manifest fact, composed of innumerable instances of suffering and death—a fact that was true in Emerson's time, but is even more true today: never before have so many men, women, and children been subjugated or exterminated on earth, never have so many human beings, that is, been transformed into guano. It is here that Emerson and Jackson join forces, as they suggest that any meditation on freedom and justice, any action taken in the name of these two experiences, should take its point of departure from this mournful and deadly fact.

If I have begun this way, then, it is because I have wanted to suggest that there is a way in which, before us, in advance of us, Jackson already will have read Emerson's essay, "Fate," even if his eyes never once cast their glance on even one of its pages. He will have taught us how to read Emerson, how to understand the reasons why, like him, Emerson is perhaps one of America's greatest mourners, which is to say one of its most significant and aggressive defenders. In asking us to remember the dead, to engage an inheritance that, even today, belongs to what we still call our future, Jackson and Emerson demonstrate that there can be no thought of the future, no experience of hope, which is not at the same time an engagement with the question "How shall we conduct our life?" We can only begin to answer this question, they suggest, by learning to read historically, by learning to mourn, by exposing ourselves to the vicissitudes of a history in which we are inscribed and to which we remain urgently and dangerously responsible because it is we who are at stake.

I begin again, this time with Emerson, although, as Jackson reminds us, time has perhaps faded nothing.

Emerson opens his essay, "Fate," by noting the chances, the coincidences, that have led to several discussions in Boston, New York, London, and elsewhere, on the theory of the age or the spirit of the times. For him, however, "the question of the times resolved itself into a practical question of the conduct of life. How shall I live? We are incompetent to solve the times. Our geometry cannot span the huge orbits of the prevailing ideas, behold their return, and reconcile their opposition. We can only obey our own polarity. 'Tis fine for us to speculate and elect our course, if we must accept an irresistible dictation" (*W*, VI: 3). As Stanley Cavell has rightly suggested, the question of the times is here the question of slavery.[6] What has yet to be noted, however, is the extent to which Emerson's essay is really less a challenge of the institution of slavery—although it is this, too—than an attempt to engage and make manifest the "huge orbits of prevailing ideas" without which this institution could never exist. In particular, it is an essay about the idea of fate that prevailed in mid-nineteenth-century America— American "manifest destiny"—and all the discursive and material means whereby this concept was supported, maintained, and mobilized in order to sustain slavery. Emerson explicitly points to the role of the idea of fate in the justification of slavery in a journal entry from 1852 entitled "*Abolition.*" There, he writes: "*Abolition.* The argument of the slaveholder is one & simple: he pleads Fate. Here is an inferior race requiring wardship, —it is sentimentality to deny it. The argument of the abolitionist is, it is inhuman to treat a man thus."[7] What Emerson seeks to alert us to in this passage but also within his essay is the way in which fate (whether it appears as "manifest destiny," "providence," "natural law," or "predestination," to name only a few of the terms under which this ideologeme was circulated) served to inform and shape a racial ideology that could be used to describe and hierarchize the world's peoples. "Fate" therefore seeks to delineate the conditions under which—given the uncertainty with which we must struggle with the past in order to give the future a chance, with prevailing ideas, for example, that irresistibly move us, as if by a kind of dictation, in the direction of slavery—we may experience freedom—a freedom from fate, perhaps, but even so, a freedom that, taking its point of departure from the transit between the past and the future within which something new is produced, passes through what it inherits in order to invent its future.

Viewing "fate"—in a first sense—as another name for limitation, as another name for what limits us, Emerson directs his writing against not only the rhetoric of unlimited privilege and expansion that informs the idea of manifest destiny but also the blindness of such rhetoric to the death, the violence, and the injury it precipitates. "Let us honestly state the facts," Emerson writes, "Our America has a bad name for superficialness. Great men, great nations have not been boasters and buffoons, but perceivers of the terror of life" (*W*, VI: 5). Providing us with a list of the disasters and catastrophes—diseases, the elements, earthquakes, and all manner of accidents—that so often remind us of our finitude and mortality, he then proceeds to hint at the disasters and catastrophes that are of our own violent making. "The way of Providence is a little rude," he tells us, "The habit of snake and spider, the snap of the tiger and other leapers and bloody jumpers, the crackle of the bones of his prey in the coil of the anaconda— these are in the system, and our habits are like theirs. You have just dined, and however scrupulously the slaughter-house is concealed in the graceful distance of miles, there is complicity,—expensive races,—race living at the expense of race" (W, VI: 7). This passage about human carniverousness, and the gracefulness with which its conditions are concealed from itself, is, in Cavell's words, "a parable about the cannibalism, as it were, in living gracefully off other *human* races."[8] Emerson already had made this point in his 1844 address on the tenth anniversary of the emancipation of the British West Indies. Anticipating the figure of the slaughterhouse he will later use in "Fate," he writes: "From the earliest moments it appears that one race was victim and served the other races. From the earliest time, the negro has been an article of luxury to the commercial nations. So has it been, down to the day that has just dawned on the world. Language must be raked, the secrets of slaughter-houses and infamous holes that cannot front the day, must be ransacked, to tell what negro-slavery has been."[9] This is why so much of Emerson's effort in "Fate" is directed at evoking and analyzing this language. As is so often the case, however, this work of analysis can be read more easily in the *practice* of Emerson's writing, in its staging and treatment of the rhetoric of manifest destiny, race, and slavery, than in any explicit and straightforward arguments. This perhaps is also why, in an essay that is throughout concerned with all the violence committed in the name of America's "manifest destiny," Emerson takes the remarkable risk of never once using the term "manifest destiny." Suggesting in this way that there is nothing manifest about "manifest destiny"—nothing natural or obvious about it—he instead seeks to exhibit what are for him its as yet "unpenetrated" causes, the various arguments that, made in its name, make it possible.

The term "manifest destiny" was first coined by the editor of the *Democratic Review*, John O'Sullivan, in an 1845 essay arguing for the annexation of Texas. Simply entitled "Annexation," the essay predicted "the fulfillment of our manifest destiny to overspread the continent allotted by Providence for the free development of our yearly multiplying millions."[10] But the idea of the providential character of America's expansionism was scarcely new. Not only did it rely on arguments drawn from both Puritan claims for the preordained, divine purpose of their mission and Calvinist conceptions of predestination, but O'Sullivan himself already had written of America's "boundless futures" in his 1839 essay, "The Great Nation of Futurity."[11] The extension of American boundaries, he suggested, would secure the extension of democracy, or, as Andrew Jackson had put it in his justification for Indian removal, the extension of the "area of freedom." As Emerson reminds us, however, these arguments—motivated by what he once referred to as the Anglo-Saxon's "Earth-hunger," his "love of possessing land" (*W*, 12: 135)—only ensured the deadly fact that the territorial and economic expansion of the United States would be achieved at the expense of Native Americans and other minority communities. In his 1856 speech on the Kansas-Nebraska act, describing the way in which proponents of American "manifest destiny" disguise cruelty with euphemism, he writes: "Language has lost its meaning in the universal cant. *Representative Government* is really misrespresentative;...*the adding of Cuba and Central America* to the slave marts *is enlarging the area of Freedom. Manifest Destiny, Democracy, Freedom*, fine names for an ugly thing. They call it otto of rose and lavender,—I call it bilge water. It is called Chivalry and Freedom; I call it the taking of all the earnings of a poor man and the earnings of his little girl and boy, and the earnings of all that shall come from his, his children's children forever" (*AS*, 113-14).

The resulting cruelty and violence of such language was naturalized, however, by arguments that, gaining their strength from closely related Enlightenment ideas of progress, suggested, in the wording of Eric Sundquist, "that the exploration of foreign lands and the conversion of alien peoples through political and economic expansion took place according to organic laws of growth." Within the context of such arguments, the narrative of "a relentless conquest in which the march of one civilization destroyed or utterly changed many others through dispossession and absorption" was supported by what Sundquist goes on to call a "political and cultural medium in which conquest could be naturalized, or set within a panoramic elaboration of predestined history."[12] In many respects, Emerson's discussions of race and manifest destiny during the 1840s and 50s should be understood as his analysis of this medium—a medium that, including all the discourses of scientific racism, physiognomy, geology, ethnology, and evolution that worked together to consolidate the racial privilege and hegemony of white America, belongs to Emerson's inheritance. Emerson's analysis here follows not only the political implications of his antislavery discourse but also his attempt to measure and limit determinist explanations for human achievement. Emerson's essay "Fate" is in fact a kind of anthology of all the various determinisms at work in mid-nineteenth century debates over the relations among the races. Arguing in the essay that "a good deal of our politics is physiological," Emerson ventriloquizes nearly every scientific explanation for racial difference available to him. The entire essay can be read as an evocation and analysis of the various kinds of discourses that have throughout history—but especially throughout the eighteenth and nineteenth centuries—worked to enable one race to live, as Emerson tells us, "at the expense of other races," at the expense, that is, of what he elsewhere calls "the guano-races of mankind."[13]

The emergence of ethnology by the late 1840s as a recognized science of racial differences, for example, presumably offered scientific validation of black inferiority and thereby reinforced the claims of southern slavery. "The mission of Ethnology," as one southern writer declared, "is to vindicate the great truths on which the institutions of the South are founded."[14]  Following the scientific ethnology of Samuel Morton's *Crania Americana* (1839) and *Crania Aegyptiaca* (1844)—works that sought to define mental capacity in terms of skull size and shape—the Alabama physician Josiah Nott notoriously defended and promoted polygenesis. Basing his claims on a wide range of biblical and ethnographic materials, he argued that, because the races had different origins and different degrees of development, they could be classified and hierarchized according to their general capacities. "Dr. S. G. Morton," he wrote in 1849, "by a long series of well-conceived experiments, has established the fact, that the capacity of the crania of the Mongol, Indian, and Negro, and all dark-skinned races, is smaller than that of the pure white man."[15]  As he explained five years later in the *Types of Mankind*—a book he co-wrote with the Egyptologist George R. Gliddon and which sought to justify the enslavement and eventual extinction of nonwhite peoples—the Caucasian races were fulfilling a law of nature. They were as "destined eventually to conquer and hold every foot of the globe," he argued, as the inferior races were destined to extinction: "Nations and races, like individuals, have each a special destiny: some are born to rule, and others to be ruled....No two distinctly marked races can dwell together on equal terms. Some races, moreover, appear destined to live and prosper for a time, until the destroying race comes, which is to exterminate and supplant them."[16]  Or, as he put it in his introduction to the book, "Human progress has arisen mainly from the war of the races. All the great impulses which have been given to it from time to time have been the results of conquests and colonizations."[17]  Considered natural or organic, expansion and enslavement were justified by claims that they guaranteed freedom and independence, encouraged the development and regeneration of resources and land, and confirmed a fated and future-oriented historical process that could be supported by scientific models of racial difference.

Emerson's most remarkable passage in "Fate" about the deterministic languages with which slavery was justified—a passage that encrypts the entire history of the rhetoric of American colonization and imperialism, that seeks to provide a genealogy of the rhetoric that served to justify the living of one race at the expense of another—occurs soon after he refers to the role of physiology in American politics and history. I cite the passage in its entirety:

> The book of nature is the book of Fate. She turns the gigantic pages,—leaf after leaf,—never re-turning one. One leaf she lays down, a floor of granite; then a thousand ages, and a bed of slate; a thousand ages, and a measure of coal; a thousand ages, and a layer of marl and mud: vegetable forms appear; her first misshapen animals, zoophyte, trilobium, fish; then saurians,— rude forms, in which she has only blocked her future statue, concealing under these unwieldy monsters the fine type of her coming king. The face of the planet cools and dries, the races meliorate, and man is born. But when a race has lived its term, it comes no more again.
>
> The population of the world is a conditional population; not the best, but the best that could live now; and the scale of tribes, and the steadiness with which victory adheres to one tribe, and defeat to another, is as uniform as the superposition of strata. We know in history what weight belongs to race. We see the English, French, and Germans planting themselves on every shore and market of America and Australia, and monopolizing the commerce of these countries. We like the nervous and victorious habit of our own branch of the family. We follow the step of the Jew, of the Indian, of the Negro. We see how much will has been expended to extinguish the Jew, in vain. Look at the unpalatable conclusions of Knox, in his "Fragment of Races,"—a rash and unsatisfactory writer, but charged with pungent and unforgettable truths. "Nature respects race, and not hybrids." "Every race has its own *habitat*." "Detach a colony from the race, and it

deteriorates to the crab." See the shades of the picture. The German and Irish millions, like the Negro, have a great deal of guano in their destiny. They are ferried over the Atlantic, and carted over America, to ditch and to drudge, to make corn cheap, and then to lie down prematurely to make a spot of green grass on the prairie. (*W*, VI: 15-17)

There would be much to say about this passage, but here I only wish to signal four indices of the contexts in which it should be read, and to which I believe it responds.

First, Emerson's passage, with its innumerable layers and strata, comes to us in the form of the very geological strata of which he is writing. Like the earth that bears the traces of the entirety of its history, Emerson's language inscribes, within its very movement, the traces of all the texts that have informed his own. As such, it demands that we rake his language, that we reckon with it in order to see how it often ventriloquizes language that has been used to justify what, for him, goes in the direction of the worst, in the direction, that is, of the sentences that close this passage. The link between geology and language was pervasive during Emerson's day and we need only recall his claims in "The Poet" that "language is fossil poetry" or that "as the limestone of the continent consists of infinite masses of the shells of animalcules, so language is made up of images or tropes, which now, in their secondary use, have long ceased to remind us of their poetic origin" (*W*, III: 22) or Whitman's claim that "the science of language has large and close analogies in geological science, with its ceaseless evolution, its fossils, and its numberless submerged layers and hidden strata, the infinite go-before of the present."[18]

Second, Emerson's effort to relate the history of natural, geological processes to the theory of the evolution of man borrows its terms and figures from his readings in the geological sciences—readings that included the writings of, among others, Buffon, George Cuvier, Charles Lyell, and Robert Chambers.[19] For Emerson, in bringing together time and space, geology seeks to make the past legible to the observer. Borrowing a figure from Chambers' *Vestiges of the Natural History of Creation*, he goes on to suggest that geological layers are "leaves of the *Stone Book*."[20] He extends the metaphor even further when he describes Cuvier studying before a broken mountainside: "In the rough ledges, the different shades and superposition of the strata, his eye is reading as in a book the history of the globe."[21] If the book of Nature is the book of Fate, then, it is because the history of the processes of nature is also a study of the irresistible processes that have led to the emergence of man.

But, if present geological formations can be explained by studying the history of geological transformations, the study of previous changes in the earth also predicts the succession of deaths that, for Emerson, composes the movement of history itself. "Every science is the record or account of the dissolution of the objects it considers," he writes, "All history is an epitaph. All life is a progress toward death. The [sun] world but a large Urn. The sun in his bright path thro' Ecliptic but a funereal triumph...for it lights men & animals & plants to their graves" (*J*, III: 219-220). To say that human history belongs to the history of nature, then, is to say that human history is a history of death, or, more precisely, a history of the life and death of innumerable generations, all of whom have left their traces in the earth's strata. The lessons of geology are the lessons of one species or race succeeding or surviving another. As John Harris writes in his 1850 *The Pre-Adamite Earth*, referring to the time required to produce the earth's sedimentations and strata: "How countless the ages necessary for their accumulation, when the formation of only a few inches of the strata required the life and death of many generations. Here the mind is not merely carried back, through innumerable periods, but, while studying amidst the petrified remains of this succession of primeval forests and extinct races of animals, piled up into sepulchral mountains, we seem to be encompassed by the thickest shadow of the valley of death." Referring to geological strata as

152

"monuments" or "platforms of death," he confirms Lyell's sense of the endless mutations and fluctuations that, characterizing both the organic and inorganic worlds, help account for the sudden extinction of whole organic creations, and the introduction of others.[22]  These "catacombs" or "charnel-houses," "crowded with organic structures which lived and died where they are now seen; and which, consequently, must have perished by some destructive agency, too sudden to allow of their dispersion," bear the traces of "the thousands, not of generations, but of species, of races...which have all run through their ages of existence and ceased."[23]  This is why, as Thoreau would put it, the world is to be considered a vast compost heap. The hieroglyphic of nature, he writes, "is somewhat excrementitious in its character, and there is no end to the heaps of liver, lights and bowels, as if the globe were turned wrong side outward; but this suggests at least that Nature has some bowels, and there again is mother of humanity."[24]

Third, in linking the rhetoric of a natural development that gives birth to man to the related processes of colonization and capitalism, Emerson alerts us to the rhetoric with which, as I already have suggested, the violent colonization and appropriation of land and peoples for political and economic reasons often was justified.  This history of conquest and colonization, it was argued—in which "victory adheres to one tribe, and defeat to another," in which "the English, French, and Germans" could plant themselves "on every shore and market of America and Australia" and monopolize their commerce—was as natural as the successive superposition of one geological stratum upon another.  As Lyell himself notes, in a passage from The Principles of Geology that Emerson may very well have had in mind here, "When a powerful European colony lands on the shores of Australia, and introduces at once those arts which it has required many centuries to mature; when it imports a multitude of plants and large animals from the opposite extremity of the earth, and begins rapidly to extirpate many of the indigenous species, a mightier revolution is effected in a brief period, than the first entrance of a savage horde, or their continued occupation of the country for many centuries, can possibly be imagined to have produced."[25] Having pointed to this process of dispossession, however, Lyell goes on to emphasize that it belongs to the economy of nature:

> The successive destruction of species must now be part of the regular and constant order of Nature....We have only to reflect, that in thus obtaining possession of the earth by conquest, and defending our acquisitions by force, we exercise no exclusive prerogative. Every species which has spread itself from a small point over a wide area, must, in like manner, have marked its progress by the dimunition, or the entire extirpation, of some other, and must maintain its ground by a successful struggle against the encroachments of other plants and animals....The most insignificant and diminutive species, whether in the animal or vegetable kingdom, have each slaughtered their thousands, as they disseminated themselves over the globe.[26]

Associating the violence of colonization, possession, and extermination with the progress of nature, Lyell's rhetoric here resonates with the justifications that so often gave voice to American manifest destiny. Emerson reinforces this point by describing the processes of colonization and possession as a kind of "planting." As Patricia Seed has argued, "The action of the colonists in the New World was planting; the colonists were metaphorically plants in relation to the soil, and hence their colonial settlements were referred to as plantations. Thus, when the English most commonly referred to their colonies in the New World as plantations, they were referring to themselves metaphorically as taking possession."[27] This metaphor often was literalized by one of the rituals whereby new lands were claimed: in addition to building houses and fences, settlers would assert their occupation and possession by cultivating and, in particular, fertilizing the land. Indeed, as Seed reminds us, the verb to manure in sixteenth-century England meant, among other things, "to own."[28] What is at stake for Emerson, then, is an understanding of the ways in which violence and dispossession—and the death that comes from them—are disguised by acts of naturalization. If he identifies America with these processes of dispossession (he tells us that America belongs to the same family of colonizers), the nervousness of its "victorious habit" lies in its recognition—acknowledged or not—that its drive for territorial acquisition, along with the enslavement and death this drive produces, betrays the promises of freedom and independence on which it was founded.

Fourth, Emerson's final lines should be read in relation to the context of the importation of guano into America in the 1840s and 50s—both as a fertilizing resource and as a metaphor—a context that Emerson understood to belong to the history of American colonization and imperialism. As James Skaggs has noted, "declining agricultural productivity in the United States prior to the Civil War led to an ever-increasing demand for fertilizers." "In middle and southern states such as Maryland and Virginia," he goes on to explain, "farmers (growing crops such as tobacco and cotton, both of which are especially hard on the land) faced bleak futures as soil exhaustion became increasingly pronounced."[29] In response to this exhaustion—the result of several factors, including climate, erosion, the removal of organic matter and nutrients, soil toxicity, destructive methods of cultivation, and a market that focused almost entirely on tobacco and cotton[30]—agricultural journals such as the *American Farmer*, the *New England Farmer*, *De Bow's Review, The Southern Planter,* and *The Southern Agriculturalist* urged crop diversification and rotation, along with the application of fertilizers. The demand for fertilizer was partially filled by various artificial manures, but especially by Peruvian guano. The best guano came from the Chincha Islands, just twelve miles from the coast of Peru, in the bay of Pisco. Since the islands received very little rainfall, the naturally high nitrogen content of the guano remained undiluted in a pungent, brownish-yellow concretion that was also very rich in phosphate. In some of the ravines of the islands, it was said to be nearly 300 feet deep and some speculated that it must have begun to accumulate there soon after the biblical flood.

At war with Bolivia in the late 1830s and experiencing several civil wars in the early 1840s, Peru found its economy shattered and, in order to reduce its enormous war debt, it began to negotiate with foreign companies for the selling of its guano. In 1841, Peru's President, Manuel Menéndez, formally nationalized the country's guano resources and, for the next thirty-five years, the Peruvian government would earn most of its foreign revenues from selling guano to other countries. In 1842, the London firm, Anthony Gibbs & Sons, shared a monopoly on exports for five years and, in 1847, gained sole control of British and North American markets. By 1846, Peru had received more than $1.3 million in guano advances and by the 1860s seabirds supplied more than 75% of the government's revenues. Exact figures for the first few years of what Lewis Gray has called the "guano mania" in the United States are not available because the Department of Treasury did not begin gathering import data on the commodity until 1847.[31] However, estimates suggest that between 1844 and 1851 approximately 66,000 tons per year (valued at $2.6 million, at an average price of $49 a ton) entered the United States, mostly through Baltimore and New York. In 1851, the importation of guano into North America was consigned to the Peruvian firm Felipe Barreda and Brother and, by the late 1850s, over 400,000 tons per year were coming in at $55 a ton. The first commercial fertilizer used to any significant extent in the United States, guano was advertised as a fertilizer that would help regenerate the American landscape. Horticultural journals of the period were filled with testimonials, chemical analyses, directions for its use, state-by-state statistics on its success with crops from tobacco and cotton to wheat, corn, oats, peas, potatoes, melons, asparagus, and so forth. It was repeatedly said to be more valuable than all the gold mines in California and it was regarded, in the wording of one southern farmer, "a blessing to the nation." In the mid-1850s, presumably citing a minister about to pray for the fertility of a Massachusetts farm, Emerson suggests that America's land "does not want a prayer, [it] wants manure" (*J*, XIV: 171).

High prices, however, encouraged searches for substitutes and even encouraged fraud. By 1854, several varieties of guano had been imported from Africa, Central America, the Caribbean, and assorted Pacific islands, but, according to one contemporary U.S. government study, "they were either found to be worthless or far inferior in quality" to those of Peru. Dishonest businessmen also labeled several different products as pure Peruvian in order to defraud farmers and prospective clients. There was even a thriving underground market for used Peruvian guano bags—bags with the Peruvian government stamp—that some unscrupulous dealers refilled with spurious guano and sold as genuine guano. As Skaggs notes, "such practices were so prevalent by 1846 that Maryland legislature mandated oversight of all guano sold in its jurisdiction, a charge of forty cents per ton being tacked onto the retail price by the state's 'guano inspector,' William S. Reese, who officially inspected every sack at the port of Baltimore and issued grade stamps."[32] A test was soon devised so that prospective buyers could decide in advance whether or not the guano they were about to purchase was genuine or not, genuine meaning that it came from Peru and not, say, Africa. The buyer would place a small sample of the guano on a hot iron shovel. If the guano was genuine, it would leave behind a pearly white ash and, if it was fraudulent, a colored ash.[33]

Many farmers and legislators soon argued, however, that the only way to overcome these difficulties, to make sure that Peruvian guano was available to everyone, was to challenge the Gibbs monopoly. The United States made several efforts to persuade the Peruvian government to loosen its monopoly and to lower its prices, but without success. On December 2, 1850, in his first State of the Union address, President Fillmore made special reference to guano. Amidst remarks about such pressing matters as slavery, the increasing significance of foreign trade and commerce to the national economy, and the growing significance of the United States in the international arena, he declared: "Peruvian guano has become so desirable an article to the agricultural interests in the United States that it is the duty of the Government to employ all the means properly in its power for the purpose of causing that article to be imported into the country at a reasonable price. Nothing will be omitted on my part toward accomplishing this desirable end."[34]

After several episodes in which American businessmen tried to steal guano from Peruvian islands with the help of American officials (including then Secretary of State, Daniel Webster), Senator William Seward presented a petititon to Congress in March of 1856 on behalf of the American Guano Company (a company formed in 1855 at a reported capitalization of $10 million and wishing to claim and mine the Baker and Jarvis islands in the mid-Pacific, which it believed to be rich in guano deposits). Seward hoped to make it easier for American entrepreneurs to claim global guano deposits under United States government jurisdiction. The resulting Guano Islands Act (1856) furthered Seward's drive for American commercial supremacy and resulted in America's first overseas territorial acquisitions. In the wording of the Act, whenever the government "should have received satisfactory information that any citizen or citizens of the United States have discovered a deposit of guano on any island, or other territory not within the lawful jurisdiction of any other Government," then, at the discretion of the President, it shall "be considered as appertaining to the United States for the use and behoof of the discoverer or discoverers, and his and their assigns, and may, at like discretion, be taken possession of in the name of the United States, with all necessary formalities."[35]  Within the ten years following the passage of the Guano Islands Act, American entrepreneurs sought to claim every island, rock, or key that might possess deposits of guano. They were soon followed by the French and the English, who hoped to share in the plunder—often, the enormous resources of native peoples whose cultures were violently altered or destroyed. As Skaggs tells us, "between August 1856 and January 1863 (when the Lincoln administration suspended the law by declining to process additional requests for title during the duration of the

Civil War), the U.S. Department of State accepted ten separate bonds on fifty-nine islands, rocks, and keys in the Pacific and Caribbean."[36]

When Emerson evokes the figure of guano in his essay "Fate," then, he recalls a commodity that bears the traces of the history of American imperialism and colonization, of the consequences, that is, of America's conviction in its so-called "manifest destiny." But he also wants to suggest the ways in which political liberty and economic prosperity in antebellum America are entangled with the oppression, and often the death, of millions of slaves and ethnic immigrants. As he puts it elsewhere, "in each change of industry, whole classes and populations are sacrificed" (J, XIV: 16). This point is confirmed with great force when we note that the workers involved in supporting and maintaining the guano trade included not only the German, Irish, and African Americans to which Emerson refers but also, among so many others, the Peruvian convicts, natives, and Chinese coolies that worked the Peruvian guano fields. According to Evelyn Hu-Dehart, from 1849 to 1874, as many as 100,000 contract laborers or "coolies" were transported, under deception or coercion, across the Pacific to help meet the demand for cheap labor on the coastal guano fields.[37] There would in fact have been no guano trade without these laborers. Amidst the ravages of war and the labor shortages resulting from the end of African slavery, Peru— hoping to encourage foreign investment and unable to find enough cheap labor among the small coastal peasantry, freed slaves, or the highlanders, to meet the growing demand—decided to seek it overseas.

When it was clear that European immigrants were not drawn to the lack of available land and low wages in Peru, the Peruvian government— following the example of the British planters in the West Indies and Cuba— resorted to the importation of Chinese laborers. In south China, Westerners used Chinese "runners"—just as their counterparts in Africa were called— to "recruit" poor young men, often by force but also by persuading them that they were to work the gold mines in California. Some boarded ships in Amory or other Chinese ports, but the greater number probably passed through the Portuguese colony of Macao. As Hu-Dehart points out, many of the same ships and captains used in the African slave trade "transported Chinese coolies, packing them on board in the same way as slaves, across a 'middle passage' that was even longer in distance and more arduous."[38] Mortality rates on these ships—often referred to as "floating coffins"—were as high as 30% or more, due to overcrowding, insufficient food, lack of proper ventilation, and poor hygenic conditions.

Once the Chinese laborers arrived in Peru, they were auctioned, and then housed in long, rectangular slave quarters. The working conditions on the islands were unbearable, not only because of their inhospitable nature—the climatic conditions on the islands made any work there a matter of privation and hardship, since the heat and lack of rainfall made water and food supplies very scarce—but also because of the viciousness with which the laborers were driven to dig and load the guano. In response to these harsh conditions, the coolies often chose to commit suicide in order to escape their enslavement. One contemporary account published in *The Southern Planter* in 1855 tells of mass suicides, sometimes involving up to fifty coolies at a time. These suicides were so frequent that the Peruvian government was forced to station guards around the cliffs and shores of the islands to prevent them. Stories about the atrocious work conditions in the guano fields, often similar to abolitionist accounts of the abuse and mistreatment of southern slaves, were published in several southern agricultural journals in the two decades before the Civil War. Eventually, the gross abuses in the recruitment and transportation of the coolies generated such fierce international and national criticism that the Peruvian government suspended the trade between 1856 to 1861, and only reopened it later under the more relaxed supervision of the Portuguese. But the pressure experienced by the Peruvian government to stop what often was referred to as "another African slave trade" did not prevent the deaths of tens of thousand of coolies and Peruvian laborers—many of whom, buried in the guano fields in which they died working, became, like the flesh and carcasses of birds and sea lions, part of the guano that soon would be exported to the United States to fertilize its lands and crops. To recall this history is to begin to delineate the world that made Emerson's figure possible.

If Emerson takes the risk of ventriloquizing the language of proslavery propaganda—we can find in "Fate" echoes of most of the important proslavery arguments: biological determinism, pre-Adamitism, the black's arrested evolution, and the eventual extinction of the black race, and his citations from Knox often have been understood as signs of his own latent racism—he seeks to recontextualize this language not only within an antislavery argument but also within a more general reflection on the nature of race and the violence that takes place in its name. In regard to the citations from Knox, for example, we need only register the adjectives he uses to introduce and describe the English anatomist's language. Far from endorsing Knox's evolutionary theories, Emerson states that the book's conclusions are "unpalatable," that its writer is "rash and unsatisfactory," and that its truths are "pungent and unforgettable." With this last phrase, in particular—referring as he does to the one adjective that always is associated with guano: "pungent"—he suggests that Knox's book is a piece of guano, a book to be condemned, but a book that, fertilizing racist soil, enables the transformation of minorities into guano. The strength of Emerson's criticism becomes clearer if we recall that Knox's claims for the racial superiority of the Anglo-Saxon are made in the name of its racial purity. What kind of purity can there be, Emerson suggests, if America's prairies and crops are composed largely of foreign bodies: the seeds that are imported from England, the fertilizer imported from Peru and elsewhere, the bodies and blood of peoples from Africa, Germany, Ireland, Peru, China, and so forth—all of which will become part of the "American" body? What his extraordinary figure tells us is that the American body should be understood as neither "American" nor even entirely human.

If Emerson's identification between ethnic minorities and guano encourages us to rethink our relation to the violent enterprise of slavery, however, this identification does not belong to him alone. From Melville's allegorical assault on American imperialism, "The Encantadas," in which the white imperialist's desire to occupy the enchanted isles is associated with the whitish remains of the various seabirds that nest on them, the guano that covers and dominates the island's rocks and earth, to Thoreau's *Walden*, which tells us in its first pages that "men labor under a mistake" and that, "by a seeming fate" or "necessity," their "better part...is soon ploughed into the soil for compost," to Douglass's famous 1852 "Fourth of July" speech, which depicts a group of slavers headed for the slave-market and mourns for those "wretched people" who "are to be sold singly, or in lots, to suit purchasers" and who will soon become "food for the cotton-field, and the deadly sugar-mill," to Faulkner's *Absalom, Absalom!*, which, in an extraordinary passage that describes the spot of earth on which Charles Bon was born, refers to "a soil manured with black blood from two hundred years of oppression and exploitation until it sprang with an incredible paradox of peaceful greenery and crimson flowers and sugar cane sapling size and three times the height of a man," the figurative association between laborers and manure works to exhibit the violence of oppression and of colonialist and imperialist expropriation, the injuries and scars, the deaths, murders, and sometimes collective assassinations that have supported capitalist expansion.[39]

If such rhetoric offers a graphic rendering of the familiar trope of the black "blood and tears" that nourish the land (implicitly in the context of agriculture) that appears so often in abolitionist writing, it does so in order to work against proslavery arguments that, asserting a similar identification between slaves and the material bases of America's growth and development, argued for the necessity of slavery. Perhaps the most celebrated example of this proslavery position—a position that takes its point of departure from the tension between the twin imperatives of democracy and capitalism—is offered by James Hammond's famous "Mud-Sill" speech, delivered to the United States Senate in March 1858. There, aligning himself with the earlier proslavery rhetoric of Henry Clay, John Calhoun, and others, he claims that "the greatest strength of the South arises from the harmony of her political and social institutions"[40] and he goes on to explain that "in all social systems there must be a class to do the menial duties, to perform the drudgery of life. That is, a class requiring but a low order of intellect and but little skill. Its requisites are vigor, docility, fidelity. Such a class you must have, or you would not have that other class which leads progress, civilization, and refinement. It constitutes the very mud-sill of society and of political government....Fortunately for the South, she found a race adapted to that purpose to her hand. A race inferior to her own, but eminently qualified in temper, in vigor, in docility, in capacity to stand the climate, to answer all her purposes. We use them for our purpose, and call them slaves."[41] The relation between Hammond's metaphor and that of the "guano-races of mankind" that are fertilizing the land is reinforced when we remember that the mud-sill of a structure—the lowest part of the structure—is generally embedded in the soil. As Sundquist notes, "the spread of the Cotton Kingdom into the Deep South from the 1820s to 1850s (resulting in a tenfold increase in production, to a peak of nearly five million bales per year, three-fourths of the world's cotton, by the outbreak of the Civil War) guaranteed the survival and expansion of slavery."[42] Marx already had confirmed the South's dependence on slavery in 1847. "Without slavery you have no cotton," he tells us, "without cotton you have no modern industry. It is slavery that gave the colonies their value; it is the colonies that created world-trade that is the pre-condition of large-scale industry. Slavery is an economic category of the greatest importance."[43]

But what is the status of the principles of freedom and autonomy to which Hammond has recourse here? If Anglo-Saxon freedom and equality are achieved through slave labor, then what possibilities exist for this conduit of Saxon identity? In what way do emancipatory discourses of rights, equality, and citizenship depend on forms of racialization and on the

invisibility of the practices of domination and discipline? As Marx explains—
and here he points both to the history of racial subjugation and enslavement,
and to the entanglement of slavery and freedom—despite the presumed
universalism of such principles, the democratic rights to self-determination
Hammond proclaims depend on the success of a violent politics of
oppression, of economical and ideological enslavement, and thus of the
destruction of autonomy. In Werner Hamacher's words, "the process of the
practical universalization of individual and social liberties"—the dream
articulated by the rhetoric of manifest destiny—"often has gone hand in hand
with a process of oppression, disenfranchisement, and the massacre of
countless persons and peoples. And this process—one hesitates to call it a
process of civilization—has to this day continued to thrive on the massive,
capitalist exploitation of individuals and peoples."[44]  The process of
civilization and refinement to which Hammond refers has always been a
process of capitalization. As Hamacher goes on to explain, "the formation of
cultural ideals, which is supposed to culminate in the *autonomy* of the self, is
at the same time a process of the *automation* of the mechanism of capital. It
is a process of the obliteration of labor, the obliteration of a violent history and
of the particularity of the socio-economic and politico-cultural forces that
sustain this autonomy, a process of the erasure of those who are always
insufficiently paid and of that which cannot be counted. Whoever invokes the
universalism of *this* freedom and *this* equality always invokes, whether or not
he acknowledges it, *this* history of automatization, colonialization, and
exploitation."[45] Whoever appeals to equality, Emerson would say, does so
within a history of inequality, within a history in which the America that was
to be the realization of the promise of the right to representation for everyone,
perhaps can never exist, perhaps can only exist in the form of a promise, but
a promise which must be enacted and performed with every breath we take.

     This is why, we "must call to mind the history of the
universalization of the principle of autonomy...not in order to discredit the
universalist ethics of the claim to freedom—this claim can never be simply

fulfilled and never completely discredited—but rather to see the paradoxes of its principles clearly whenever they become political realities in history, that is, where they make history."[46]   As Emerson reminds us in his essay "Man the Reformer," in a passage that again seeks to tell us why we must learn to mourn, in order to be the Americans that we are, in order to be the Americans we are still not: "We are all implicated...in this charge; it is only necessary to ask a few questions as to the progress of the articles of commerce from the field where they grew, to our houses, to become aware that we eat and drink and wear perjury and fraud in a hundred commodities. How many articles of daily consumption are furnished us from the West Indies....The abolitionist has shown us our dreadful debt to the southern negro. In the island of Cuba, in addition to the ordinary abominations of slavery, it appears, only men are bought for the plantations, and one dies in ten every year, of these miserable bachelors, to yield us sugar" (*W*, I: 232).

Learn to mourn, then, remember the dead, keep the memory of the dead alive, think your relation to a past that, never behind you, haunts you, tells you for what you are answerable. As Walter Benjamin would have it: "To articulate the past historically does not mean to recognize it 'as it really was.' It means to seize hold of a memory as it flashes up in a moment of danger....Only that historian will have the gift of fanning the spark of hope in the past who is firmly convinced that *even the dead* will not be safe if the enemy wins. And the enemy has not ceased to be victorious."[47]

**Philipp Misselwitz:** Since the September 11th attacks, the Western world is in the grip of the proclaimed "War on Terrorism." It is now clear that the days of the Clausewitzian definition of warfare as a symmetrical engagement between state armies in the open field are over. War has entered the city again—the sphere of the everyday, the private realm of the house, sacred to Western societies. We find ourselves nervous when we use public transport systems or mingle in crowds, due to frequent bomb scares. Our parliaments are debating whether to grant powers to our armies to maintain internal security, powers that were previously held by the police, while violent clashes with the anti-globalization movement take place on main public squares and shopping streets. Do we need a new definition of warfare in relationship to our cities?

**Eyal Weizman:** Cities were always exposed to war and organized according to the logic of defense. Each period's urban form related to the available technologies of destruction. Changes in the technologies of warfare during the last decade radically changed the relation between war and the city.

Having said that, some of the roots of what is now widely discussed as "urban warfare" can be traced to the nineteenth century. At that time, European powers were fighting insurgencies and rebellions within urban and rural areas at the fringes of their colonial empires while protecting their exploding capital cities against homegrown rebellions and revolutions nourished by class struggles. The battleground shifted from the open fields to the city walls and further positioned itself within the heart of the city, as a fight for the city itself.

If historical siege warfare ended when the envelope of the city was broken and entered, urban warfare started at the point of entering the city. It is worth examining how the city grew to be perceived from military and security perspectives. This perspective might help explain some of the radical transformations that occurred and are still occurring within the fabric of contemporary cities, from New York to Ramallah to Kabul.

Cities are security nightmares. The military forces feel threatened by the huge increase of big cities and their ineptness at dealing with them. It is the very nature of urban areas and their tendencies to density, congestion, diversities, heterogeneity, and formal diversity that makes them hard to invade and conquer.

The military tends to deal with the problem of taking over a city in a way similar to the way a planner deals with issues of development. Both look for ways to control an area by manipulating its infrastructure, reshaping and replacing the built fabric, or attempting to manage the local population's various cultural sensitivities.

**PM:** Can you give a historical example that illustrates the shift of warfare into the cities?

**EW:** The Israeli architect and writer Sharon Rotbard lectured about the French 1840s invasion of Algiers by Marshall Thomas Robert Bugeaud. In a typically colonial attitude of zero tolerance and total disregard for the complexity of the historical structure, Bugeaud set out to break popular support for the resistance leader Abdel Kader by attacking the fabric of cities, towns, and villages.

His actions were so extreme and brutal that they managed to raise parliamentary criticism in nineteenth century Paris. Bugeaud, commanding more than one-hundred thousand troops, had taken seven years to subdue Abdel Kader's ten-thousand man army. He finally regained control over Algiers' dense kasbahs by destroying entire neighborhoods in reprisals for guerrilla attacks, sometimes breaking centers of resistance by reshaping cities, widening roads for military movements.

These were some of the first demolitions used as military planning: Kader's resistance was broken, but the European project in Africa sought to further civilize the local population by replacing their primitive habitat in accordance with the rules of modern design.

It is a historical irony that the captured fighters of Kader's guerille and their families were deported by the French to Palestine which was then a province of the Ottoman empire and were settled just north of the Sea of Galilee. There they prospered until the war of 1948—where, this time as Palestinians, they were made to flee their villages and turned refugees. Some went to Syria but most ended up in the refugee camp of Jenin. Jenin is an important site for the urban warfare that we may like to talk about later.

But the relationship between Algiers and Paris was far more symbiotic. Algiers became a laboratory for another war. The ardent Royalist Bugeaud personified the anti-urban attitudes of the French restoration. Opposed to the industrial revolution, which he thought was physically and morally toxic, he believed that he could reverse the trend of migration to cities by making land cultivation more efficient. It is not surprising that the person who first carried out the destruction of cities was a strong advocate of rural life.

The re-emerging aristocratic and bourgeois elite feared, above all, the densely populated, desperately poor, and rapidly growing capital of Paris. As mass migration from rural France led to the dramatic overcrowding of cities' outer districts, new strategies to maintain stability and state control had to be developed.

Rotbard tells how, with his experience of Algiers, Bugeaud returned to Paris in 1847 and published the treatise La Guerre des Rues et des Maison, which is described as the first manual for the preparation and conduct of urban warfare. As a preventative measure against civil unrest in Paris, Bugeaud proposed a radical reorganization of the city. Much like in Algiers, he said, new routes for military maneuvers should be cut through the city and military regiments positioned within it.

Bugeaud understood that there is a direct relationship between the organization of the urban terrain and the ability to control it militarily and that this logic, when extended into the urban area, means that military thinking has to guide urban design. If strategic urban design previously focused on strengthening the city's peripheral walls and fortifications to keep out the enemy, here, since the enemy was already inside the city, the city had to be controlled from within. It is the city fabric itself, its streets and houses, that were now weapons in a warfare turning urban.

**PM:** The anti-urban experiments of the French Royal Army seem to coincide with the emergence of modern town planning. The idea of the Romantic Gesamtkunstwerk is embodied in the great beautification projects of Peter

Joseph Lenn, and Frederick Law Olmsted's planned extension of New York. Both were attempts to fuse urban and rural landscapes, to control and tame the emerging megalopolises through design. As with the experimental city models developed by the English utopian modernist Robert Owen, they seem to reveal a deep-rooted suspicion of the density and chaos of the emerging industrial metropolis. Are there any links between military experiment and modernist design projects in the nineteenth century?

**EW:** Modernization and the hygienic project are tightly linked. The hygienic obsession of the nineteenth century became operative at the level of urban design. Both conservative and progressive elites considered the city congested, filthy, decadent and, above all, dangerous. The modernization of cities was carried out by inserting infrastructure and public services. The modern city relied on the growing fragmentation and classification of space, carried out under the pretext of hygiene and social reform. Urban population was dispersed via the underground and railway systems into new towns whose contemporary descendants are today's suburbs and gated communities.

But, on the other hand, urban regeneration served the interests of the government, helping to turn the city into a governable and controllable apparatus, allowing for quick military deployment into the heart of potentially troubled areas.

Napoleon III's bureaucratic government machine conceived Paris' serpentine medieval fabric as a place that had to be subdued, tamed, and civilized.

Georges-Eugène Haussmann, the spirit behind the great modernization project of Paris in the early 1870s, was one of Marshall Bugeaud's readers. Thus it seems that the experiment of Algiers led, ironically, to one of the most influential and admired urban projects of the modern era. Haussmann

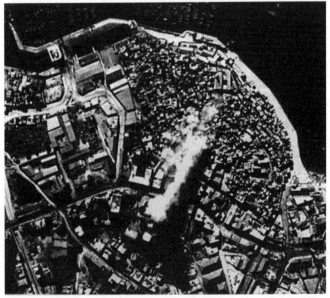

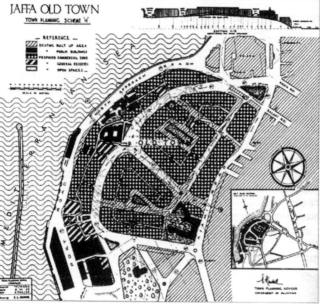

Before, during, and after *Operation Anchor* to clear paths through the old city of Jaffa, Royal Air Force, 1936

created wide boulevards down which the cavalry could charge against rioting crowds and artillery would have straight lines of fire to break barricades, while leveling many labyrinthine slums. Military control was exercised on the drawing board, according to the rules of design, fashion, and speculative interests.

In the nineteenth century, one can perhaps still differentiate between kinds of destruction: while urban warfare is tested at the periphery of Western civilization, the modernization policies in city centers employ the same tools, but camouflage themselves with different rhetoric.

The tandem of modernization and urban destruction is carried into the twentieth century in many corners of the colonial world. In Palestine "Operation Anchor," a "designed" destruction of Old Jaffa, was carried out by the mandatory British forces in 1936—a time later known as the first Arab rebellion—perhaps the first Intifada. British forces and Jewish civilians suffered casualties from stone throwers and snipers protected by Jaffa's winding roads and dense urban fabric. In response, the British government decided to cut a large anchor-shaped "boulevard" through the old city, destroying between 300 and 700 homes. This boulevard is still apparent today—it is where most of old Jaffa's cafes and restaurants are located, but at the time it allowed deep patrols into the very heart of the city and put an end to resistance with a combination of design and military force.

When serious concerns were voiced in the British parliament about these actions, the destruction was defended as urgent measures of regeneration and public hygiene in an area lacking basic services. Indeed, soon after the destruction, infrastructure began to be laid out under the path of the ruins.

**PM:** The reprisal tactics of colonial armies seem to be based on the instrument of the plan, revealing a two-dimensional understanding of the city as a functional diagram that can be manipulated and controlled at will. This imposition of Western thinking seems to demonstrate an inability to register the complexity of urban structures. Were the strategies of Algiers and Jaffa really effective in the long run?

**EW:** During the colonial wars, Western powers' understanding of colonial cities was very rudimentary. All complexities were flattened out, intellectually and physically. Attempts to "understand" local cultures were distorted by an Orientalist and Romantic vision of the Mediterranean kasbah—a place that can be considered aesthetically fascinating, but that remains suspect, deceptive, treacherous, and violent. It was the double-edged fear and fascination that led to a desire to flatten and rationalize it.

Knowledge and power are closely linked, and colonial knowledge of foreign places was largely reproduced on maps. Cities were measured, mapped, and charted. Obviously, Western cartography could capture Mediterranean urban life only with the crudest simplification. The military endeavored to stamp out the differences between the reality of urban life and the charted information. The desire to make the terrain resemble the map is typical of military ambitions—mapping, as much as it represents the world, also creates it. Representation of the city and military action became inextricably linked.

The evolution of modern surveillance technology also mirrors this two-dimensional perception of the city. At the beginning of the twentieth century, aerial photography—first with air balloons, later with airplanes—became one of the most important tools available to the military. This was due to its ability to produce "ready-made maps" that register fast changes and sometimes even movements across the territory. Yet, in urban combat, extending the battle ground into the third, aerial dimension was of limited use. Cities have a syntax that is not apparent from above. The defending party, whose city is its home, knows how to use this principle to the full and moves through secret routes and passageways, roof connections, and undergrounds. Colonial armies found themselves exposed to situations that are not dissimilar to contemporary "asymmetrical warfare."

One contemporary military analyst went so far as to describe the developing city as "the post-modern equivalent of jungles and mountains—citadels of the dispossessed and irreconcilable."

**PM:** Did the techniques of urban destruction during World War II have a similar effect on the radical reorganization of cities in post-war urban planning, as could be seen in the relationship between Bugeaud's Algiers and Haussmann's Paris? Can an understanding of military strategic thinking offer a new perspective on the post-war rejection of urban density?

**EW:** During World War II, for the first time, cities became targets of a systematic airborne campaign of destruction. Later, the phobia of nuclear destruction became engrained in post-war public consciousness and became one of the most influential features of post-war planning. Military strategic thinking tried to counter the tendency to dense urban centers and instead encouraged systematic suburbanization and regionalization. In Europe, this phenomenon is apparent almost everywhere and is well illustrated by the construction of a ring of new towns around London in the 1950s and by the planning of post-war Hanover. Further down the design scale, the design of particular building types—like Le Corbusier's safe skyscraper for late variations of the Ville Radieuse—included measures against bombing and chemical attacks.

On the other side of the Atlantic, the American suburb owes its existence as much to the fear of nuclear war as to the presence of the freeway. This was a preconceived and pre-planned scientific experiment in population dispersal, which relied on the mobilization of huge public funds (or massive subsidies to corporations) investing in new infrastructure. There was, as well, an unprecedented reliance on wartime engineering practices and technologies, which generated yet another generation of American utopias.

Just like the urban destruction programs of the previous century, the radical reorganization of post-war cities was justified with the middle-class values of hygiene and regeneration.

Two decades later, some American city centers underwent extreme processes of degeneration. In 1967, Detroit was taken over by inner city riots, with pitched gun battles between the black communities and the National Guard—and Detroit was not the only such city.

**PM:** But this anti-urban logic did not stop global urbanization in the second half of the 20th century. Hasn't the model of the city proven more durable than ever before?

**EW:** From a global perspective, it is true that urbanization processes have not halted at all. The majority of the world's population will soon live in cities. Today, cities are the exclusive nuclei of political, economic, and cultural power. The global order is composed of a matrix of nodal points with cities as the centers of its nervous system. But it is precisely the concentration of technologies, infrastructure, and capital that makes cities ever more vulnerable to attack by both foreign militaries and terrorist organizations. Seizing control of cities is now perceived as the only effective way to control a state. Control of territory has ceased to be the primary objective of warfare.

From the military point of view the city is a social or physical obstacle that must be reorganized to be controlled. Beyond being a conflict that takes place within the city, urban warfare is fought by transforming it.

NATO's campaign of "bombing for peace" in Serbia in 1999 demonstrated that attacking symbolic buildings within cities became an effective and acceptable tool to exercise considerable psychological pressure on both the regime and the civilian population. All parties clearly realized which buildings are located in "target banks"—as the air force calls them—and as a result these buildings were deserted long before the first bomb was dropped. This is true for Belgrade's empty ministries, the Palestinian authority installations in the West Bank, and palaces of Baghdad. In the whole Kosovo campaign, very few Serbian tanks, or any other essential military installations, were actually destroyed from the air.

The effect sought in bombing campaigns is purely psychological and as such it looks for symbols rather than for military effects. Realizing that cities will be the primary sites of warfare, militaries around the world have become acutely aware of their failure to develop suitable doctrines and technologies. The existing military arsenal of weapons is better suited for "classical" armored warfare on the great Russian plains than to urban combat. The trauma of house-to-house battles in World War II, as waged between the Wehrmacht and the Red Army over Stalingrad, led to an acceptable military doctrine which avoided urban warfare at all costs. The 1991 Gulf War was perhaps the last of the purely territorial wars. In the most recent war, Saddam positioned most of his forces around and within the major cities, with particular units even planted in hospitals or housing blocks and dressed in civilian clothes. In many ways, the drive to Baghdad was just a logistical deployment for a war that started at the city gates and was won as much through psychological manipulations as through the precise air campaign that preceded it.

**PM:** Cities have radically changed over the last 50 years. The spatial and technological complexity of the vast 21st-century megalopolises bears little resemblance to the compact colonial cities of the 19th and early 20th centuries. What impact does the contemporary city have on military operations today?

**EW:** The contemporary city has developed complexity, especially along the vertical axis. Its infrastructure—sewage systems, electric telecommunications, water mains, and underground transport system—is buried in the subsurface. Supersurfaces of very high roofscapes have emerged, while the air between and above them is cluttered with complex electromagnetic fields. Besides growing vertically, cities now sprawl horizontally across vast territorial regions.

Within this type of environment, high-tech military equipment is easily incapacitated. Buildings mask targets or create urban canyons, which diminish the capabilities of the air force. It is hard to see into the urban battle space; it is very difficult to communicate in it, because radio waves are often disturbed. It is hard to use precision weapons in it because it is difficult to obtain accurate GPS satellite locations. And it is becoming more and more difficult (but not impossible) for the military to shoot indiscriminately into the city. For all these reasons, cities continue to reduce the advantages of the technologically superior force.

**PM:** A main influence on contemporary warfare seems to be the constraints imposed on military operations by the world media and the accepted standards of warfare in international law. How does the military respond to these political and ethical constraints?

**EW:** International media reports on the atrocities committed by Western forces have great effect on public opinion. But often enough, the media tends to collaborate with the military. Focusing on psychological warfare and public relations as a key element in urban warfare, the military has a clear interest in promoting maximum cooperation from the media and often uses it to disseminate information or disinformation and to maintain political support at home. In Iraq, we saw a lot of reporters attached to military units, essentially doing what military propaganda did generations before. It is revealing that the US military calls these methods a "strategy of reprogramming mass consciousness."

Moreover, the existence of international courts, an extensive network of NGOs, the development of cheap recording equipment, and the availability of satellite communication greatly limit military operational methods. The military term "strategic corporal" characterizes the huge ramifications of the actions of the individual soldier.

Another component in the psychological environment of warfare is international humanitarian law. Since World War II, we have seen the rise of international institutions and the elaboration of customary law and the laws of war. The inauguration of the ICC (International Criminal Court) in the Hague this March made it possible to examine and prosecute individuals for war crimes, but the court's jurisdiction extends only to member states—and still needs to demonstrate its effectiveness. Since military planners are acutely aware that the methods required for urban warfare will make soldiers potentially liable to prosecution for war crimes, American and Israeli governments cancelled their memberships in the ICC. Besides fearing prosecution, the military wants to preempt possible restrictions to military freedom of actions. These reassurances, provided to the American and Israeli armed forces, indicate that they may be considering in advance some of what international humanitarian law defines as war crimes. The effectiveness of international courts has to be proven. I think that as long as the world armies serve nations and are not under the authority of a single world government, the "rule of law" between these nations is impossible. Some "war criminals" may be taken to court while others not. The question of who will face trial will be dictated by power politics. But, in the end, the mere knowledge that the ICC exists might help deter war crimes.

**PM:** How does the army deal with an ever more complex reality?

**EW:** Military academies across the world show great interest in urban studies, in gaining more understanding of the ways cities work. Simon Marvin, Professor of Planning at the University of Salford, has shown how armies set up many new urban research programs and allocate huge budgets for the study of cities. As urban warfare increasingly resembles urban planning, armies study the complexity of cities and train their own urban practitioners. Suddenly, architects and planners are in high demand as a valuable source of knowledge.

I have actually witnessed some of the conferences set up for this purpose. These are surreal events where military personnel, arms dealers, and academics from different corners of the globe exchange views on urban military operations and essential equipment—over dinner. I was amazed that my attendance as an architect did not raise any eyebrows. When asked, I explained my presence in terms of a research project, and my conversation partners—instead of being more cautious—were very curious to hear more about the relationship between my work on human rights planning and architecture. This embrace made me feel uncomfortable.

Unlike in earlier periods, the city is no longer studied only in terms of its formal and material dimension, but also as a techno-social apparatus— a complex "system of systems." This is an approach that understands the city in terms of a relationship between software and hardware, between performed and built culture. "Cultural intelligence" tries to understand the social fabric of a city and the way it relates to the built fabric, as well as the logic of social groupings, local politics, and local rivalries, in order to take full advantage of them.

The city can be understood as a composite of three parts, the "urban triad": the physical structure which includes buildings and roads; the urban infrastructure; and the population itself.

All layers are considered equally available for military manipulation. Obtaining strategic control of key infrastructure systems such as roads, power supplies, water, and communication networks can be more effective than controlling an urban space by conventional means. By temporarily shutting down electricity and telephone connections in particular parts of a city, the military can paralyze the enemy. The infrastructure available for military manipulations also includes a series of mechanisms that allow capital to flow, credit to be granted, and investment to be channeled—and these institutions, as September 11th clearly showed, are prime targets for manipulation.

The military methods of dealing with a city are thus similar to those of a planner. If in the last century military planning dealt with the organization of the city and its physical fabric, today's planning is more complex; military personnel seek to learn how cities work so that they may control them by manipulating their various components.

"Design by destruction" increasingly involves planners as military personnel in reshaping the battle environment to meet political and strategic objectives. Bombing campaigns rely on architects and planners to recommend building and infrastructure as targets and in order to evaluate the urban effect of their removal. The overall effect of urban planners in battle is evident. The destruction in Bosnia of public functions—mosques, cemeteries, and public squares—followed a clear and old fashioned planner's logic; social order cannot be maintained without its shared functions. The manipulation of key infrastructure—roads, power, water, and communication such as in Ramallah—seeks to control an urban area by disrupting its various flows.

182

Karel Zwanefeld, Urban Warfare training Site in the Netherlands, 2002

The destruction of monuments and heritage sites, such as in the bombing of Belgrade and Baghdad, as we discussed earlier, seeks a psychological victory over "enslaving" architectural projects.

**PM:** What case studies are available?

**EW:** Information is retrieved from the study and analysis of historical and contemporary precedents: Chechnya, Belgrade, and Mogadishu have been discussed at length in military magazines and websites. But perhaps the most important precedent was set with the Israeli incursion into the refugee camps of the West Bank in April 2002. In view of the expected invasion of Baghdad, Jenin not only supplied a valuable source of information, but was also considered a live model for this emerging type of urban warfare. While governments and human rights organizations strongly condemned the acts of the Israeli army, militaries were eager for every piece of information provided by Israeli generals, through open and classified channels. The American army, a long-time ally of the Israeli army, actually dispatched officers on the ground. I have testimonies from several sources claiming that American military personnel were in Jenin at the time of the battle. Dressed in IDF uniform and walking without weapons, they were observers examining military tactics and methods of combat in the dense fabric of the Arab town.

**PM:** What, in Jenin, was of such interest to the Western military?

**EW:** I spoke to an Israeli reserve soldier shortly after the battle of Jenin. I was interested in the relationship between planning—not physical planning, but the attempt to foresee scenarios and act accordingly—and urban warfare. What he said was not surprising in its essence, but in its intensity. He spoke of his perception of total chaos, where all the plans and preparations became irrelevant, the battle completely unexpected, dense, full of contradictions, with characters changing their role from woman to man, removing the dress to reveal a gun or explosive belt, from civilian to combatant and back again, from friend to foe. Chance played a more important role than the ability to calculate and predict. It has become impossible to draw up scenarios, plan next steps, or draw up single-track plans to follow through.

This really shows that, as far as the military is concerned, urban warfare is the ultimate post-modern warfare: beyond the ambiguity of characters, the belief in a logically structured, single-tracked and pre-planned approach is lost in the complexity and ambiguity of the urban reality.

The officer's disorientation mirrors that of Western armies when facing the complexities of the city in urban combat. In Jenin, a few dozen Palestinian fighters managed to hold back a whole army division as long as fighting took place between the homes and streets. The Israelis only "won" the battle when bulldozers collapsed the city on its defenders. The complexities of urban warfare were then finally erased in the last days of the battle, when the center of the refugee camp, an area about 300 meters square, was flattened. 350 buildings, mostly homes, were destroyed or severely damaged, and about 4,000 people were left homeless.

**PM:** Were these acts of demolition a form of "design by destruction"?

**EW:** Yes. American and Israeli military jargon call these acts "reshaping the battle space," organizing the city in a way that serves the attacking force.

In a recent conference in Manchester organized by Simon Marvin and Steve Graham, the American General Keith Dickson defined campaigns of planned destruction as the "re-orientation of the built fabric to create conditions favorable for operational movement and maneuver." It looks as if military jargon is accustoming itself to a cleaner, publicly defendable language in which technical terminology is used to dress up the actions which include the leveling of buildings to improve transportation, and the destruction of infrastructure to deny water, electricity, and other systems to the defenders.

In Jenin, the IDF, considering physical design, used armored bulldozers to break paths through narrow and winding alleys to enable military vehicles to penetrate deep into the camp's interior. It is clear that the destruction has its own inherently military-design logic—rather than an approach which simply seeks total destruction. The aerial photographs taken after battles and published in various places allow for a close inspection of the form of destruction. Another type of inspection is needed in addition to counting homes and the size of the area destroyed. The investigation of the formal aspects of the destruction reveals the design logic and the military intentions of controlling the camp by means of the radical and brutal reorganization of its urban form. Architects and planners can realize and judge this matter.

The logic of designed destruction and the reorganization of the built fabric's own urban syntax is pursued as well on a smaller architectural scale. IDF Lt. General Eyal Weiss (who was later killed when a wall collapsed and buried him) developed a routine of moving through walls by cutting routes through the buildings. This technique was initially tested by the undercover "Arabist" unit Duvdevan [Cherry]. During operations, the soldiers of this unit never entered a house through the door but rather through an opening blasted in one of its walls.

Realizing that about 70-80 percent of the military casualties occurred outside buildings, Israeli infantry adopted this technique and started moving through the refugee camps by tunneling their way through the urban fabric, like worms in apples. Soldiers traveled through walls, from one home to the next, cutting openings with hammers or explosives. This type of movement ignores the existing urban syntax of streets or internal stairs, replacing it with another circulation system.

The paths of these cuts were not pre-planned, but determined in response to necessities, problems, and opportunities. Soldiers progressed mainly through the second-floor level because the entire ground floor was booby-

186

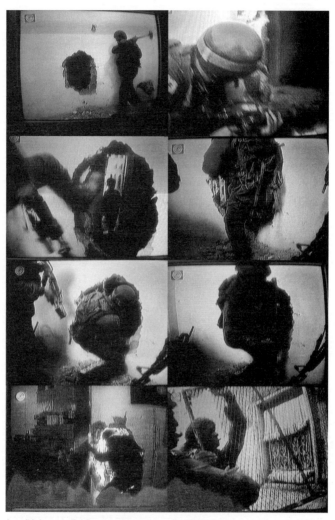

Israeli Infantry in Tul-Qarem refugee Camp, Israeli Channel One, April 2002

trapped. The technique has a long tradition that appropriated the ability of defenders to navigate the dense city in this manner, through alternative routes, secret passages, and trap doors. In Jenin, both soldiers and the Palestinian defenders moved through tunnels cut through solid city fabric, often crossing each other's route at a few meters' distance. Some buildings were like layered cakes with Israeli soldiers both above and below a floor where Palestinians were trapped.

The architecture of the camp was perceived like a solid through which "free" paths were carved out. A Palestinian family might have sat in the living room when a group of soldiers appeared through the wall.

**PM:** If advanced strategic planning is no longer relevant, how does one manage and coordinate the campaign of urban warfare?

**EW:** Complex ways of mapping which communicate the position of each combat unit and minimize collisions and friendly-fire casualties are now a standard part of Western military equipment. Each unit worked with the same aerial map, on which all building roofs were numbered. Central command could thus receive a group's position within the built fabric in terms of the X, Y (position), and Z (floor) coordinates. Rapidly updated information was achieved using helicopters, unmanned aerial vehicles [UAVs], or unmanned balloons positioned above the battle field, day and night. They delivered constant live updates on the rapidly developing situation on the ground and the transformed urban fabric. What was experimented with during this battle was the complete and synergetic integration of all parts of the military, with every unit commander on the ground able to receive information from all available sources. At night, the whole camp was so strongly lit from above with projectors and bombs that diurnal rhythms were confused. The ten-day battle turned into one long day.

Nir Kafri, IDF infantry in Tul Qarem, 2003

The military is increasingly adopting partisan and guerrilla tactics in regular military strategic thinking. Sometimes, strange zoological metaphors find their way into military jargon: after the worms came the bees. A standard military terminology for describing operations in urban terrain talks about "swarming"; instead of the old-school military column, soldiers move as a swarm—without the direction or logic of movement being apparent to the enemy—for minutes at a time, they are "everywhere," moving through alleys, cracks, walls, and then pulling out. The idea of "swarming" seeks to activate a large number of small forces. In this way, defenders find it hard to predict the attacker's next move. This is a part of the military's non-linear warfare— a method which adapts itself to the chaos and unpredictability of the city.

**PM:** Has military strategic thinking surrendered to the complexity and unpredictability of the city? While force has been used to change the form of the colonial cities of Algiers or Jaffa to sustain control, is it now military tactics that are being changed by the city?

**EW:** I do not think we can talk in terms of surrender to complexity, but in terms of different ways of dealing with complexity. In a sense, we should no longer speak of war in the city, but of war of the city, by the city. The city has become no longer the locus, but the apparatus of warfare.

**PM:** In the Israeli-Palestinian conflict, urban and architectural form have become instruments in the military occupation. This is possible due to Israeli authority over planning and construction. The campaign against the refugee camps is at the heart of this battle. Is it just military resistance that needs to be broken, or are there other more symbolic factors that give this battle such intensity?

**EW:** Steve Graham, Professor of Urban Technology at the University of Newcastle mentions the term "urbicide"—the destruction of the condition of plurality that defines a city—in this context. He claims that the main objective behind the destruction of Palestinian cities was to deny the Palestinians access to an urban modernity, and that the deliberate destruction of the central district of the Jenin camp was carried out with the preconceived ideological background of Israeli fear of the refugee camps.

Israel sees the control of the West Bank's fast-expanding, complex, and interconnected refugee camps as an attempt to secure Israel's control over Palestinian urban culture. Israeli military planning prohibits the expansion of the camps by tight zoning laws, while their internal fabric is regulated by periodic destructive attacks.

It is important to understand the symbolic quality of the camps in the eyes of the Palestinians. For Palestinians, it is important that the temporary "camp" should never be allowed to become a permanent city, in all the mundane normality that it may imply. The refugee camps are the spaces of exception, extraterritorial enclaves outside normal reach and beyond the rule of the law.

As emergency-governed extraterritorial places, the camps were serviced by different NGOs and UN agencies, not by the states in which they were located. In some cases the camp's inhabitants do not pay taxes or follow planning regulations of the host country. Although the initial temporary encampments were gradually replaced by built structures, their layout reflected an imagined geography of displacement, one that recreated the refugees' places of origin, and left the camps in a state of permanent temporality.

The camps are thus the footholds of Palestinian urban memory. Their very layout sometimes includes quarters referring to Haifa and Jaffa—places the refugees were evicted from—at times recreating geography by memory. All these factors reinforce the camp's emergency-governed, placeless temporality, which allows for it to lie outside of the law. But this temporality is only an illusion, nourished by the urge for the return. The camps have in effect been temporary for the past 50 years. In a cruel reversal, it was at the moment of a second confrontation with the Israeli army that the camp's inhabitants finally accepted it as a permanent city.

The Israeli-censored film *Jenin Jenin*, by Muhammad Bakri, describes the aftermath of the battle from the Palestinian perspective. The feeling is that when the threat of destruction and dispossession arose for a second time (the first being their eviction from their pre-1948 villages), the camp was finally accepted and embraced as a city. The home is that which is lost.

While restricting Palestinian urban development in general, Israelis also have a fundamental interest in transforming the temporary camp into a permanent city, because this is perceived as reducing the threat that the refugees will return to their homes within Israel proper. In the 1970s and 1980s, the IDF tried to achieve this goal by constructing permanent homes for the Palestinians in and around the camp. It is a bitter irony that large-scale construction did not turn the camp into a city; destruction has.

**PM:** You have already mentioned how military strategists have used the skills of architects and planners to facilitate a "design by destruction." If architects as experts of urban issues become willing informants and collaborators for the military—indirectly and directly—this action seems to touch upon fundamental ethical issues.

**EW:** Architects and planners are and have always been service providers working for all sides. Some architects engage with urban warfare to develop and elaborate tools for the military, others to understand, expose, and oppose their methods.

I think that this new military "science" and these methods must be looked at and studied very carefully. NGOs and humanitarian organizations must understand that war crimes have clear spatial dimensions and that there is therefore a role for the professionals of space—architects and planners—in their analysis.

The aftermath of the Battle of Jenin, various sources, April 2002

For example: until recently, the destruction of urban warfare was reported and analyzed as a purely statistical issue, relating to numbers of destroyed homes, the extent of economic damage, etc. Current human rights research, as well as International Humanitarian Law (IHL), has tended to divert attention away from space and urban form. People argue whether the destruction of Jenin amounts to a war crime because of the number of homes destroyed. But besides a quantification of destruction, we can see a much more serious phenomenon in which the urbicide of Jenin was an attempt to subjugate a population on the basis of redesigning its habitat, on the basis of denying it the advantages of urban life. To rightly report and understand it, we need to examine how the design aspect of the destruction functioned to achieve this. When human rights organizations go to Jenin and count destroyed houses, they ignore a component essential to understanding what kind of crime the IDF committed. "Human Rights Watch" dispelled the rumors of a massacre that were associated with the battle of Jenin, by showing that casualties were much lower than initially expected. This report reduced criticism of the Israeli government, but the story of the crime of urbicide was only later told by someone like Steve Graham.

Architecture and planning intersects with contemporary warfare in ways that the semantics of international law are still ill-equipped to describe. International Humanitarian Law is predicated on a now obsolete distinction between civilians and combatants in a low-intensity urban conflict, one that can no longer be understood according to the law's clear dialectic of war and peace.

The removal of urban matter must not only be quantified as a statistical problem relating numbers of buildings destroyed, or be valued by heritage site status as IHL sees them, but must also be understood as an active form of design having a cumulative effect in the creation of new spaces.

Architects and planners have the responsibility to use their ability to help make people understand the repercussions involved in formal aspects of warfare—and the crimes of an attack on urbanity.

The large bulldozers employed by the Israeli army in the West Bank and Gaza to destroy homes were the most effective strategic urban weapon. Each one of these mammoths is manned by a crew of three, including an engineering officer—usually a civil engineer or an architect on reserve duty. The reason is that they best know how to topple a building, to which side the debris must fall, etc. This is similar to a medical doctor's engagement in torture. Architecture has no equivalent of the Hippocratic oath, but if we accept urbicide and destruction as war crimes, architects may in principle end up in jail. The application of international law as the most severe method of architectural critique has never been more urgent. Crimes relating to the organization of the built environment call for placing an architect/planner for the first time on the accused stand of an international tribunal.

**PM:** The situation in the occupied territories of the West Bank is an extreme clash between First and Third World cultures and economies. Why do military strategists pay such attention to this peripheral frontier, so infinitely complex and specific?

**EW:** In many ways, the West Bank can be seen as an extreme model—perhaps a laboratory—of a territorial and urban conflict that can take place in other places. Globalization takes the periphery straight into the center, the frontier between First and Third Worlds starts running through the middle of world cities. The historical relationship between Paris and Algiers finds its analogy in the relationship between Baghdad and NYC.

Violations of articles of war crimes, as discussed above, do not legally require a declaration of war. The source of the term "urbicide" did not originate in Belgrade, Mostar, Grozny or Gaza but in the total regenerations and "hygienic" practices of American urban planning as described by Marshall Berman in the case of the destruction of the Bronx.

Internal security forces and the police borrow army knowledge. The difference between the terms "urban warfare" and "riot-control" are geographical rather than methodological—a matter of center and periphery. In both cases, the powerful authority attacks urbanity itself, not only its physicality, but the diversities and heterogeneity of urban life. Western states are in equal fear of losing control. Popular, carefully nurtured fears relate to terrorism and the threat of immigration as the new enemy from within. They lead to the protection of the center and attempt to preserve it from flux and change.

Human rights are routinely violated in the slow and seemingly benign processes of planning, development, and the allocation of resources. We can thus understand the design of a closely knitted fabric of homes and infrastructure—as in San Paulo, Mexico City, or California—as acts of spatial exclusion creating wedges that separate the habitat of a population marked as a political "outside" and perceived as a political threat.

Generally speaking, cities are apparatuses of social organization and control. The technologies of control take on complex physical and electronic form. A lot of attention has already been paid to how optical or electronic means dematerialize surveillance technologies. But the fabric of the city—its bricks and mortar—changes in accordance with that. And it is the physical fabric of cities that ultimately interests me.

Cities are organized by the fear of, and preparation for, violence. Consider how world leaders today meet either outside cities or, as was the case with the 2002 NATO meeting in Prague, the city is shut down in an act explicitly

196

Bethlehem 2002, anonymous Palestinian activist

designed to prevent protest and violence.

**PM:** Since September 11th, Western powers seem not only to have waged new military campaigns on the periphery. At home, public fear and disorientation is exploited to justify the build-up of gigantic apparatuses of control whose databases will begin to invade and control our daily lives. We can observe how the "war on terror" is used to justify the build-up of surveillance of US citizens to a level never before experienced. We have heard that soon, intelligence will be gathered on what Americans read and watch and on whom they communicate with. These measures seem to be part of far-reaching preparatory or pre-emptive strategies. What influence will this development have on the shape of our cities in the future? What importance will be assigned to notions of borders and frontiers? What is the connection between the changing nature of warfare and political changes on a larger scale?

**EW:** In the Western world, an understanding of borders as lines has given way to a new understanding of frontiers as a series of disconnected and estranged points across a surface. The contemporary city is exploding spatially, but in essence is fractalized into a collection of interlocking, internally homogeneous, and externally alienating synthetic environments. The separation between the affluent, established populations from the poorer immigrant populations can no longer be understood as a continuous line across the map. Internal city borders will be further reinforced, forming local enclaves scattered across the city and its suburbs. Point-based security systems fractalize borders and turn them from a defined object into a condition of heightened security whose presence is manifested in electronic or physical barriers at entry points to office buildings, shopping malls, or transport infrastructure—from midtown to suburbia.

On a larger scale, as the open terrain loses its strategic, demographic, and economic importance, international borders are becoming increasingly irrelevant, because even the entry point into cities is no longer via the periphery of a nation-state border, but through airports.

As for the last part of your question, I can only speculate about a connection between the heightened state of fear, the organization of violence, and developments of a new political order. The nature of warfare has always affected the organization of politics and power. In this case, I think that the relationship between city and sovereign territorial states will radically change. While states define themselves by means of internationally recognized borders, urban warfare will render this physical border redundant. When the line of the border and the surface of the state ceases to matter strategically, the political order will cease to be line-based—i.e., dependent on a homogeneous state territory—and become increasingly point-based, dependent on a networked system of cities. This is obviously going to help in accelerating the erasures in the economic viability and spatial coherence of the state. The city model already dominates the global markets. With the influence of urban violence and warfare, we might find ourselves back with the political system of the city-state.

Nir Kafri, balata refugee camp, the site of urban warfare in April 2002

**MOBILIZING SHAME**

Thomas Keenan

What difference would it make if human rights discourse took the photo-opportunity seriously?  Not the ones they themselves organize, and often quite well, but the ones coming from the other side, the other sides.  What would it mean to come to terms with the fact that there are things which happen in front of cameras which are not simply true or false, not simply representations and references, but rather opportunities, events, performances, things that are done and done for the camera, which come into being in a space beyond truth and falsity that is created in view of mediation and transmission?  In what follows, I wish to respond to these questions by focusing on what, within human rights activism and discourse, has come to be known as "the mobilization of shame." *

## Shame and Enlightenment

It is simply accepted that governments, armies, businesses, and militias are exposed in some significant way to the force of public opinion, and that they are (psychically or emotionally) structured like individuals in a strong social or cultural context which renders them vulnerable to feelings of dishonor, embarrassment, disgrace, or ignominy. Shame is thought as a primordial force that articulates or links knowledge with action, a feeling or a sensation brought on not by physical contact but by knowledge or consciousness alone. And it signifies involvement in a social network, exposure to others and susceptibility to their gaze—"a painful sensation excited by a consciousness of guilt or impropriety, or of having done something which injures reputation, or of the exposure of that which nature or modesty prompts us to conceal" (*Webster's Unabridged*, 1998).

Those with a conscience have no need of shame; they feel self-imposed guilt, not embarrassment which comes from others. Shaming is reserved for those without a conscience or the capacity for feeling guilty—and is required only where an external, enforceable law is absent. Indeed, publicity and exposure are at the heart of the concept. Webster's hypothesizes that the word, which is consistent as far back as Old High German and before, descends "perhaps from a root *skam* meaning to cover, and akin to the root (*kam*) of G. hemd shirt, E. chemise. Cf. *Sham*."

In this regard, "mobilizing shame" has Enlightenment roots, as many have pointed out. But they are contradictory ones. Kant defined Enlightenment as the release or exit from heteronomy, from dependence or reliance on the opinions of others, and as growing up out of shame and into courage, reason, and conscience. But the sign of an accomplished Enlightenment is, he adds, the use of that reason in public, so as to engage with others and change their opinions. The Kantian moral subject is fully realized only when his or her reason is liberated from the guidance, surveillance, pressure, or context of others, but at the same time when it is destined for public exchange, exposure, or enlightenment. Reason must be employed in public, says Kant, if there is to be any possibility of progress or social transformation; beliefs and institutions have no hope of survival if they are not exposed to reason, to judgments sparked by its critical force in public. Reason works when it exposes, reveals, and argues.

## Mobilizing Shame

No one seems to be able to pinpoint the moment when the phrase "mobilizing shame" entered our lexicon. Robert Drinan, in his recent book titled *The Mobilization of Shame*, credits what his footnote calls "Turkey campaign documents, Amnesty International" as the source of the phrase, but fails to supply a date or a title.[1] The first published references, though, go a long way toward sketching the essential elements of the concept as it is practiced today. The earliest citation I have found is from Judge B.V.A. Roling, who already put the phrase in quotation marks in an article on war crimes published in 1979:

> A weak form of enforcement can be seen in the influence of public opinion. If mass violations become known, the world reacts, as it did in the Vietnam war. That same Vietnam war demonstrates the power of this "mobilization of shame."[2]

The lockstep logic of if-then, in which knowledge generates action (reaction), seems to suggest a wishful fusion of an Enlightenment faith in the power of reason and knowledge with a realistic pessimism that retreats to the shame appropriate to the unenlightened. This pattern repeats itself as the concept develops.

The earliest mentions in news articles, at least those archived in Lexis-Nexis, quote the lawyer Irwin Cotler in his campaigns on behalf of Soviet Jewry and dissidents. Announcing in 1983 a plan to create a center to prepare amicus curiae briefs on behalf of political prisoners, showing how governments have violated their own laws, Cotler argued that exposing the gaps between self-professed norms and behavior could actually change that behavior. "We intend," he stated, "in the language of human rights lawyers, to bring the mobilization of shame against the Soviet Union, to expose the Achilles heel of their human rights violations."[3]

But the obscurity of its origins only strengthens the self-evidence of the phrase. Today it is the watchword of the international human rights movement. Here are some examples of this contemporary consensus at the level of tactics. In a recent summary article on the state of things, Louis Henkin, the dean of human rights law in the United States, writes that:

> The various influences that induce compliance with human rights norms are cumulative, and some of them add up to an under-appreciated means of enforcing human rights, which has been characterized as 'mobilizing shame.' Intergovernmental as well as governmental policies and actions combine with those of NGOs and the public media, and in many countries also public opinion, to mobilize and maximize public shame. The effectiveness of such inducements to comply is subtle but demonstrable.[4]

In practice, this modesty ("under-appreciated," "subtle") is rather false. Mobilizing shame is the predominant practice of human rights organizations, and the dominant metaphor through which human rights NGOs understand their own work, as in this response from William Schulz, president of Amnesty International USA, to an interviewer who asked, earlier this year: "How do you exercise your power?":

> Our power is primarily the power of mobilizing grass-roots people to speak out. "The mobilization of shame" is one way to put it. The eyes of the world shining on the prisons and into the dark corners of police stations and military barracks all over the world to try to bring international pressure to bear upon governments which are committing human rights violations.[5]

The pervasiveness of this consensus cannot be overstated, nor can its special relationship to the mass- and especially the image-based media. The

204

concept gathers together a set of powerful metaphors—the eyes of the world, the light of public scrutiny, the exposure of hypocrisy—as vehicles for the dream of action, power, and enforcement. "In the absence of effective enforcement mechanisms" means: we do not have a machine, a real law or an institutionalized apparatus that can deliver reliable results, but we have an informal system that attempts to approximate it.[6] It ought to function automatically. Light brings knowledge, and publicity brings "compliance," even if it works by shame and not reason or conscience. Precisely because the perpetrators are immature, dependent on the opinions of others, as are the governments that might challenge them, they are vulnerable to shaming. Judge Roling's sentence expresses the faith most simply: "If mass violations become known, the world reacts."

### Becoming Shameless

The dark side of exposure is over-exposure. Sometimes we call it voyeurism, sometimes compassion fatigue, sometimes the obscenity of images or "disaster pornography." If shame is about the revelation of what is or ought to be covered—"perhaps from a root *skam* meaning to cover, and akin to the root (*kam*) of G. hemd shirt, E. chemise"—then the absence or failure of shaming is not only traceable to successfully remaining clothed or hidden in the dark. Today, all too often, there is more than enough light, and yet its subjects exhibit themselves shamelessly, brazenly, and openly.[7]

Obviously, this "crisis" has important implications for the struggle for human rights, especially in an age when its traditional allies—the camera and the witness—have acquired unprecedented levels of public access, bordering at times on saturation, and when it increasingly finds new allies, intentional or inadvertent, like them or not, in the armies of the world's most powerful nations.

But the crisis is not simply on the side of the audience or the public, as even the most sophisticated commentators seem to assume, nor is it merely one of indifference or denial or even enjoyment (voyeurism). To leave it at that would be to leave the general structure of the shaming hypothesis or strategy intact. But the crisis is in fact far more profound: the enjoyment or the exposure is now, at least often enough to consider it non-accidental, on the side of those who appear on camera. In the age of the generalized photo-opportunity—whether the suicide-bomber's videotape, made-for-television ethnic cleansing, or embedded reporters and videophones—what role can publicity, the exposé, and shame (still) play?

I am not sure I can answer this question, but I can offer a pair of examples which underline the difficult situation faced by the traditional paradigm. I want to turn to a couple of photo opportunities, media events, made for television moments.

Before I do so, a word about Iraq: to hear the breathless talk from the media-on-media commentators over the last six months or so, you would think reporters and photographers had never gone along for a ride in a plane or a tank before, never stood at an intersection and waited for someone to get shot at, never done a standup during a firefight, never had to coordinate their logistics and movements with those of the military, never shared meals and camped out with the soldiers about whom they were reporting, and never reported favorably on the conduct of their country's armies. Needless to say, they have, and they have also complained bitterly about not being able to do those things.

"We've never had a war like this, and we got inundated by close-ups," said *Nightline* producer Tom Bettag in March, about the war which his aging correspondent covered from a tank.[8] While it is certainly true that we have never had a war *quite* like this, especially not to the extent that it happened on television, we do have many precedents for it. It is worth revisiting some of that televisual history—here, two moments from the last decade in Somalia and Kosovo—to think about the assumptions underwriting most discussion about the ethics and politics of human rights struggles, including wars, in the media.

## Somalia

Elsewhere, I have written about the televising of "Operation Restore Hope," the first serious post Cold War "humanitarian intervention," in Somalia. There, I was interested in the images of the soldiers in humanitarian action, especially on the first night of the operation, along with the images of starvation which preceded it and the images of military debacle which eventually followed it. I wrote then that the point of Somalia was the pictures, the transmission and archiving of a new image for a military-aesthetic complex recently deprived of the only enemy it could remember knowing.

The tenth anniversary of the events recreated in *Black Hawk Down* has just passed, and all we really have left is the movie, which impressively omits both that opening night and the critical role of a camcorder in the ultimate conclusion of the battle on October 3, 1993.[9]

And we all skipped right past the anniversary of the opening night's landing last December, so let me recall it for you, prime-time (EST) of December 8, 1992, as the first groups of what would ultimately be a 25,000-soldier force began to arrive in Mogadishu to take control of transport facilities and enable a massive humanitarian relief operation to proceed securely. (I leave aside many important questions here about the wisdom of this intervention, its timing, its actual relation to the famine which was its pretext, and so on.)

Reporting from the Mogadishu airport within (night-scope) sight of the landing beaches, CNN correspondent Christiane Amanpour narrated the goings-on rather economically: "it was a classic media event—lights flashing—people desperately trying to ask the marines some questions."

The Marines—a small group of Special Force-style commandos called a Marine Reconnaissance Unit, the vanguard of the landing—were not so enthusiastic about answering questions on the beach. They had come, with Navy SEALs, directly out of the water onto the beach, and seemed a bit perplexed to be met by reporters and cameras. As an after-action report put it later: "The team on the beach were surprised to meet members of the news media who made their job difficult with crowds of cameramen using bright lights to get footage of the wet, camouflaged Marines who were now brilliantly lit up in the dark night."[10] Crowds of cameramen? Surprised? It seems that the commandos were inadequately briefed on the full extent of their mission. Or a little too isolated there on the *USS Juneau* offshore: the headline that morning in *USA Today*, after all, was "Somalia landing airs live," and the instructions for the viewing public were clear: "NBC and CNN plan to air the scheduled troop landing live at 10 pm ET/7 pm PT."

A few minutes after the initial landing, a Marine spokesman "came ashore," as he put it, "in a rubber boat," in order to deal with the questions. The assembled journalists—some estimates put the total in Mogadishu that night at about 600, or roughly the same quantity as were "embedded" with all of the U.S. and U.K. troops in the war against Iraq—interviewed Lt. Kirk Coker not so much about the landing itself as about the scene of the landing, and about what they were all doing there at the moment. It was not quite live, but within a few minutes CNN was playing the tape:

> Q. Sir, don't you think it's rather bizarre that all these journalists are standing out here during—
> A.—Yes, it really was, and you guys really spoiled our nice little raid here. We wanted to come in without anybody knowing it—
> Q.—Like it was a surprise we were here—
> A.—Well, we pretty much knew that. [...]
> Q. So far everything's going well, sir?
> A. Everything seems to be going well right now. We're not being

shot at and I'm standing here talking to all of you.

Needless to say, it was no surprise to anyone. Michael Gordon of the *New York Times* reported merely the obvious on the day after the landing: the cameras and lights were already on the beach because the Pentagon had told them to be there. "All week the Pentagon had encouraged press coverage of the Marine landing," he wrote, "reporters were told when the landing would take place, and some network correspondents were quietly advised where the marines would arrive so that they could set up their cameras. [...] But having finally secured an elusive spotlight, the marines discovered that they had too much of a good thing.[11] Or, as the Joint Task Force commander Marine Brig. Gen. Frank Libutti had told reporters in Mombassa (his HQ) earlier that day: "I recommend all of you go down to the beach if you want a good show tonight."[12]

There was grumbling, though, about the way the media—or the briefers who advised them—had perhaps exposed the Marines to the risk of hostile fire. As one analyst put it later: "the event was benign only because no gunman decided to take advantage of the illuminated target area containing both the U.S. Marines and the news media whose coverage had helped to bring them there." The key words are the last, though, not about the media but about the Marines: "the news media whose coverage had helped to bring them there."[13] What Operation Restore Hope taught us was that war today—hard war as in Iraq, both times, and soft war as in Somalia— was and remains (among other things, to be sure, but crucially) a battle of images.

A CBS television producer who was there later told me that one of the first SEALs on the Mogadishu beach had shouted to his cameraman: "kill the lights, we're tactical." The allegory seemed to suggest that lights were only appropriate at the strategic level. But he missed the point: the imagery was not just strategic—even if the very strategy of the operation did depend on reporters, cameras, uplinks, and the rest. The imagery, and the production and transmission of imagery, was also a tactic, a ground-level move in the prosecution of the operation.

One need not look behind or beneath the images it produced, as if they concealed some lurking geo-strategic ambition or agenda. What was most deeply significant about the operation was that it had no depth. It was an operation on the surface, of the surface. The agenda, the tactics and the strategy, was the imagery: the creation of images.

Of course, the Somalis could watch television too, and it was obvious very quickly that the battlefield was one of pictures. The Americans used satellite uplinks, the forces of General Aidid a camcorder, but the war of images could and was fought with skill and craft by both sides. After all, the disaster of October 3rd (Black Hawk Down)—a disaster not only for the 18 dead Americans but more so for the perhaps 1000 Somalis who died that night—was also a photo opportunity and a media event. Bodies were presented—as they had been on earlier occasions as well—for the scrutiny of the cameras, not simply dragged around for fun. As British journalist Richard Dowden tells the story:

> Television pictures brought US troops to Somalia and television pictures will pull them out. [...] The pictures raise serious questions about the nature of news-gathering in Somalia, especially since the gunmen clearly perform for the camera.[14]

It is tempting to talk about these "photo-ops" and "made-for-television" events—both the December and October ones—in dismissive terms, as if the pre-arranged presence of the camera somehow renders the events it witnesses less serious or less real. But the second set of images reminds us why we have to take the first set seriously. The stakes of this mediatic scenario are high; we cannot understand, nor have a properly political relation to, invasions and war crimes, military operations and paramilitary atrocities—both of maximal importance for human rights campaigners—in the present and future if we do not attend to the centrality of image production and management in them. We will be at an even greater loss if we do not admit that the high-speed electronic news media have created not just new opportunities for activism and awareness, but also for performance, presentation, advertising, propaganda, and for political work of all kinds.

## Kosovo

Just a week before the war over Kosovo began, in mid-March 1999, the Yugoslav and Serbian forces operating there taught the world a lesson about publicity, exposure, the politics of information, and what Michael Ignatieff called, in his book about Kosovo, "virtual war." They taught it using those very media.

As the week of March 15, 1999 began, a set of villages about 20 km north of Pristina on the road to Vucitrn (7km further north) were under assault, ostensibly, as the OSCE's monitors later reported, in retaliation for the presence of KLA guerillas. Reporters from around the world were in place throughout Kosovo, and it was to this area (a short drive in the morning) of operations between Pristina and Vucitrn that many of them gravitated. They found much to see and to report on, but the reports from the area of Mijalic from those couple of weeks share one dominant self-referential trope. Reporters seemed determined to underline that they could not see everything, that things were being hidden from them, that the warring factions were interested in concealing the full extent of their activities. Their reports further underlined the nature of the problem—and of the self-understanding—by brandishing the evidence of their successful evasion of these restrictions and repressions. The paradigm of revelation, exposure, and shaming were in full operation. Their reports were important in the run-up to the war, NATO's first full-scale combat, and one undertaken not in the name of national interest, imminent threat, regional stability, or control of territory but rather of human rights, and a war which in the minds of its authors in Washington and London and Brussels was a de facto apology for their years of inaction in Bosnia and Croatia.

On the 11th, an AFP correspondent wrote from along the shifting front lines:

> "Get out! You're in a war zone," barked a Kosovo Liberation Army (KLA) commander named Labinot in Mijalic village, where the rebels and security forces were less than 500 meters (yards) apart. Several armored vehicles closed in on the village, as did Serbian special forces wearing masks and bullet-proof vests for protection against the Kalashnikov-armed guerrillas.[15]

The next day, Friday March 12th, two Serb policemen were shot and wounded in Mijalic, and the confrontation intensified over the weekend. AP's Anne Thompson reported:

> With the villages empty of civilians, army troops and Serb police started looting Mijalic and Drvare and burning down houses Saturday, said diplomatic monitors whose mission is led by the Operation for Security and Cooperation in Europe. While much of the shelling was aimed at driving the rebels west over the mountains and into their traditional Drenica region, monitors said the burning was sheer vengeance.[16]

By Sunday, wrote Julius Strauss in the The Daily Telegraph:

> [In Drvare] The charred remains of some houses were still smoldering. All the locals had fled. The only sign of life was a large and nervous horse who snorted as the army trucks rolled past. The Serb police turned us back with a swear-word and a

universal gesture. Skirting round the position through scrubby fields to the west gave a clearer vantage point. Smoke could be seen rising from Mijalic, the next village, which locals said had been completely torched by the Serb forces. On top of a ridge-line a Yugoslav army half-track with a heavy machine-gun mounted and an armored personnel carrier could be seen. Some nearby gardens and small trees had been shredded by the passage of tanks. One could be heard rumbling into a new position just out of our view.[17]

And Reuters reported on the same day:

Reporters who reached the centre of Mijalic, about six kms (four miles) southwest of Vucitrn, found the village a smouldering ruin, empty save for Serbian police in armored vehicles who warned of sniper activity.

"Turn around. Get out of here. This is a military zone and there are snipers firing in this area," a police officer in a flak jacket ordered.

He spoke amidst shell-shattered, burned-out houses at an intersection strewn with downed electric and telephone lines.

Houses on the ridge-line above the village centre were still smoking and at least one was in full flame. Occasional automatic weapons fire ripped the air above the ruins.[18]

The next day, March 15th, Carlotta Gall reported for the *New York Times*:

The OSCE has watched as a string of villages has come under tank and mortar fire for more than a week now. Yugoslav army forces took over the Albanian village of Mijalic and were guarding the entrance with a tank and several troop trucks, keeping journalists and monitors away. "This is a war zone," said a young Serbian soldier guarding the road, an automatic rifle at the ready across his chest. "It is dangerous and you must leave."[19]

This is a rather traditional war story: war means no access. And more often than not, no access is taken as a sign of the reality, the authenticity, of the war. It is the job of reporters, monitors, and human rights advocates to "skirt around the positions" and expose the violent reality. No photo ops here: only serious business. But in fact, on March 16th, the next day, something rather different happened. Correspondent Bill Neely of Britain's Independent Television News reported from that very village of Mijalic, where his camera crew—along with another crew from the BBC with reporter Angus Roxburgh in tow—was video-taping, from the ridge-line, no doubt, as Serbian policemen and nearby villagers looted and destroyed it.

Of course it was very good—and brave—reporting. But what was interesting, or especially interesting, about it was what was remarkably different from the experiences reported by Gall and the other reporters. The men destroying Mijalic were not surprised in the act of destruction. They were not exposed, caught on tape unawares. They did it for the cameras. As both television reporters noted, the men "cleansing" the village were watching the cameras that watched them, and acted in full knowledge of the fact that their deeds were being recorded. Neely spoke, simply and eloquently, about this knowledge:

> As we are filming from afar, three men come to burn the village of Mijalic, which until a week ago was full of Albanians. It is now being looted by Serbs: one man, stealing a television, is a policeman. The five men move from house to house and with a matchbox wipe Mijalic from the map, one, a Serb civilian, robbing his Albanian neighbor's television. The men are making it difficult for Albanians ever to return. The Serbs know we are filming them,

but they make the law here, and they break it. So they burn Mijalic to the ground.

The BBC's Roxburgh said something similar: "The village was razed before our eyes; they knew we were filming them, they didn't care." The ITN video log, which catalogs the film shot by shot, also reports the scene succinctly: "Looters out of house waving to cameras."

On March 19th the OSCE observer mission withdrew, unable to do its work. NATO's air campaign began a week later.

## A Wave

With this simple gesture of the hand, not simply cynical or ironic, not simply nihilistic, no matter how destructive, these policemen announced the effective erasure of the fundamental axiom of the human rights movement in an age of publicity: that the exposure of violence is feared by its perpetrators, and hence that the act of witness is not simply an ethical gesture but an active intervention.

Mobilizing shame presupposes that dark deeds are done in the dark, and that the light of publicity—especially of the television camera—thus has the power to strike preemptively on behalf of justice. With a wave, these policemen announced their comfort with the camera, their knowledge of the actual power of truth and representation.

How should we read this wave, this repeated succession of hand gestures quite different from the other "universal gesture" with which correspondent Strauss of *The Daily Telegraph* had been greeted just a few days earlier? It is a mark of recognition and acknowledgement—a kind of wink, as one anthropologist pointed out to me—first of all, it says, "we know you're there, we see you, we witness your presence." Implicitly then it also communicates a feeling of comfort with that presence, not simply permission to remain but encouragement, endorsement, benevolence toward the crews and their cameras. And the wave acknowledges—after all, these men know about televisions—as well that it is directed not just to people but to cameras, to being recorded, transmitted, archived, repeated. Waving to the cameras is never just for the cameras but for the others, for the public, for elsewhere, or the future and many futures. The wave announces itself as a performance, marks not just the camera but the space defined by the viewfinder—surrogate for the screen—that it opens up for performance or demonstration.

The wave announces—it performs, it enacts—that there's no hiding here, nothing in the dark, nothing to be ashamed of. And it demonstrates this for the very instruments which are known for their revelatory abilities—the wave says "expose this, this that I am exposing for you." Like the writing or the hand at the end of Keats' strange little fragment "This living hand," the waving hands of Mijalic each say "see here it is, I hold it towards you," and they do what they say.[20]

Is it a gesture of contempt? A statement of power over against the powerlessness of the witnesses? Or is it an announcement of impunity? Or just a happy wave of contentment, that of a satisfied shopper? Does it imply superiority, or the overcoming of a feeling of inferiority? Is it cynical, or desperate, or wanton, as the reporter suggests?

All these interpretations are possible, but I prefer to try to read the act *as an act* and not simply as a message. In that sense, it challenges the Enlightenment presuppositions I have been following. It suggests that the camera does not simply capture what happens and convey that elsewhere in the form of knowledge or information, of something to be acted on. Rather, the wave is an action, not only a fact to be revealed (although it is that as well) but an event that takes place, for the camera, as if to demonstrate to it, through it, something about it and its actual force in the world. The wave sends its message by doing it: we know you are watching, we know that you know that we know you are watching, but...and then it turns out that there is no But. If the classic formula of denial is "we know very well, but nevertheless [we do it anyway]," then this is not a matter of fetishism or denial. Here, we all know everything, and there are no second thoughts, no buts. We know, and hence we enact our knowledge, our status, our sense of the complete irrelevance of knowledge. We are news, information, knowledge, evidence, yes, because we are doing it, making it. In this sense, the Croatian theorist Boris Buden is right to adopt Baudrillard's slogan about the "transparency of evil": "If there is a lesson to be learned from the Yugoslav disaster, it is about the transparency of evil. Nothing has happened in these ten years of war that wasn't 'entirely predictable'—if it wasn't announced outright and in advance."[21]

## Conclusion

*Nightline* producer Bettag's comment, quoted earlier, that "we got inundated by close-ups" has an unexpected resonance now. Close-up means no distance, and self-exposure. So what difference does it make, for those of us who have to respond, when the technologies of exposure become opportunities for performance, exhibition, self-exposure? What becomes of shame? One does not have to sympathize with Karl-Heinz Stockhausen to suggest that aesthetic categories are relevant here. The aesthetic finds itself in extreme proximity to the ethico-political now; the proximity is perhaps discomforting to some, but it is also the condition of any serious intervention. That intervention, though, will have to enter into political dispute, not from the safety of a distance or the ethical certainty of a good conscience. The closer we get the more uncertain things are. What difference does all this exposure make, here and there? Only time and force will tell. The time and the force of those images will surely have something to do with it. That is why we have a responsibility—ethical and political—to attend to them.

* A few sentences in this talk were drawn from pieces I have written about similar topics: "Publicity and Indifference: media, surveillance, 'humanitarian intervention,'" in *CTRL [SPACE]: Rhetorics of Surveillance from Bentham to Big Brother*, ed. Thomas Levin et al (Karlsruhe: ZKM and Cambridge: MIT Press, 2002): 544-561; "Looking like flames and falling like stars. Kosovo, the first Internet war," in *Mutations*, ed. Rem Koolhaas et al (Barcelona: ACTAR and Bordeaux: arc en reve centre d'architecture, 2000): 84-95; revised version in *Social Identities* 7.4, "The Other Europe" (2001): 539-550; and "Live from..." in *Back to the Front: Tourisms of War/Visite aux armées: Tourismes de guerre*, ed. Elizabeth Diller and Ricardo Scofidio (Caen: F.R.A.C. Basse-Normandie, 1994): 130-163.

Unhampered by the red tape of the nation-state, embodying her own cultural identity and stowing its accessories in a carry-on bag, the modern nomad wandered out of the romantic landscape of Goethe's *Young Werther* and into the property-less states of work and leisure of Le Corbusier's bucolic Radiant City before descending into the global network. We encountered her, perhaps for the last time, in a recent design competition sponsored by Alessi who was looking to furnish those perpetually on the move. We designed her a utility belt for personal tools and a portable computer station that would both now fail to make it through airport metal detectors. Detained in the airport lounge since September 11—or perhaps since the most recent global summit—she sits and contemplates the flow of capital as it passes by, siphoning off resources in its wake and forcibly pushing people along with it. By now we are all familiar with Deleuze and Guattari's depiction of nomadology, which sets up two moments: the state asserting its authority through the "striated" spatial grids of power and the nomad using a war machine to expand its "smooth" territory. The tribes left out of this Nietzschean dualism of conquest are the displaced who would not choose to be either nomadic or stationary in their given circumstance.

First-Step Housing, Van Alen Institute, Fall 2000. View of two attached units oriented at 180 degrees. Three sliding panels of interchangeable position and function and varying degrees of transparency compose the front wall. They are set back from the exterior edge of the closet to create a zone of transition and identity like a porch.

The subject/clients of this article are the displaced, the döppelgangers of Alessi's urban nomad, the other product of post-cold war geo-politics inhabiting a society of scarcity beneath our cultures of abundance. Whether the result of internecine struggle, foreign war, famine, or mass unemployment, their displacement has a root cause in patterns of investment that date from the Cold War superpowers' aid to contested territories—such as continuously destabilized Afghanistan—and exist today in public and privatized form.[1] Neither foreign powers seeking control over natural resources nor foreign companies interested in a "cash crop" production like sneakers have tended to invest in the infrastructure or future of their host nation, with the consequence of underdevelopment and displacement more often than the showcase success of towns like Hyderabad, India. One typical pattern of migration in relation to investment begins with the move of subsistence farmers to the local city in pursuit of new jobs, and then to the world city-at-large when the jobs disappear as foreign investment moves on. The accrued mass of individual movement has large

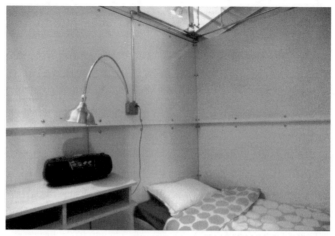

Common Ground's brief requested single rooms for single men, but we conceived a system capable of different occupancies and configurations. The units can be combined to have multiple bedrooms or shared and contiguous living arrangements.

consequences such as the reduced agricultural production and environmental degradation of abandoned land, and the overstressed physical and social infrastructure of rapidly expanding cities. Competition for increasingly scarce rural and urban resources and the political control over them can then fuel the strife that leads to ethnic struggle, regional war, and mass displacement. In its drive to expand, and in its ability to do so without sovereign limits, capital spurs these related human displacements: de-ruralization, migration, emigration, and flight.[2]

As quantified by the United Nations, the number of people subject to scenarios of displacement are vast—one in every 297 persons on this planet, including a new category officially recognized by the UN, the Internally Displaced Person (IDP), who is forced from home but not region or country. There are at least twenty-five million refugees, the population equivalent to double the world's largest metropolis. The imagined specter of such a vast urban receptacle for the dispossessed haunts an understanding of the real impact of displacement on existing cities. As they wane with attack, wax through immigration, or emerge suddenly in the debased form of the refugee camp, cities register the phenomena of displacement, and displacement describes the temporality and permanencies of cities. Any strategy for housing the displaced ultimately must envision the new or recuperated urban culture.

The dominant architecture of displacement, that of a refugee camp, seems a dark legacy of an International Style of military operations unaffected by all our postmodern lessons regarding the disruption of regions, cultural memory, and patterns of daily life. There are still few alternatives to the economies and apparent rationality of blue tarp tents arranged *cartus* and *decumana* in relation to group latrines and delivery routes, a plan that dates from nineteenth-century military manuals, which in turn model themselves quite self-consciously on Caesar.[3] This arrangement expedites both the surveying and surveillance of the camp. It offers effective protection from military attack and epidemic. The blue tarp is extremely cheap and tough—tougher than even pre-sewn tents, which tend to give at the seams under environmental stress like wind. It is efficient to transport and distribute, even in circumstances with fragile roads that cannot be passed by heavy trucks.

Most importantly, the tarp tent is the sign and the goods of the temporary. In the first months of conflict, the message of the tent, shared by their displaced inhabitants, the camp hosts, and the Non-Governmental Organizations (NGO) alike, is that the conflict will be brief and resettlement imminent. The investment in both tents and land matches the expected duration of stay. When the conflict persists, the temporality of the tents takes on the quasi-military signification of resistance to the enemy's expanded borders and the political signification of the host's opposition to local resettlement. A tent city in Azerbaijan for 10,000 people who share the ethnicity of their hosts has persisted for a decade, under conditions that the local government admits to be unacceptable, because more permanent accommodations would signal the military acceptance of reduced borders and the local acceptance of a burdensome population.[4]

It is a more than ironic coincidence that the other most popular refugee site is an abandoned military camp. It is in the nature of current warfare, ideally fought by a virtual infantry with cyber intelligence and fast moving deployable structures like inflatable barracks, that the retardataire military setting loses its value. On the other hand, the adaptive reuse of its regulatory structure has a brutal clarity reminiscent of Michel Foucault with a disturbingly appealing ecological twist. The military compound of Nagyatád, Hungary opened as a Bosnian refugee settlement for 3,000 people in 1991 without any dramatic physical change to the original mess hall, infirmary, or four-story barrack buildings of large undivided rooms and gang bathrooms built to accommodate fifty soldiers each. The original barbed wire fence remained, officially to protect the refugees but also to control their movement and to maintain balance with the deprived local population of 12,000, who both coveted and resented the stockpiled cigarettes and fruit that the refugees traded at the local market. The camp's school, mosque, and other formal and informal social structures earned it the epithet "refugee village" but could not overcome its liminal existence, such that after three years the refugees wanted only to go home rather than become Hungarian—and the citizens of Nagyatád would have them go.[5]

To those responsible for displacement planning, the ecology implicit in reusing the military barrack as a refugee village is not a trivial advantage. Refugee camps can be the size of small cities with physical impacts at the environmental and bio-regional level so profound that the United Nations High Commission on Refugees (UNHCR) describes them as "eco-disasters."[6] The problems include: deforestation as refugees collect fuel wood and building material, consequent soil erosion and loss of bio-diversity, poaching of wildlife, over-cultivation of soil, water depletion, soil and water contamination from waste, air pollution from cooking fires, and the production of vast amounts of garbage, including shipping and construction materials. The conditions of scarcity that fuel displacements in the first place recur at the sites of relocation.

Taken together, the environmental policies now emerging to control the camps' impact describe a planning vision almost Vitruvian in its combination of quasi–military techniques and ideality. Sophisticated satellite mapping and imaging of the geography determine sites that can accommodate the settlements of 20,000 people with minimal environmental damage.[7] The rule of thumb is a 15 km radius buffer zone between campsites and natural areas to be protected based on the circumference of refugees' search for fuel. Within the camp, the rule of "no clear felling" of trees and shrubs and the demarcation of areas of protected growth extend the principle of forestation. To accommodate the need for agricultural land while maintaining "bio-mass," planners have developed systems like "taungya" in which crops are planted between trees.[8] The recommended plot size is a generous 400 square meters per household minimum, in order to encourage management responsibility of the immediate site and the addition of bio-mass through household planting. The cluster of four to six shelters around a shared central space is the favored device of balance between the social benefit of eating and preparing meals within the family unit and the environmental advantage of collective cooking. Collective facilities such as markets and infirmaries are distributed according to criteria of walking distance and room for expansion. In sum, the emergent planning principles of eco-friendly refugee camps bear uncanny resemblance to enlightened urbanisms, such as the New Bombay of Charles Correa or the Majorca Technopolis of Richard Rogers, that challenge the culture of the car by using the pedestrian radius of travel as the basic module for planning, reformulate the modernist garden city tradition as a productive landscape, and envision an equitable society based on equal dwelling plots.

In theory, the socio-political attitude implicit in the new physical planning of the camp extends to its operation by involving the refugees as decision makers. In a form of "grassroots organization" they elect leaders who help to organize the distribution of food, shelter, and jobs. The reality, however, can come closer to social engineering because of the needs for protection and the effort to modify cultural practices that are not sustainable. While stressing the use of educational workshops to promote good environmental practice, the UN guidelines also suggest economic incentives to shape behavior. UNHCR commonly exacts a fee for firewood, seeds, and solar stoves because they find that the cost of the item creates its value in the minds of the refugees. Cooking practices are often sites of intense negotiation between camp efficiency and cultural mores, seen for example in the resistance of many populations to fuel-efficient solar cooking from the belief that evil spirits will enter the uncovered food; a common compromise is the use of very large heavy-lidded pots. While clusters of tents arranged with the assistance of a refugee representative can offer a closer approximation to tribal or neighborhood structure than the military row, ultimately the opportunities for physical, economic, and social self-determination are limited. The isolated camp exists in a suspended spatio-temporal moment, which defeats the possibility of urbanism.

The approach to camp organization that best mitigates the problem of self-determination and in doing so explores an expanded range of physical settings is that of permaculture.[9] Permaculture, a neologism of permanent and culture from the 1970's, refers to settlement patterns that minimize waste, maximize diversity, and choreograph mutually supportive relationships among the elements of the system—houses, animal units, streams and forests and the like. In the context of refugee camps—which have neither permanence nor culture—the goals of permaculture pertain to the larger lifecycle of the camp and to the roles of its refugee population as stake holders in their current condition and agents in the future of the place. The intention is for camp residents to manage first their internal and ultimately their extended environmental affairs, as occurred, for example, in the Umpium camp in Thailand, where residents first negotiated the allocation of land and fruit trees for home gardens and then participated alongside local villagers in a public representative body that deals with the Thai authorities on environmental matters.[10] Ideally, camps and villages become political

Interior Perspective of a unit inserted into house ruins where it acts as service core, structural support and scaffold for the construction of a larger dwelling.

and economic partners, as in Jhapa, Nepal, where refugee and local residents first collaborated on erosion controls and then on land reclamation for commercial agro-forestry.[11]   The strict, ecological vantage point of permaculture requires the camp to be understood as a fragment of a region, the region to be held to the same environmental standards as the camp, and the refugee and host to jointly shape the identity of the place.

The permaculture camp echoes the vision of eco-idealists and green economists in their post-industrial alternatives to corporate globalization.  The society outlined is one of small-scaled, decentralized, and self-reliant communities that join together in municipal networks of shared laws and standards in order to maintain bio-regional balance.  In the eco-service economy, service replaces commodity through the concept of use-value, such that products are mobility not cars, nutrition not food, cooking not fuel, and—one might add in the context of refugee camps—planting not crop production.  As in the closed economy of the camp, the green marketplace uses an eco-incentive system of barter that extends to the recycling of objects.  It relies on local currency and exchange values that prevent the siphoning off of capital to remote locations.  Granted by an

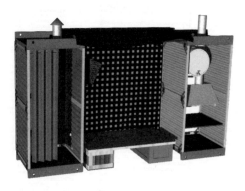

Assembled Single Unit: At a distance from one another, the separate privy and hearth can initially frame a habitable space between them protected by a photovoltaic tarp.

authority other than the nation state, shaped by its inhabitants for sustained development rather than expansive growth, operated as a service use-value economy with a system of exchange credit based on energy consumption, the permaculture refugee camp aspires to an experiment in the eco-idealist manner with populations that far outsize any of the current eco-idealist communities.[12]

This spatial blurring of the permaculture camp and village, refugee and host, is likewise a temporal blurring in which the site of refuge becomes the site of resettlement, and the settlement a self-determined village where the refugee has, in fact, cultivated her own garden. Still, the underlying condition of displacement remains. Temporized by the idea of return, all such sites are diasporic.

The unending desire of the displaced is to return home, even when acknowledging that home consists of a set of conditions that will never recur or, perhaps, never quite existed. "Were our customs really beautiful or am I just imagining things," is one such refrain.[13] More than unmet desire, however, the idea of return is a *realpolitik* solution to halt the erosion of the social as well as physical fabric and the loss of property rights. Basically, the longer one waits the worse things get. UNHCR aids voluntary repatriation by evaluating towns according to criteria of *inter alia* (access to housing, freedom of movement, police protection) and through gifts of tools, seeds, and tarps; but it lacks a strategy for the recuperation of the physical city needed to make return a real possibility.

The problem of urban recuperation drove our thinking in a competition for disaster relief housing for Kosovo. The competition called for an alternative to the tent—that most telegraphic sign of displacement—to be erected within 48 hours from an absolute minimum of materials and to remain in place for as long as two years. Considering the projected duration of the camp set-up, the fundamental issues lay beyond the scope of the tent in questions of infrastructure, planning, and the environment. Rather than create better sites of dislocation, our strategy considered the reuse of the city to avoid the physical and mental waste inherent in building refugee camps. The challenge was to develop a physical device that could reconstitute an urban fabric without the support of a civic scale of infrastructure and that could, as an auxiliary consequence, retool a refugee camp as if it were a city. The proposal employs a condensed infrastructure of a privy and a kitchen with hearth/heat source and integral cistern/shower housed in de-mountable yet load-bearing enclosures.

The design negotiates among issues of cultural specificity, using both the locally available, such as insulating straw, and the imported, such as high-performance ceramic sheathing. It juggles the need to preserve the camp ecology from a strip search for building materials or fuel and the need to minimize the material value of the shelter as resale scrap with the demands of a structure suitable for reuse on the sites of return. Given the variety of refugee lifestyles, the plan required flexibility such that, for example, the kitchen could face the privy, or garden, or not. The style of this object is largely irrelevant; embedded deep within the permanent house, it has little impact on an outward appearance determined largely by the inhabitant. The boxes aspire to the universality of the tent through their

230

instrumentality alone. To this end, the photovoltaic tarp and its battery supply not just heat or light, but also a TV hookup, the ultimate link from nowhere to everywhere, more desired in the camps of Chechnya, the streets of Calcutta, and the shelters of New York than square footage or a full kitchen.[14]

The boxes are seeds of the new city containing all the goods immediately needed, with husks that can be transformed and eventually absorbed within the growth of the house. While they allow the renewed operation of a site, these objects remain incomplete and ultimately dependent on their host city as a form of economy. The urban situation takes on their trace along with that of the pre-existing city but remains somewhat fluid, with the possibility of new kinds of buildings, new relations among them, and the hope of a lush second growth.

The tents still in place ten years after the civil strife in Azerbaijan demonstrate that temporary solutions are not distinguishable from the permanent on the basis of duration. What makes dwelling temporary is its dislocation from site, from political and economic community, and from one's own history. Underlying our project to retool the ruined or limited city so that it can perform in new ways is a belief that the ultimate check to the progress of dislocation is not the literal act of return but urbanity itself. As Scott Anderson suggests, the "historical cosmopolitanism" of Sarajevo and Belgrade, Pristina and Mostar and the Dalmatian Coast was such a cultural and economic urbanity undone by events resembling the pattern of de-ruralization, migration, and flight: "The gulf of experience between city and village in the Balkans is an awful chasm. The cities are emblems of cultural fusion; the typical Balkan village a hard and pitiless place with ancient feuds and primitive blood laws. The leader/villains (Milosevic, Karadzic) are country boys who, when faced with the economic crises, shed their urbanity and return to their village ways."[15] We cannot undo globalization or certain continuing economic crises, but we might imagine a new hybrid city that is more resistant to the epidemics of dislocation.

## Coda: A True Story

With the collapse of the Soviet block, a small town on the Dalmatian coast bounced back from a progressive decline in its agricultural economy to emerge as a tourist haven for Europe in the 1980's. Residents eagerly gave up small farms, vineyards and fisheries, moved to town and opened hotels, cafés, and restaurants. They claimed their villas were worth half a million dollars each. The war eventually stopped the tourists, decimated the economy, and drove out the resident Bosnians, destroyed much of their property and with it some coastal beauty, and the real estate value. But because the tourist economy had depended on the scenic appeal of the permanent culture of the area, namely the vineyards, farms, and harbor, traces of the agrarian economy remained. Those who closed their hotels replanted their orchards; those who lost their villas again launched their boats. First they fed themselves with the produce and now they even begin to prosper. Still, they would prefer for the tourists to return and for their houses to be worth half a million dollars. But they know that day will come only after some of the Bosnians return and reconstruct their homes and businesses along the coast so as to calm the fears of the multi-ethnic tourists. Then there will be hotels and cafés, but also working vineyards, fruit groves, and fisheries, in an unpredictable and lush second growth, which they will never be so foolish as to abandon again.

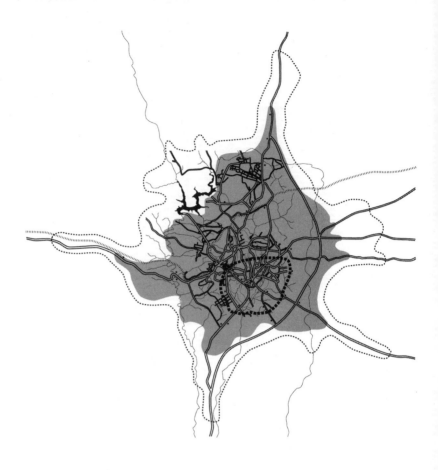

\* Exhibited in "Cities Without Citizens" at The Rosenbach Museum & Library, July 8-
September 28, 2003. Installation shots are available in Section III (Documentation).

## Ibadan, Nigeria

The refugee camps of today are the cities of tomorrow. The evidence lies in the colonial settlements and forced displacements of previous centuries that have become the metropoli of today. The trading companies of Europe considered themselves temporary occupants of undeveloped territories focused on the extraction of wealth without the long-term investment of city building. They did not intend their forts, residential cantonments and roads as foundational plans for the exponential growth of the sprawling contemporary cities of Madras or Calcutta. The African cities of Ibadan, the second largest city of Nigeria, and Mbuji-Mbayi the third largest city of former Zaire, originated in the displacements of population from colonial wars among indigenous as well as European empires. The proverbial epithet, "slum of Calcutta," and the Rough Guide quip "the hell hole of Ibadan," should be our call to halt the nonstrategized urbanization of the world through displacement.

"Present Ibadan started as a refugee camp in 1829." Founded in the late eighteenth century by a group of Yorubu adventurers from the ancient city of Ife, Eba Odan (City Situated Near a Grove) was a colonial settlement among other tribal peoples. In all their urbanizing and colonizing practices, the Yorubu spread to both vacant and already inhabited areas absorbing the indigenous population into their administrative reach but not necessarily physical structure. They then established long distance trade routes from their city to other regional markets. During the nineteenth century, various Yorubu kingdoms battled for control of the territory and its slave trade routes causing not only the internal displacement of Yorubu but the actual physical displacement of the city itself to a camp site. Now called more simply Ebadan or Ibadan, as if to trace the loss of its original grove with the corruption of its name, this remnant of Eba Odan expanded rapidly as it became a permanent settlement for the wandering soldiers of Ile-Ife, Ijebu and the Oyo. This amalgam of refugee soldiers seized territory and prominence from the competing Oyo Yorubu Empire, and then solidified the political and military eminence of their phoenix city Ibadan with the growth of trade routes from the interior to the coast. From 1865 onward Ibadan has been the single most important city of Yorubuland.

In spite of its size, there is a controversy as to whether Ibadan is truly a city because of its dual structure whereby its core is inhabited by indigenous peoples who spend half the week in the surrounding villages. It remains as at its founding, a temporary settlement with some permanent physical characteristics. Ironically, the most stable urban presence are its contemporary immigrants, and a literate elite linked to the renowned University of Ibadan, established by the British in 1949.

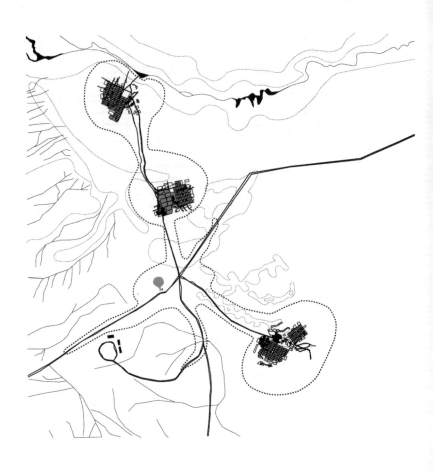

236

## Dadaab, Kenya

Dadaab is a refugee camp on the Somalian border established in 1992 in response first to the civil warfare and then to the natural disasters effecting that country. Its three compounds of Ifo, Dagahaley, and Hagadera are currently home to over 300,000 refugees—most of whom have lived at the camp for over a decade. Prior to the establishment of the camp, the local town and region of Dadaab was largely nomadic and pastoralist, with a permanent village population of less than 5000. Today its regional population is more than 10,000, many of whom have settled in relation to the wells, bore holes, and other infrastructure of the refugee camps. These settlers are either former pastoralists attracted by the constant supply of water and food for their herds, or traders capitalizing on the new market economy of the camps. The demographic and physical structure of Dadaab region is further blurred by the shared ethnic descent of the refugees and local population such that, while the refugees are officially confined to the fenced compounds and have no civic rights, there are Somalis of undefined origin living both in town and in camp. The familial reach of the refugees extends even further beyond the town and its immediate desolate landscape to Nairobi and Canada and it has instigated "mutatus" bus routes, trade connections, phone and communication networks across all of Kenya and beyond.

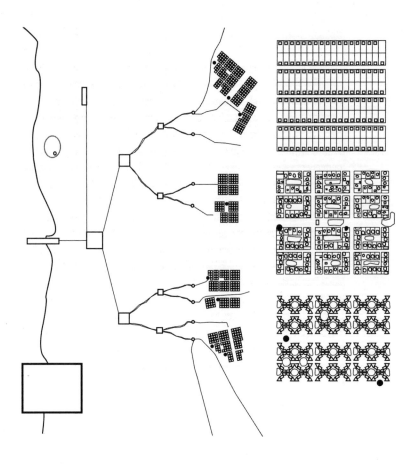

**Refugee Camp: Components of a Logistics Systems**

While the host government has ultimate authority over the existence of a camp, The United Nations High Commission on Refugees takes responsibility for its organization and structure, much of which is standardized. The diagram is infrastructural, focused on the procurement, ordering, packaging, dispatch and delivery of goods as the foundation for the plan of the camp and the map of the larger landscape. Not surprisingly, the linguistic and physical logics of this refugee network bears strong resemblance to military operations, especially in the period immediately following disaster. As prospects of speedy return fade, the military character softens somewhat under the paths worn by quotidian events, the spontaneous assertion of customary patterns, and the conscious cultivation of both literal and cultural natures on the barren site. However, the initially inscribed plan of rigid grid with rows of tents precludes the radical spatial transformation of camps and its trace will dominate the structure of the virtual city for decades after its reasons for being have faded.

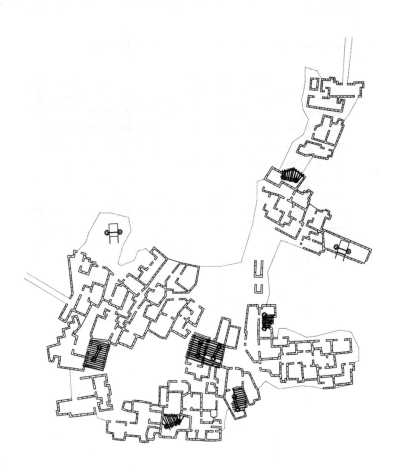

240

## Urban Camp

Even in our dream of the 'good camp that became a city' the underlying condition of displacement remains; for, temporized by the idea of return, all such sites are diasporic. People want to return home and reproduce their lives. Sometimes the socio-political situation precludes this return, but often it is more simply a question of infrastructure, of fractured water mains, power lines, and tarmacs. Replacing the monumental city can take years, during which time the displaced languish, desiring only their own backyard with a TV hookup.

Why not recuperate sites of return rather than create better sites of dislocation? Why not develop a physical device that can reconstitute an urban fabric without the support of a civic scale of infrastructure and that can, as an auxiliary consequence, retool a refugee camp as if it were a city? As an alternative to a tent, we propose a condensed infrastructure of two enclosures: one with a privy and one with a kitchen of hearth / heat source and integral cistern / shower. Both are de-mountable yet load-bearing. Placed at a distance from one another, the two boxes framed a habitable space in between wide enough to accommodate a bed. Initially protected with tarps, the distance could subsequently be framed with beams as scaffolding for the construction of the house around it such that the boxes became a structural and functional core.

Apartment houses, the opera and civic buildings remain in ruins; but houses and shops have been rebuilt. The nature of the destruction lends itself to small-scale reconstruction because it often occurs as a conscious dismantling of buildings by components, like windows and even bricks. Those who flee take them along, and those who return bring them back, or scavenge them from the abandoned stock. There is a continuing supply of recycled local material and prefabricated components that can be used in relation to new structural armatures and cores.

1 out of every 300 people on earth face some form of displacement. Displaced persons are previously settled ones, who bring expectations, desires and values of living with them, and attempt to enact them in ways that often address not only their extreme situation but also emerging conditions that will eventually face us all.

## I. LIVING BODY MUSEUMEUM:

## A Laboratory of Self-Invention

### Request

The team of Arakawa/Gins requests public land upon which to erect a museum of ALIVENESS that will be dedicated to the LIVING BODY just as it is, fully forthright yet completely perplexing to itself, despite its being the source of all that can in any way be clear. Certainly a museum devoted to ALIVENESS must exceed its own bounds, and no sooner has such an idea been hatched than it recombinantly stretches some distance beyond the name with which it first came into the world to come alive as (a) MUSEUMEUM. Within LIVING BODY MUSEUMEUM all that will be on display will be the LIVING BODY whose actions sculpt its future. LIVING BODY MUSEUMEUM ought, then, to be classed as a museum of the future on two counts. First, it will have on display a body-wide, a community-wide, sculpting of the future, a presentation of the germinating of the not-yet as that which waltzes or careens, is engineered into view. Second, MUSEUMEUMS are the next generation of museums. Obliged to display what does not yet exist, a museum of the future weighs in more as a contradiction in terms than as a realizable institution; filled with depictions of another time by those who can only be of this time, it would exhibit many futures, each a work of fantasy or science fiction. MUSEUMEUM bridges this contradiction; a group of architectural nurturing grounds designed to help the body self-invent to the maximum, it will be an architectural invitation ever directed toward getting the future to happen perspicuously; a place to visit that is tumultuously alive with process, MUSEUMEUM will turn the present into the future before the eyes of, under the noses of, and throughout the entire bodies of its visitors. Replete with life-investigating technologies, MUSEUMEUM will be for the LIVING BODY this much and more: a laboratory, a field station, and a super-duper nursery. An in-house group of medical personnel will show visitors what their bodies know and can learn to know about self-healing.

244

LIVING BODY MUSEUMEUM will be constructed in a series of three stages over a period of several years and will, when complete, offer a large array of urban spaces that will guide a thoroughgoing reinventing of life: affordable experimental housing; a think-tank retirement community; a cluster of satellite nursery schools; a research center-cum-hotel; several office suites. MUSEUMEUM will be built at no cost to its host city.

**Purpose**

LIVING BODY MUSEUMEUM will concentrate attention on and give architectural emphasis to the body as the living and breathing and moving source of terrestrial, to say nothing of urban, events. It will be through a quintessential urban context that the LIVING BODY will be able to wrest itself free from that unconscious fatalism which has haunted it forever. A classic oddity without parallel, the LIVING BODY needs to be given a chance to live and breathe on its own account. No sooner has it grown to encompass its own fullness as the means to all ends than does it begin to make honest note of its communal upbringing and underpinnings—all individual life has its basis in the group. LIVING BODY MUSEUMEUM will be a site for collecting and coordinating shared communal life and will become the means for constructing life on a new basis.

Beginning with their research project, *The Mechanism of Meaning*, Arakawa and Gins have sought to identify and highlight the operative set of tendencies, qualitative states, and coordinating skills necessary and sufficient to human thought and behavior. LIVING BODY MUSEUMEUM will elicit from and make apparent to a visitor this set of tendencies and skills; which means to say, it will show her all that she must and does draw upon in order to be able to be a person, the set of everything that makes her tick, her composite mechanism of meaning through which she can form (read *co-form*) the world and recognize herself to be doing so.

245

In much the manner in which an infant will suddenly giggle with surprise upon catching a glimpse of its own hand or foot in motion before it, a visitor to MUSEUMEUM will frequently be startled and delighted upon receiving the distinct impression that she has come across her own body as if for the first time. Tactically posed architectural volumes function as well-tooled pieces of equipment that help organize the body and put an *organism that persons* directly and indirectly on the track of what needs to be felt or known.

## Elements and Features

+ The product of a highly systematic, reflective approach to architectural design that holds the scientific method in high esteem, MUSEUMEUM, a work of procedural architecture, will address, in the context of the workaday world, and by virtue of how it is structured, all major thus far intractable philosophical problems, either reframing or suggesting solutions to them; it is believed that this wisdom-generating urban landscape will also—and this might be seen as a tenet-in-the-making of procedural architecture—be a kindness-nurturing one. Having the built-in capacity to put all that happens within it into the interrogative mode, MUSEUMEUM steers a human being to reconsider and, as it were, recalibrate his confidence in himself and his actions, causing him to launch a series of investigations into what it means to feel confident that he can successfully perform an action. A human being comes to know throughout his body a more self-questioning and therefore more accurate type of confidence; no longer able to be unquestioningly confident of actions he performs in the moment, and aquiver instead with an unsteadying tentativeness, he can nonetheless countenance more broadly and with more assurance actions and events that need a long time to reach fruition because he can and does now hold fast to *an end in sight*; working toward a fixed purpose, he becomes more confident of his ability to figure out what is happening around him; in other words, he acts with a well-tempered conviction that makes him able, despite having grown considerably less sure of just about everything, to be suitably totally unrelenting when it comes to a long-term goal. This wholly new type of architecture, whose purpose far exceeds that of shelter, promises to be a means by which to resolve our species' dilemma. Elaborate setups invite the body to perform sequences of actions that are beneficial to it; within the volumes to which they give shape, these setups hold sway as a new breed of thing/concept known as *architectural procedure*. An increasing number of people will acquire the ability to invent and assemble *architectural procedures*, and together they will construct a closely argued built-discourse, a collaborative effort that will continually put the crucial notion of urbanity up for on-the-spot critical analysis. MUSEUMEUM should be seen as both example and herald of *the urban landscape as critical discourse*.

+ The ecological balance to be desired more than all others must be the one capable of providing human life with the longest lifespan; what the composition of this most desirable of all ecological landscapes needs to be remains to be determined. To begin with, living bodies themselves surface as portable, favorable (to life as *homo sapiens* know it and hope to know it) ecological landscapes. LIVING BODY MUSEUMEUM will be wholly devoted to this subject matter upon which the continuation of our species depends.

+ The architectural core of LIVING BODY MUSEUMEUM will be an assembled group of basic-generative units. A basic-generative unit is an enclosure designed to give maximal architectural support and guidance to the body. The result of decades of research, MUSEUMEUM's basic-generative unit incorporates within it recent findings in physiology, biophysics, and experimental psychology and is structured so as to be able to accommodate many future findings as well. The basic-generative unit consists of six distinctive wall-facets, and it rotates to stand posed in each of its seventeen placements at a different orientation. A placement of the unit that has been rotated 180 degrees in relation to another will have for its floor expanse a wall-facet identical to the one that serves as ceiling in the placement of which it is, one might say, a flip version. The unit also undergoes a dramatic change in size from one placement to another; stretching out in a series of three successive expansions, it ends up, in its fullest expansion, measuring four times its original length.

+ LIVING BODY MUSEUMEUM will showcase new materials; in addition, it will have on permanent display the environmentally responsible building materials out of which it is formed. On a biyearly basis, a call will be issued for hard-to-find or yet-to-be-invented materials. Andrew Dent, director of Material Connexion, an internationally known materials library, has offered to help conduct this research.

+ It is anticipated that all those who step into LIVING BODY MUSEUMEUM will immediately know how to make use of it, but even so each visitor will receive a set of *Directions for Use*. This document instructs visitors in how best to go about positioning themselves so as to make what underlies their actions more salient, leading them to have a better sense of the overall dynamics of the efforts they make; it urges them to compare what they have gathered to be the case within one part of the *architectural surround* with what they have surmised to be so in another, thereby causing certain hitherto unknowable constituent factors of world and self to become manifest. These easy-to-understand directions show people how best to benefit from what

248

MUSEUMEUM's gardens and enclosures offer them. MUSEUMEUM's set of *Directions for Use* plays such an important role in its architecture that it should be thought of as all of a piece with it, an architectural element in its own right.

**✦** LIVING BODY MUSEUMEUM'S DWELLINGS—Do we want to speak of an outdoorsy and fragrant thought-provoking urban landscape? It seems we do. Architectural volumes communicate briskly and lingeringly with those who enter them. Each neighborhood entered and each apartment stepped into, whether for hours or years, "speaks" volumes bodily to you who enter and, more often than not, passes on information vitally important to well-being. Dwelling units will be for rent on a daily, weekly, or yearly basis. A stay at the REVERSIBLE DESTINY HOTEL will give people a taste of how daily life might be lived on new terms.

**✦** TODDLER UNIVERSITY, aka UNIVERSITY OF INCISIVE LAUGHTER AND VITAL COORDINATING SKILLS—Of course critical thinking needs to be introduced to people during their earliest years. Toddlers will receive a university-level education as they move about within and learn to negotiate architectural settings. A school of invention as well as a school for architecture, the university will be constructed as a "built discourse" that shows children, by "conversing" with them, how to structure into their existences an ever sharper critical ability. Toddlers need to be given a solid grounding in what it means to form oneself as an architectural body. Anyone wishing to enter TODDLER UNIVERSITY need only self-issue a birth certificate that shows her to be either still in or just out of diapers.

**✦** THINK-TANK RETIREMENT COMMUNITY (WISDOM CIRCLE OF ELDERS)—Members of this retirement community will certainly not be content to be retirees. Community members will be as adept at perspicuous bodily thinking as birds in the sky and fish in the sea, but even more so. Residents will develop and test *architectural procedures* that can help them with their chosen task, which is to stay alive for an indefiniiely long amount of time so as to infuse into the sorry happenstance known as the human condition a happier fate.

+ SITE OF ACCELERATED EVOLUTION—A place in which to consider all that underlies *the having of a life*, LIVING BODY MUSEUMEUM will, in effect, operate as a site of accelerated evolution, a place within which to brighten our species' prospects, a repository of the set of coordinating skills that a considerably brighter version of our species will need to master, a conduit to the transhuman or posthuman.

## About Arakawa + Gins

Arakawa and Madeline Gins started collaborating in 1963. Their collaborative art work *The Mechanism of Meaning* was published in 1971, and a sequel to that, *To Not To Die*, appeared in 1987. Gins and Arakawa have exhibited jointly throughout Europe, Japan and the United States. Their exhibition, *Site of Reversible Destiny*, was on view at the Guggenheim Museum Soho in December 1997 and won the College Art Association's Exhibition of the Year and Distinguished Body of Work award.

Arakawa's large-scale paintings are in the permanent collections of museums throughout the world. Gins's published works include the avant-garde classic *What the President Will Say or Do!!* and an innovative art-historical novel, *Helen Keller or Arakawa*.

## A Proven Track Record

The team of Arakawa/Gins has already proven itself adept at designing and organizing the construction of a highly successful and profitable project. Their project *Site of Reversible Destiny,* a seven-acre park commissioned by the Gifu Prefecture, in central Japan, and which was built at a cost of 16 million dollars, has succeeded in earning back, within the first two years of its existence, the total sum expended for its construction! *Site of Reversible Destiny,* which charges an admission fee of seven dollars, has continued over time to attract ever larger audiences, serving as a major tourist attraction and turning a profit for its sponsoring prefecture.

## II. EXECUTIVE SUMMARY

### The Industry

In the history of museums, there has never been a museum in which the visitor's body is the main focus of the exhibit. There is no precedent for a museum that heals its visitors.

### Admission Fee

There will be a $7.00 charge per person. This is comparable to most art museums, and costs 50 percent less than typical urban science museums, for example the American Museum of Natural History.

## Attendance Projections

| Time | Year 1 | Year 2 | Year 3 |
|------|--------|--------|--------|
| Visitors Per Week | 1,500 | 2,250 | 2,750 |
| Visitors Per Year | 78,000 | 117,000 | 143,000 |

These are conservative figures based upon typical urban science museums.

## Operating Schedule

The MUSEUMEUM will be open seven days a week, 10:00am to 9:00pm. During this time all automated exhibits will be open to the public. The healing team will work with the public 11:00am to 6:00pm, Monday through Saturday.

## Staff

The MUSEUMEUM will require the following staff to commence operations:

*Full Time Staff*

| | |
|------|--------|
| Director | $70,000 |
| Security Officer | $28,000 |
| Administrative Assistant | $35,000 |
| Admission Booth Attendant | $22,000 |
| **Total** | **$155,000** |

*Part Time Staff*

| | |
|------|--------|
| Cleaning | $9,500 |
| Maintenance | $15,000 |
| Financial/Accounting | $13,000 |
| **Total** | **$37,500** |

The MUSEUMEUM will rely heavily on volunteer teams, as is common for science museums. The doctors and nurses that make up the healing team have already agreed to work on a volunteer basis.

*Volunteer Staff*

| | | |
|---|---|---|
| Doctors | Nurse/Medical Assistants | |
| Nutritionist | Other Healers | Tour Guides |

## III. MARKETING PLAN

The multi-disciplinary aspect of the MUSEUMEUM will earn the attention of a wide range of general and trade-specific media outlets. Even during the planning and construction phase, before the general public is contacted, the MUSEUMEUM is certain to attract attention from architecture + design media, scientific media, art magazines, health care practitioners and organizations, city-specific press, and many others.

Then, once the MUSEUMEUM construction is near completion, a public relations firm will be hired to launch a marketing plan designed to:

+ Attract local, national, and international media attention for the ribbon-cutting
+ Draw visitors of all ages and backgrounds
+ Promote the healing effects of the state of the art medical component
+ Inform and educate the public about the relationship between architecture and the body/consciousness, and motivate them to further investigate this idea on their own and in community with others
+ Encourage scientists, architects, philosophers (bio-ethicists in particular), health care professionals, artists, and others to experience the house
+ Publicize scheduled lectures or exhibitions

**Elements**

*Direct Mail:* Glossy brochures will highlight the MUSEUMEUM, its services and staff. The MUSEUMEUM will also periodically send out mailers highlighting lectures, promotions, special events, etc.

*Advertisements:* Subway, local NYC press, art and museum publications, and outdoor billboards

*Internet:* The MUSEUMEUM will have a comprehensive website, and promote it through advertising banners and web sites within Web MD, About.com and other health-based internet sites. The MUSEUMEUM will use strategic meta-tags for maximum exposure on various search engines including Google, Yahoo, Lycos, Alta Vista, and Ask Jeeves.

**Preliminary Advertising Budget (Year One)**

| Month | Budget | Print | Outdoor | Direct Mail |
|---|---|---|---|---|
| January | $25,000 | $10,000 | $10,000 | $5,000 |
| February | $25,000 | $10,000 | $10,000 | $5,000 |
| March | $10,000 | $5,000 | $5,000 | -- |
| April | $10,000 | $5,000 | $5,000 | -- |
| May | $10,000 | $5,000 | $5,000 | -- |
| June | $10,000 | $5,000 | $5,000 | -- |
| July | $5,000 | $5,000 | -- | -- |
| August | $5,000 | $5,000 | -- | -- |
| September | $5,000 | $5,000 | -- | -- |
| October | $5,000 | $5,000 | -- | -- |
| November | $5,000 | $5,000 | -- | -- |
| December | $5,000 | $5,000 | -- | -- |
| **Total** | **$120,000** | **$70,000** | **$40,000** | **$10,000** |

## IV. CAPITAL FORMATION

### Sources of Revenue

The MUSEUMEUM expects to derive revenues from multiple streams:

1. Ticket revenue  2. Apartment rentals  3. Donations

In addition, a group of distinguished physicians has proposed that they be given a 10 year lease for six thousand square feet of office space; and has offered to offset the operating expenses of the MUSEUMEUM through a yearly donation of 50% of its profits.

### Goals & Supporting Objectives

The following chart shows the anticipated cash needs for the start up phase:

| | |
|---|---|
| Construction | $30 million |
| Year One Operating Expenses | $1.5 million |

### THREE YEAR PROJECTED INCOME STATEMENT

| Gross Revenue | Year 1 | Year 2 | Year 3 |
|---|---|---|---|
| General Admissions | $546,000 | $819,000 | $1,092,000 |
| Membership | $75,000 | $100,000 | $100,000 |
| Special Events | $75,000 | $100,000 | $100,000 |
| Space Rental | $50,000 | $75,000 | $75,000 |
| Medical Services | -- | -- | -- |
| Low-Income Apartment Rentals | $180,000 | $180,000 | $180,000 |
| (10 apartments @ $500/month) | | | |
| **Gross Revenue Subtotal** | **$926,000** | **$1,274,000** | **$1,547,000** |

255

| General & Administrative Expenses | Year 1 | Year 2 | Year 3 |
| --- | --- | --- | --- |
| Accounting | $10,000 | $10,000 | $10,000 |
| Benefits/Payroll Taxes | $22,000 | $22,000 | $22,000 |
| Computer/Office Equipment | $75,000 | $10,000 | $5,000 |
| Insurance (inc. malpractice) | $100,000 | $100,000 | $100,000 |
| Furniture (office) | $50,000 | -- | -- |
| Legal | $25,000 | $25,000 | $25,000 |
| Medical Equipment (purchased) | $50,000 | $10,000 | $10,000 |
| Medical Furniture | $25,000 | -- | -- |
| Medical Supplies (including lab) | $10,000 | $10,000 | $10,000 |
| Miscellaneous | $100,000 | $100,000 | $100,000 |
| Office Supplies | $10,000 | $2,000 | $2,000 |
| Salaries/Wages - Full Time | $155,000 | $155,000 | $155,000 |
| Salaries/Wages - Part Time | $62,500 | $62,500 | $62,500 |
| Telecom Equipment | $5,000 | -- | -- |
| Utilities | $100,000 | $100,000 | $100,000 |
| Landscaping/Grounds | $12,000 | $12,000 | $12,000 |

| Sales & Marketing Expenses | Year 1 | Year 2 | Year 3 |
| --- | --- | --- | --- |
| Advertising/Marketing | $120,000 | $100,000 | $100,000 |
| Brochures | $50,000 | $50,000 | $50,000 |
| Design Services | $50,000 | $25,000 | $15,000 |
| Meals/Entertainment/Travel | $50,000 | $50,000 | $50,000 |
| **Total Expenses** | **$1,081,500** | **$843,500** | **$828,500** |

## CONSTRUCTION BUDGET

| Materials and Services | Estimate | In-kind | Actual Expenditures |
|---|---|---|---|
| Surveyor | $75,000 | -- | $75,000 |
| Excavate/ clear site, rough grade | $175,000 | $37,500 | $137,500 |
| Cabling (computers & telephone) | $175,000 | $37,500 | $137,500 |
| Concrete | $2,250,000 | $225,000 | $2,025,000 |
| Plumbing | $1,200,000 | $120,000 | $1,080,000 |
| Electric | $750,000 | $75,000 | $675,000 |
| HVAC | $1,500,000 | $150,000 | $1,350,000 |
| Cladding (misc. materials) | $600,000 | $60,000 | $540,000 |
| Material (Steel & Wood) | $6,750,000 | $675,000 | $6,075,000 |
| Kitchen cabinets, Counter tops | $750,000 | $75,000 | $675,000 |
| Sheetrock/Spackle | $600,000 | $60,000 | $540,000 |
| Insulation | $150,000 | $15,000 | $135,000 |
| Paint/Plaster | $525,000 | $52,500 | $472,500 |
| Labor | $5,250,000 | $525,000 | $4,725,000 |
| Roof | $175,000 | $37,500 | $137,500 |
| **Total** | **$20,925,000** | **$2,145,000** | **$18,780,000** |

# III. DOCUMENTATION

We learn place from place, and place from fleeing; fleeing from fleeing, and fleeing from border; border from border, and border from beyond.

—Talmud, Eiruvin 51a

James Adaire's *History of the American Indians*, first published in 1775, sought to systematically document Indian life and customs. In a short passage entitled "Cities of Refuge," Adaire argued that Indians had constructed cities of refuge so that men "subjectively innocent" of a capital crime might escape punishment or retribution through exile. Adaire might have found a precedent for these peculiar Indian cities in the Talmud, which devotes an entire section, Tractate *Makkot*, to such discussions. Cities of refuge for inadvertent killers are introduced not just as a form of punishment of the guilty party, or protection from the injured party, but also as a form of expiation or rehabilitation.

The importance ascribed to cities of refuge in everyday life in the Talmud should not be underestimated. Six cities of refuge are expressly mentioned in the Bible; forty-eight additional cities are used as such with the consent of the inhabitants. The Talmud stipulates that all roads leading to these cities be well-maintained, clearly marked, and wide: "A private road is four cubits wide, a public road six cubits wide, a road leading to a City of Refuge thirty-two cubits wide." Roads leading to cities of refuge are over five times as wide as public roads, and eight times as wide as private roads. According to one interpretation, a tower with a statue pointing the way to the nearest city of refuge must be constructed on every mile of every public road.

For Emmanuel Levinas, the modern individual is as compromised as any individual sent to a city of refuge in the Talmud. The modern individual is in need of protection and refuge for being negligent in the face of social inequality, and for being insensitive and oblivious to human suffering. "There must be cities of refuge where these half-guilty parties, where these half-innocent parties," Levinas argued, meaning us, "can stay shielded from vengeance." "Does not this make all of our cities...cities of refuge or cities of exiles?"

Taking its cue from Levinas, "Cities Without Citizens," an exhibition I organized at The Rosenbach Museum & Library from July through September 2003 as their artist-in-residence, examined the displaced and the disenfranchised in Early American cities and settlements through historical materials in the Rosenbach collections. These materials were juxtaposed with contemporary works as diverse as documentary photographs of orphans from post-war Europe, and architectural studies addressing refugee cities in Africa. Although the exhibition coincided with the opening of the new US Constitution Center in Philadelphia, it attempted a less sanitized reading of our nation's past.

As a commentary on art, archiving, and human rights, this exhibition re-indexed Rosenbach holdings according to four social parameters: settlement, citizenship, discipline, and liquidation.

The exhibition explored theories of curatorial innovation, prompting the question of how one might renew or reinvent an archival collection. Visitors to the exhibition were invited to consider curatorial questions such as the following: Is The Rosenbach Museum & Library simply a repository of material culture in need of preservation? How is this museum and library responsible to the events that gave rise to these books and documents? In working with historical collections, to whom or what is a curator or artist responsible today?

Visitors were also invited to assume critical stances in the future: Who gets to be a citizen? How does a society discipline its citizens? How does one liquidate a city of its citizens? How does one build a city anew?

**Settlement**

504m

[VESPUCCI, AMERIGO, 1451-1512.]
   Mundus nouus.
   Colophon: Magister johañes otmar; vindelice
impressit Auguste anno millesimo quingentesimo
quarto.
   [8]p. illus.(diagr.)  20½cm., in case 22cm.
   A letter addressed to Lorenzo Pietro Francesco
di Medici describing Vespucci's third voyage;
translated from Italian into Latin by Giovanni
Giocondo.
   Sabin 99330; Harisse 31; Ruge 25; Church 20.

                              R56-144

# Mundus Nouus

PENN, WILLIAM
  Information and direction to such persons as are
  inclined to America, more especially those related
  to the Province of Pennsylvania.
  [London, 1684]                    (leaflet)

Wing P1302

[1st ed.]

1 of 4 mended copies.

4 p. (4o.)                    ( )    Americana documen
                                              case

# Information and Direction

## TO

## Such Persons as are inclined

## TO

# AMERICA,

## MORE

## Especially Those related to the Province

## OF

# PENNSYLVANIA.

That the Value and Improvement of *Estates* in our Parts of *America*, may yet appear with further clearness and Assurance to Enquirers, I propose to speak my own Knowledg, and the Observation of others, as particularly as I can; which I shall comprise under these Heads.

I. The *Advance that is upon Money and Goods.*

II. The *Advance that is upon Labour, be it of Handicrafts or others.*

III. The *Advance that is upon Land.*

IV. The *Charge of Transporting a Family, and Fitting a Plantation.*

V. The *Way the Poorer sort may be Transported, and Seated, with Advantage to the Rich that help them.*

VI. The *easier and better provision that is to be made there for Posterity, especially by those that are not of great Substance.*

VII. *What Utensels and Goods are fitting to carry for Use or Profit.*

For the first, Such *Money* as may be carried, as pieces of eight, advances *Thirty*, and *Goods* at least *Fifty per cent.* Say I have 100 *l. sterl.* If I am but six in Family, I will pay my Passage with the advance upon my money, and find my hundred pounds good in the Country at last. Upon *Goods*, well bought and sorted, there is more profit: but some money is very requisit for Trade sake; for we find it gives Goods a better market; so that considering the great quantity of Goods already carried, it were not amiss at present, if one half were in Money, and the other in *Goods.*

Thus in General. But it particularly encourages Merchants, because the profit by *advance*, is seldom less then 50 *l. sterl. per cent.* which is very considerable; and we have already got some things for returns, as *Skins, Furrs, Whale-Oyle, Tobacco,* &c.

II. For *Labour,* be it of *Handicrafts,* or *Others,* there is a considerable Encouragement by advance of price, to what is here, because the Goods Manufactured there, advance equal to those the Merchant sells, and where Provision is at least as cheap, and there is such additional gain, to the first Gain of Handicrafts here (of whom the Merchant buys) the *American Handicraft must have an extraordinary time of it.* The like may be said of *Under Labourers* for some time, until the Country be better replenished with People.

III. The *Advance* upon Land is Encouraging, which will be best apprehended by an English understanding in a Comparison with the Lands of *England,* that he is familiarly acquainted with.

If 500 Acres of *unclear'd* Land there, indifferently chosen, will *keep as many Milch Cowes,* or *fat as many Bullocks* for the market in Summer, as 50 Acres of improved Land in *England,* as chosen aforesaid, can do; then by Computing the value of the Summers Grass of such fifty Acres of Land here, we shall the better find the value of 500 Acres of Land in *America;* for within that compass, the same quantity of Cattle may be well kept. Admit this then, that the Summers Grass of 50 Acres of middling Land in *England,* is worth 15 *l.* I conceive that makes 20 *l,* which is the price of the Inheritance of the 500 Acres, no dear Purchass. The cost to go thither is no Objection, because it is paid by the *Advance* that is upon the Money and Goods at the rate aforeforesaid. If the hazard of the Seas be Objected, we see that the *five hundreth* Ship using those parts, does not miscarry, and the Risk is run for themselves only. However, except in Winter, Passages are pleasant, as well as safe.

But this Comparison draws an Objection upon us that must be obviated. *What becomes of your stock in the Winter?* I say our *Woods* usually keep them for the Market till *December,* and unless it be a more then ordinary Winter (which is observed to happen but once in four or five Years) or that they are young stock, or Cattel big with Young, they mostly shift for themselves. But if Fodder be wanted, we have a supply by *Hay,* we mow in the *Marshes* and *Woods,* or the *Straw* of the English Grain we use, or the *Tops and Stalks* of Indian Corn, and sometimes that it self; a Thing hearty, *and easily rais'd,* and is good to fat as well as keep, and answers to *Oats, Pense, Beans* and *Fetches* here, tho we have of them also.

This *Scheam* of *Grazing* and keeping of Stock, may inform Inquirers what the Woods and unbroken Lands of those Countrys in some sort will do, in proportion to Lands here, and consequently, what they are worth to Lands here, allowing equally for Care and Fodder on both sides.

To be short, the produce of wild Land there in this respect, is within less then ten to one, of what our cleared Land is here, and the purchase here, is an hundred to one Dearer, which must needs make *American Lands* no hard Bargain to the Purchasers.

Now for *clearing* of our Wood-lands in order to corn;

WASHINGTON, GEORGE, pres. U.S., 1732-1799.
 Washington's farewell address, to the people of the
United States.  Published for the Washington benevo-
lent societies in New-Jersey.
 New-Brunswick:Printed by Lewis Deare.1813.
 6p.*l*.,[5]-48p.  front.(port.)  15cm.
 Page 14 misnumbered 41.
 "Constitution of the Washington benevolent society
of Mount-holly ...":3d-6th p.*l*.
 Printed blank certificate of membership: 2d p.*l*.
 Signatures: A-C$^8$, with [-]$^4$ inserted after A2.
 Running title: Washing          ton's legacy.
 "Extract from a biogra          phical sketch of ...
                                 See next card
                                 R57-1682

270

# WASHINGTON'S

# FAREWELL ADDRESS.

---

Friends and Fellow-Citizens :

THE period for a new election of a citizen to administer the executive government of the United States, being not far distant, and the time actually arrived when your thoughts must be employed in designating the person who is to be clothed with that important trust, it appears to me proper, especially as it may conduce to a more distinct expression of the public voice, that I should now apprize you of the resolution I have formed, to decline being considered among the number of those out of whom the choice is to be made.

PTOLEMAEUS, CLAUDIUS.
  Claudii Ptolemaei alexandrini Geographiae libri
octo graeco-latini; latinè primùm recogniti &
emendati, cum tabulis geographicis ad mentem auc-
toris restitutis per Gerardum Mercatorem: iam verò
ad graeca & latina exemplaria à Petro Montano
iterum recogniti, et pluribus locis castigati.
Adjecta insuper ab eodem nomina recentia et aequi-
pollentia ex varijs auctoribus veteribus et recen-
tiorih magna cura collecta, in gratiam et usum
geographiae studiosorum.
  · Iodocus Hondius excudit       sibi et Cornelio
Nicolai, in cujus offici          na prostant,
                                        See next card
                                        R59-1997

272

Mercator, tractusque nouos, terræque, marisque

Mons Gessæ, et magnum quod continet omnia cælum.

Magna tibi priscum rurlem sorrasse laborem:

Vrbna Pelusiacis debetur grana chartis:

I. Houer. fecit.

GERARDI MERCATORIS RVPELMVNDANI EFFIGIEM ANNOR.
DVORVM ET SEX — AGINTA, SVI ERGA IPSVM STVDII
CAVSA DEPINGI CVRABAT FRANC. HOG. CIƆ. IƆ. LXXIV.

## In Effigiem carmen.

GErardus Mercator erat sic cognitus orbi,
  Duysburgi raperet cum sera parca virum.
Otto nos dicies, binosq́, exegerat annos,
  Et menses octo, tresq́, nouemq́ dies.
Doctus erat verè, pius, integer, omnibus aquus,
  Ingenio dexter, dexter & ipse manu.
Sidera cum terris coniunxit, sacra prophanis
  Addidit, at rectè fecit vtrumque tamen.
Astra Mathematicus radio descripsit acuto,
  Et dedit in paruo conspicienda globo.
In tabulas terræ spatiosum contulit orbem,
  Inq́, globo mundi regna videnda dedit.

Et ne quid cæli studijs, terraq́, deesset,
  Historiam docuit tempora certa loqui.
Sacraq́, detexit vatum mysteria, Christi
  Præcones iussit quatuor ire simul.
Atque ea sic fecit superos vt vinceret omnes
  Artifices, proprio marte, manuq́, sua.
Fœlix prole sua, natisq́, nepotibus ex se,
  Spem gratæ certam posteritatis habet,
Ad quod Christe tuum sestatus ouile, beatus
  Perpetuo tecum pascua latè capit,
Et quamuis placuisse Duci non sit mala sit,
  Attamęn est maior laus placuisse Deo.

Beneuolentiæ ergo Bernardus Furmerius Leouardiensis
Licentiatus Iuris, mæst us scribebat.

[JOHNSON, ROBERT, fl. 1586-1626, supposed author.]
  Nova Britannia.  Offering most excellent
fruites by planting in Virginia.  Exciting all
such as be well affected to further the same.
  London,Printed [by W.Stansby] for Samvel
Macham,1609.
  [35]p.  18½cm.
Woodcut of ship on t.-p.
Dedication signed: R.I.
  STC 14699; Church 338 (var. 4, but with "thinke"
in line 28 of D4v).
  Signatures: A-E$^4$     (A1 & E4 blank want-
ing).

274

*IV.*

Nova Britannia.

# OFFERING MOST

Excellent fruites by Planting in
Virginia.

Exciting all such as be well affected
to further the same.

London
Printed for Samuel Macham, and are to be sold at
his Shop in Pauls Church-yard, at the
Signe of the Bul-head.
1609.

[THOMSON, CHARLES, 1729-1824.]

An enquiry into the causes of the alienation of the Delaware and Shawanese Indians from the British interest, and into the measures taken for recovering their friendship. Extracted from the public treaties, and other authentic papers relating to the transactions of the government of Pensilvania and the said Indians, for near forty years ... Together with the remarkable journal of Christian Frederic Post ... With notes by the editor explaining sundry Indian customs, &c. Written in Pensylvania.

London:Printed for   J.Wilkie.MDCCLIX.

See next card

# AN
# ENQUIRY

## INTO THE

## Causes of the Alienation

### OF THE

## *Delaware* and *Shawanese Indians*

### FROM THE

## *BRITISH* INTEREST,

And into the Measures taken for recovering their
FRIENDSHIP.

Extracted from the PUBLIC TREATIES, and other Authentic Papers relating to the Transactions of the Government of *Pensilvania* and the said *Indians*, for near Forty
Years; and explained by a MAP of the Country.

Together with the remarkable JOURNAL of *Christian Frederic Post*,
by whose Negotiations, among the *Indians* on the *Ohio*, they were
withdrawn from the Interest of the *French*, who thereupon
abandoned the Fort and Country.

With Notes by the EDITOR explaining sundry *Indian* Customs, &c.

## Written in *Pensylvania.*

## LONDON:
Printed for J. WILKIE, at the Bible, in St. Paul's Church-yard.
MDCCLIX.

[PENN, WILLIAM, 1644-1718.]

A brief account of the province of Pennsilvania
lately granted by the King, under the great seal
of England, to William Penn, and his heirs and
assigns.

London,Printed for Benjamin Clark,MDCLXXXII.
1p.*l*.,14p.  20½cm.

Signed at end: William Penn.

"An abstract of the patent granted by the King
...":p.2-6.

"The King's declaration to the inhabitants and
planters ...": p:7-8.

Signatures: A-B$^4$

This 1682 edition in      to is not in Wing or
Church.

R57-146

## An Abstract of the

# PATENT

### GRANTED BY THE

# KING

### TO

# William Penn, &c,

### The Fourth of *March*, 1681.

I. WE do Give and Grant for Us, Our Heirs and Successours (upon divers considerations) to William Penn his Heirs and Assigns for ever all that Tract of Land in America with all Islands thereunto belonging That is to say from the beginning of the fortieth Degree of North-Latitude unto the forty third Degree of North-Latitude whose Eastern bounds from Twelve English miles above New-Castle (alias Delaware Town) runs all along upon the side of Delaware River,

II.

A trve declaration of the estate of the colonie
in Virginia, with a confutation of such scandal-
ous reports as haue tended to the disgrace of so
worthy an enterprise.  Published by aduise and
direction of the Councell of Virginia.
  London,Printed for William Barret,1610.
  1p.l.,68p.  18½cm.
  Woodcut device (McK 352) on t.-p.
  STC 24833; Church 348.
  Signatures: A-I⁴ (A1 blank? wanting; sheet G
signed F).

                              R56-200

# A TRVE DECLA-RATION OF THE

estate of the Colonie in
VIRGINIA,

With a confutation of such scan-
dalous reports as haue tended to the dif-
grace of so worthy an enterprise.

Published by aduise and direction of the
Councell of VIRGINIA.

LONDON,
Printed for *William Barret*, and are to be sold
at the blacke Beare in Pauls Church-yard.
1 6 1 0.

[WATERHOUSE, EDWARD, fl. 1622.]  A declaration
    of the state of the colony and affaires in
       Virginia ... 1622.                (Card 2)
    Dedication signed: Edvvard Waterhovse.
    Signatures: A-H$^4$ (H4 blank wanting).
    "Faults in printing": A4v.
    STC 25104; Church 396.
    "The inconveniencies that have happened to
some persons ..." with imprint of Felix Kyngston,
previously issued separately (STC 24844): fold.
brs.

                                R56-166

                                   *detail, opposite*

282

# THE INCONVENIENCIES
## THAT HAVE HAPPENED TO SOME PER-
### SONS WHICH HAVE TRANSPORTED THEMSELVES

from *England* to *Virginia*, vvithout prouisions necessary to sustaine themselues, hath greatly hindred the Progresse of that noble *Plantation*: For preuention of the like disorders heereafter, that no man suffer, either through ignorance or misinformation; it is thought requisite to publish this short declaration: wherein is contained a particular of such necessaries, as either priuate families or single persons shall haue cause to furnish themselues with, for their better support at their first landing in Virginia; whereby also greater numbers may receiue in part, directions how to prouide themselues.

### Apparrell.

|  | li. | s. | d. |
|---|---|---|---|
| One Monmouth Cap | 00 | 01 | 10 |
| Three falling bands | — | 01 | 03 |
| Three shirts | — | 07 | 06 |
| One waste-coate | — | 02 | 02 |
| One suite of Canuase | — | 07 | 06 |
| One suite of Frize | — | 10 | 00 |
| One suite of Cloth | — | 15 | 00 |
| Three paire of Irish stockins | — | 04 | 00 |
| Foure paire of shooes | — | 08 | 08 |
| One paire of garters | — | 00 | 10 |
| One doozen of points | — | 00 | 03 |
| One paire of Canuase sheets | — | 08 | 00 |
| Seuen ells of Canuase, to make a bed and boulster, to be filled in Virginia 8.s. | — | 08 | 00 |
| One Rug for a bed 8. s. which with the bed seruing for two men, halfe is | — | 05 | 00 |
| Fiue ells coorse Canuase, to make a bed at Sea for two men, to be filled with straw, iiij.s. |  |  |  |
| One coorse Rug at Sea for two men, will cost vj. s. is for one | — | 05 | 00 |
|  | 04 | 00 | 00 |

*Apparrell for one man, and so after the rate for more.*

### Victuall.

|  | li. | s. | d. |
|---|---|---|---|
| Eight bushels of Meale | 02 | 00 | 00 |
| Two bushels of pease at 3.s. | — | 06 | 00 |
| Two bushels of Oatemeale 4.s. 6.d. | — | 09 | 00 |
| One gallon of *Aquauitæ* | — | 02 | 06 |
| One gallon of Oyle | — | 03 | 06 |
| Two gallons of Vineger 1.s. | — | 02 | 00 |
|  | 03 | 03 | 00 |

*For a whole yeere for one man, and so for more after the rate.*

### Armes.

|  | li. | s. | d. |
|---|---|---|---|
| One Armour compleat, light | — | 17 | 00 |
| One long Peece, fiue foot or fiue and a halfe, neere Musket bore | 01 | 02 | 00 |
| One sword | — | 05 | 00 |
| One belt | — | 01 | 00 |
| One bandaleere | — | 01 | 06 |
| Twenty pound of powder | — | 18 | 00 |
| Sixty pound of shot or lead, Pistoll and Goose shot | — | 05 | 00 |
|  | 03 | 09 | 06 |

### Tooles.

|  | li. | s. | d. |
|---|---|---|---|
| Fiue broad howes at 2.s. a piece | — | 10 | — |
| Fiue narrow howes at 16.d. a piece | — | 06 | 08 |
| Two broad Axes at 3.s. 8.d. a piece | — | 07 | 04 |
| Fiue felling Axes at 18.d. a piece | — | 07 | 06 |
| Two steele hand sawes at 16.d. a piece | — | 02 | 08 |
| Two two-hand-sawes at 5. s. a piece | — | 10 | — |
| One whip-saw, set and filed with box, file, and wrest | — | 10 | — |
| Two hammers 12.d. a piece | — | 02 | 00 |
| Three shouels 18.d. a piece | — | 04 | 06 |
| Two spades at 18.d. a piece | — | 03 | — |
| Two augers 6.d. a piece | — | 01 | 00 |
| Sixe chissels 6.d. a piece | — | 03 | 00 |
| Two percers stocked 4. d. a piece | — | 00 | 08 |
| Three gimlets 2.d. a piece | — | 00 | 06 |
| Two hatchets 21.d. a piece | — | 03 | 06 |
| Two hand bills 20. a piece | — | 03 | 04 |
| One grindlestone 4.s. | — | 04 | 00 |
| Nailes of all sorts to the value of | 02 | 00 | — |
| Two Pickaxes | — | 03 | — |
|  | 06 | 02 | 08 |

*For a family of 6. persons and so after the rate for more.*

### Houshold Implements.

|  | li. | s. | d. |
|---|---|---|---|
| One Iron Pot | — | 07 | — |
| One kettle | — | 06 | — |
| One large frying-pan | — | 02 | 06 |
| One gridiron | — | 01 | 06 |
| Two skillets | — | 05 | — |
| One spit | — | 02 | — |
| Platters, dishes, spoones of wood | — | 04 | — |
|  | 01 | 08 | 00 |

*For a family of 6. persons, and so for more or lesse after the rate.*

For Suger, Spice, and fruit, and at Sea for 6. men

|  | li. | s. | d. |
|---|---|---|---|
| So the full charge of Apparell, Victuall, Armes, Tooles, and houshold stuffe, and after this rate for each person, will amount vnto the summe of | 12 | 10 | — |
| The passage of each man is | 06 | 00 | — |
| The fraight of these prouisions for a man, will bee about halfe a Tun, which is | 01 | 10 | — |
| So the whole charge will amount to about | 20 | 00 | 00 |

Nets, hookes, lines, and a tent must be added, if the number of people be greater, as also some kine.

*And this is the vsual proportion that the* Virginia *Company doe bestow vpon their Tenants which they send.*

Whosoeuer transports himselfe or any other at his owne charge vnto *Virginia*, shall for each person so transported before Midsummer 1625. haue to him and his heires for euer fifty Acres of Land vpon a first, and fifty Acres vpon a second diuision.

Imprinted at London by Felix Kyngston. 1622.

U.S. Dept. of state.

Report of the Secretary of state, to the President of the United States, of the quantity and
situation of the lands not claimed by the Indians,
nor granted to, nor claimed by any citizens,
within the territory of the United States ...

[Philadelphia,Printed by Francis Childs and
John Swaine,1791.]

8p.  31½x20cm.

Evans 23913.

Signatures: [A]-B².

Read in the House of  representatives, November 10, 1791.

Signed: Th. Jeffer  son.

Remarks on the French memorials concerning the
limits of Acadia; printed at the Royal printing-
house at Paris, and distributed by the French
ministers at all the foreign courts of Europe.
With two maps, exhibiting the limits: one according to the system of the French ... the other
conformable to the English rights ... To which is
added, an answer to the summary discussion, &c.
London:Printed for T.Jefferys.MDCCLVI.
2p.*l*.,110p.,1*l*.  2 fold maps.  19½cm.
"Additions" and "Errata":p.109-110.
Sabin 69463.
Signatures: [-]²,     B-O⁴,[-]².
Imperfect: last leaf    wanting.

R57-533

Louis XIV. made answer, that he was willing to consent to cede Acadia, according to its ancient Limits, as the Queen demanded. But offered, in case she would consent to restore Acadia, the river St. George should thenceforth make the boundary*; or, in other words, the bounds of it, should be restrained to that river, as it is expressed, on a relative occasion †; for Louis extended the Limits of Acadia as far as the river Kennebek.

The English Commissaries, according to the obvious meaning of the words, explain the King of France's answer thus: that he would cede ancient Acadia, as was demanded; but if the Queen would restore him Acadia, that is, the same ancient Acadia, so ceded, he would refrain its bounds to St. George's river, besides giving an equivalent.

It is evident from the words that the ancient Acadia ceded by Louis XIV. was the same with the Acadia, required by him to be restored; and since this latter, when its bounds should be restrained to the river St. George, would be much larger than the ancient Acadia of the Commissaries; consequently, the ancient Acadia, ceded first in the preliminary articles and afterwards in the treaty of Utrecht, pursuant thereto, is very different from the ancient Acadia, of the French Commissaries, as being greatly more extended. Let them analise the words by the strictest Rules of Logic or Mathematical Reasoning, and see if they will ever be able to bring out any other but the same invariable sense.

* Pieces Justfic. Art. 32. P. 281, 282. & Art. 33. P. 391.
† Art. 25. P. 335.

To

To make the words of Louis XIV. and his Ministers, convey the sense of the present Ministers; or, to suppose the Acadia ceded by them was their diminutive Acadia, they ought to run in this form. I am willing to cede Acadia, according to its ancient Limits, as the Queen has demanded; but if the Queen will return Acadia back, I will consent to refrain or contract it, that is, modern Acadia, or the bounds of it, to the river St. George.

This would, indeed, serve their purpose. But then, it is obvious, that to accommodate his words to this sense, it would be absolutely necessary to infer the term, modern: for, they cannot possibly bear the same meaning, as they now stand; the natural and grammatical construction of the words being point blank against such a meaning. For the particle it refers to Acadia restored, (as its next antecedent) and that name is synonymous with the ancient Acadia yielded up: consequently, that particle can by no means be referred or applied to modern Acadia; unless the ancient Acadia, mentioned in the articles, be understood to be the same with the modern Acadia of the Commissaries, or with the Acadia of Louis XIV.; which, perhaps, they will not readily grant, although, in reality, it is the case, as will be shewn presently.

It may here be noted, that although the King cedes Acadia, with the addition of the words, according to its ancient Limits; in order to answer catagorically to the Queen's demand: yet, in requiring its restitution, he is content to mention it simply under the name of Acadia. This

I 2

is

**[Agreement to found Aaronsburg, Philadelphia with 40,000 acres]**
**Aaron Levy, agreement with Robert Morris and Walter Stewart, 1792**
*Manuscripts do not have card catalog entries.*

Agreement

Robert Morris of

Walter Stewart

with

Aaron Levy

respecting 40,000 acres of

Land

**[Cortez letter concerning his porters] Hernando Cortez, 1764**
*Manuscripts do not have card catalog entries.*

✝

Paredes

o q[ue] se escriuen en nonbre del marques del Valle rrespondiendo a la de mil quinientos y quarenta años hizo con q[ue] a mi p[adre] y las demas p[er]sonas por el nonbradas en rrazon y diziendo tal q[ue] a mi y a mi henrr[ique] se tomaron por su mandado çiertos yndios q[ue] yban car[gad]os a la mar del sur Aben luys de luna y fran[cis]co canelas dizen q[ue] juezes esecutores e hizieron boluer a los d[ic]hos yndios a[n]te q[ue] segun q[ue] esto yo q[ue] cosas mas largamente en la d[ic]ha su nobreda de mi naçion caguer q[ue] se contiene el tenor de la d[ic]ha q[ue] mi Aviso por el d[ic]ho q[ue] dize q[ue] v[uestra] m[erced] no deue rresçebir fasta q[ue] mi naçion ni hazer lo q[ue] d[ic]ho es por el d[ic]ho d[ic]ho fernandez por lo qual conuiene

o por q[ue] no fue rresçebida por parte del d[ic]ho d[ic]ho fernandez que de ser tal se mi nado de a mi çed[ula] que dello

yo por q[ue] no se que dieron las causas y solenidades que de mi nadas de d[e]r[ech]o se rrequieren y[te]m por q[ue] la d[ic]ha de mi nacion caguer de rrelaçion çierta y verdad y y[te]m por q[ue] ya q[ue] algunos yndios del d[ic]ho mi parte mandara cargar q[ue] fueran carg[ad]os no seria ni fue q[ue] con ynterese ni probecho p[arti]cular mi en su d[ic]ho Ante como por v[uest]ro capitan y enbi[o] q[ue] al nonbre y q[ue] v[uest]ra q[ue] al ernisse fernando y aun biendo lo que por v[uest]ras q[ue] ales...

**[Portolan chart of the Atlantic, 1575] Bartolomeu Lasso,** *detail*

*Maps do not have card catalog entries.*

**Plan of the city of New York [New York, ca. 1795]**

*Maps do not have card catalog entries.*

**Reprint of Thomas Holmes's 1683 map of Philadelphia**

*Maps do not have card catalog entries.*

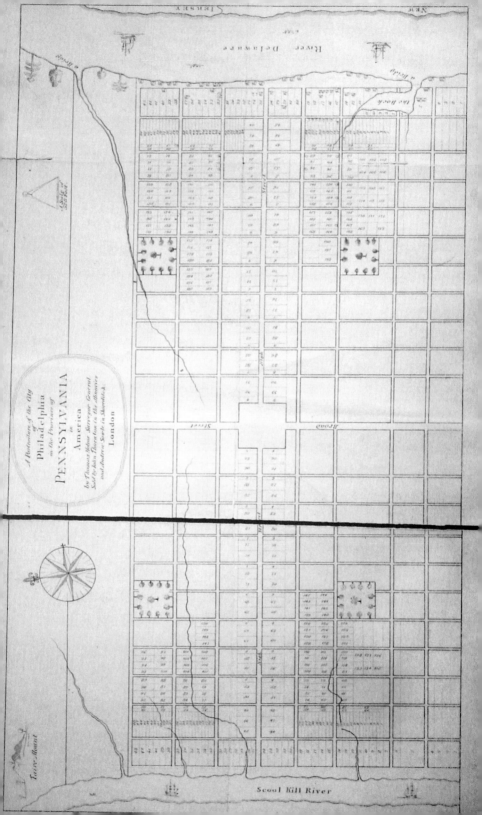

NEW JERSEY

River Delaware

a Bridge

a Brook

Angle of 33 Foot

A Portraiture of the City
Philadelphia
in the Province of
PENNSYLVANIA
in
America
by Thomas Holme Surveyor General
Sold by John Thornton in the Minories
and Andrew Sowle in Shoreditch
London

Broad Street

High Street

Faire Mount

Scool Kill River

Citizen

**Abraham Lincoln, excerpt from the "House Divided" speech, Springfield, IL, 1860**

*Manuscripts do not have card catalog entries.*

We are now far into the fifth year since a policy was initiated, with the avowed object and confident promise, of putting an end to slavery agitation. Under the operation of that policy, that agitation has not only not ceased, but has constantly augmented. I believe it will not cease, till a crisis shall have been passed, and a permanent "A house divided against itself can not stand." I believe this government can not endure, permanently half slave and half free— I do not expect the Union to be dissolved— I do not expect the house to fall— but I do expect it will cease to be divided— It will become all one thing, or all the other. Either the opponents of slavery, will arrest the further spread of it, and place it where the public mind shall rest in the belief that it is in course of ultimate extinction; or its advocates will push it forward till it shall become alike lawful in all the

**Thomas Jefferson, holograph list of slaves [ca. 1811], Monticello**
*Manuscripts do not have card catalog entries.*

| Tomahawk | Bear creek |
|---|---|

**Tomahawk**

Hall. Bess's. 67. Sep.
Hanah. Cate's. 70. Ian.
   Sally. 98.
   Billy 99.
   Iamy. 05.
   Phil. 08.
   Edmund. 09.
Lucinda. Hanah's. 91. Iune
   Melinda. 09. Aug. 8.
Kate. Cate's. 73.
Phil Hubard.
Will. ab.ᵗ 53.
Abby. ab.ᵗ 53.
Edy. Will's. 92. Apr.
Manuel. Will's. 94.
Amy. Will's. 97.
Gawen. Betty's. 78. Aug.
Sal. Will's. 77. Nov.
   Betty. 01. Ian.
   Abby. 04. Nov.
   Edy. 06. Aug.
   Martin. 09. Ian. 31.
   Moses. 11. Apr.
Milly. Sal's. 97. Mar.
Dick. 67.
Dinah. 66.
Aggy. 89.
Evans. 94.
Hanah. 96.
   Lucy. 99.
   Iamy. 02.
   Briley. 05.
Bess. ab.ᵗ 47
   Ambrose. 99.
   Prince. 04. Mar.
   Ioe. 06. May
   Shepherd. 09. Apr.
      *children of Suck Hubbard & of Bess.*
Betty. ab.ᵗ 49.
Hercules. Betty's. 94. Nov. 20.
Iesse. 72. Nov.

**Bear creek**

Iame Hubbard. ab.ᵗ 43.
Cate. ab.ᵗ 47.
Armistead. Hubard's. 71.
Cate. Rachael's. 97. Aug.
Maria. Cate's. 76. Oct.
   Nisy. 99.
   Iohnny. 04. Sep.
   Isaac. 09. Nov.
Sally. Cate's. 88. Aug.
   Billy. 08. Aug.
   Anderson. 10. Apr. 14.
Reuben. Hanah's. 93.
Austin. Betty's. 75. Aug.
Flora. Will's. 83.
   Gawen. 04. Iuly.
   Aleck. 06. Sep.
   Billy 08. Oct.
   Boston. 11. Dec. 1.
Fanny. Will's. 88. Aug.
   Rachael. 07. Feb.
   Rhody. 11. Iuly.
Caesar. Bess's. 74. Sep.
Cate. Suck's. 88. Mar.
   Davy. 06. Iune.
   Iohn. 11. Iune 1.
Daniel. Suck's. 90. Sep.
Stephen. Suck's. 94.
Cate. Betty's. 88. Mar. 8.
Mary. Betty's. 92. Ian.
Nanny. 78. Iuly.
   Maria. 98. Feb. 24.
   Phil. 01. Aug.
   Milly. 06. May.
   George Dennis. 08. May.
   Anderson. 10. Aug.

40.          35

**[Manumission papers], Jon Custis, Williamsburg, VA, 1747**

*Manuscripts do not have card catalog entries.*

To all Christian People to Whom these Presents shall Come. John Custis Esq.r of the City of Williamsburgh Sendeth Greeting Whereas John otherways called Jack my Negro Boy born of the body of my Negro Wench Young Allie was born a Slave and for such is Commonly held, esteemed and Reputed both publickly and privately, Now Know Ye That I the said John Custis for Diverse true Lawfull and meritorious Causes and Considerations me moving and so adjudged and allowed by the Governor and Council, as by a Licence from them had and obtained bearing Date the Eighteenth Day of Aprile one thousand seven Hundred and forty four Have manumitted freed from all obligation of Servitude Discharged as by These Presents I Do for myself my.t Heirs Executors and Administrators for Ever Manumit free & Discharge the said Negro boy John, otherways called Jack with all his Issue of his body born or to be born of any free Woman together with his Goods and Chattles Lands and Tenements whatsoever already obtained & acquired or hereafter to be obtained or Acquired. Know Also That I the said John Custis Have Remised Released and for me my Heirs Executors and Administrators, for Ever have quit claimed As by these presents I Do remit release and for Ever Quit Claim to the said Negro John otherways Called Jack his Heirs & all their Issue All & all Manner of actions real & personal, Suits Claims Services Traspasses Debts Dues and Demands Whatsoever which Against the said Negro John otherways Called Jack & his Heirs or their Issue or any of them, I my Heirs Executors or Administrators had now Have or any ways hereafter may Have by means of his Servitude or Slaverly aforesaid or on any other Cause or Account whatever from the beginning of the world to the Day of the Date hereof And I the said John Custis for myself my Heirs Executors or Administrators the said Negro Boy John otherways Called Jack with all his Issue born or to be born of any free Woman Will Warrant to be free Against all Persons Whatever by these Presents In Witness whereof I the said John Custis have hereunto set my Hand & Affixed my Seal this Third Day of February one thousand seven Hundred & forty Seven.

Jn.o Custis

Sealed & Delivered
in the presence of us
William Nimmo

Richard Kello

**An Essay on the Africans having been subjected to more injuries than the Indians, Benjamin Rush, 1850**

*Manuscripts do not have card catalog entries.*

An Essay
on
The Africans
having been subjected
to more injuries
than The Indians.

By W. Rush

Delivered before the Public
of the borough of West Chester,
on the evening of Monday 16th 1

CHARLESTOWN, W. Va.

Proclamation!  In pursuance of instructions from
the Governor of Virginia, notice is hereby given to
all whom it may concern, That, as heretofore, particularly from now until after Friday next the 2nd
of December, strangers found within the county of
Jefferson, and counties adjacent, having no known
and proper business here, and who cannot give a
satisfactory account of themselves, will be at
once arrested.  That on, and for a proper period
before that day, stangers [!] and especially parties, approaching under          the pretext of being

See next card

*detail, opposite*

# PROCLAMATION!

IN pursuance of instructions from the Governor of Virginia, notice is hereby given to all whom it may concern,

That, as heretofore, particularly from now until after Friday next the 2nd of December, **STRANGERS** found within the County of Jefferson, and Counties adjacent, having no known and proper business here, and who cannot give a satisfactory account of themselves, will be at once arrested.

That on, and for a proper period before that day, stangers and especially parties, approaching under the pretext of being present at the execution of John Brown, whether by Railroad or otherwise, will be met by the Military and turned back or arrested without regard to the amount of force, that may be required to affect this, and during the said period and especially on the 2nd of December, the citizens of Jefferson and the surrounding country are *EMPHATICALLY* warned to remain at their homes armed and guard their own property.

Information received from reliable sources, clearly indicates that by so doing they will best consult their own interests.

No WOMEN or CHILDREN will be allowed to come near the place of execution.

**WM. B. TALLIAFERRO,** *Maj. Gen. Com. troops,*
**S. BASSETT FRENCH,** *Military Sec'y.*
**THOMAS C. GREEN,** *Mayor,*
**ANDREW HUNTER,** *Asst. Pros. Att'y.*
**JAMES W. CAMPBELL,** *Sheriff.*

November 28th, '59.                    Spirit Print.

GODWIN, MORGAN, fl. 1685.
The Negro's & Indians advocate, suing for their
admission into the church: or Persuasive to the
instructing and baptizing of the Negro's and
Indians in our plantations ... To which is added,
a brief account of religion in Virginia.  By
Morgan Godwyn ...
London,Printed for the author,by J.D. and are
to be sold by most booksellers.1680.
7p.ℓ.,174p.  17½cm.
Pages 113-128 misnumbered 97-112.
"Errata": verso of     7th prelim. leaf.
Wing G971; Church  (     ) 663.
                        See next card
                        R57-149

# Negro's & Indians ADVOCATE,

Suing for their Admission into the

# CHURCH:

### OR

## PERSUASIVE to the Instructing and Baptizing of the *Negro's* and *Indians* in our Plantations.

### SHEWING,

at as the Compliance therewith can prejudice
no Mans just Interest; So the wilful Neglecting
and Opposing of it, is no less than a manifest
Apostacy from the Christian Faith.

which is added, A brief Account of Religion in *Virginia*.

## By MORGAN GODWYN,

*Sometime St. of Ch. Ch. Oxon.*

es 19. 30. *And it was so, that all that saw it said, There was
such deed done not seen from the day that the Children of Israel
ne up out of the Land of Egypt, unto this Day.*
4.20. *We cannot but speak the things which we have seen and heard.*

*e must answer for our idle Words, how much more for our idle
nce? St. Augustin.*

NDON, Printed for the Author, by *J. D.* and are
to be Sold by most Booksellers. 1680.

U.S. Continental congress, 1775.
  A declaration by the representatives of the
United colonies of North-America, now met in
general congress at Philadelphia, setting forth
the causes and necessity of their taking up arms.
  Philadelphia:Printed.Watertown:Re-printed and
sold by Benjamin Edes.1775.
  15p.  16cm.,in case 17½cm.
  Drawn up by John Dickinson.
  Evans 14549; Sabin 19159.
  Signatures: [A]-B⁴ ([A]1 wanting).
  Imperfect: 1st leaf      (half-title?) wanting.

)          R57-590

# A
# DECLARATION

## BY THE

## REPRESENTATIVES

### OF THE

## UNITED COLONIES

### OF

## *NORTH-AMERICA,*

### NOW MET IN

## GENERAL CONGRESS

### AT

## *PHILADELPHIA,*

Setting forth the CAUSES and NECESSITY of their
taking up

## A R M S.

---

*PHILADELPHIA:* Printed.

*WATERTOWN:*

Re-Printed and Sold by BENJAMIN EDES.

1775.

**Discipline**

[FRANKLIN, BENJAMIN, 1706-1790.]
  Poor Richard, 1733. An almanack for the year
of Christ 1733 ... By Richard Saunders, philom.
[pseud.]
  Philadelphia: Printed and sold by B.Franklin,
[1732].
  [24]p.diagr. 16cm.,in case 17½cm.
  Evans 3541; Hildeburn 448; Campbell 42.
  With Isaac Norris Sr.'s marginalia and his
diary on blank interleaves.

R57-10

*Poor Richard*, 1733.

# AN
# Almanack

For the Year of Chrift

# 1733,

Being the Firft after LEAP YEAR:

| *And makes fince the Creation* | Years |
|---|---|
| By the Account of the Eaftern *Greeks* | 7241 |
| By the Latin Church, when ⊙ ent. ♈ | 6932 |
| By the Computation of *W.W.* | 5742 |
| By the *Roman* Chronology | 5682 |
| By the *Jewifh* Rabbies | 5494 |

### *Wherein is contained*

The Lunations, Eclipfes, Judgment of the Weather, Spring Tides, Planets Motions & mutual Afpects, Sun and Moon's Rifing and Setting, Length of Days, Time of High Water, Fairs, Courts, and obfervable Days.
Fitted to the Latitude of Forty Degrees, and a Meridian of Five Hours Weft from *London*, but may without fenfible Error, ferve all the adjacent Places, even from *Newfoundland* to *South-Carolina*.

By RICHARD SAUNDERS, Philom.

PHILADELPHIA:
Printed and fold by *B. FRANKLIN*, at the New Printing-Office near the Market.

A
779 R

U.S. Continental congress, 1779.
    Report of Commissioners for settling a cartel
for the exchange of prisoners.
    Philadelphia:Printed by David C.Claypoole.
MDCCLXXIX.
    20p.  21½cm.in case  22½cm.
    Signed: William Davies, Robert H. Harrison.
    Evans 16631; Hildeburn 3946.
    Signatures: [A]-B$^4$,C$^2$.
    Unbound, untrimmed, stitched as issued; in hf.
green mor. case.

)

R57-653

shall only be rated as you propose, at six men, though we think the appreciation inadequate.

" 7th, In case either party, from motives of generous confidence, and to accelerate relief, should be induced to dispossess themselves of a portion of prisoners, before circumstances admit of receiving an equivalent, the plighted honors of the generals, or some adequate security must guarantee the delivery of the said equivalent, so that no pretence whatever may be assumed to evade or delay it.

" 8th, We are not unwilling to frame regulations to establish and facilitate future periodical exchanges upon terms of mutual advantage, and which can leave no room for altercation or misconstruction. Whether such an instrument shall be called a general cartel we will not dispute, and we shall be contented with powers on the part of the American commissioners of a like tenor with our own. But we can, neither in the present nor in any future case, admit, that officers and soldiers of militia, when not in service, shall be exempted from being made prisoners of war.

Signed,      W E S T   H Y D E,
              J O H N   A N D R E,
             Commissioners for an exchange
             of prisoners on the part of sir
             Henry Clinton.

| T A R I F F. | Men. |
|---|---|
| General commanding in chief, | 5,000 |
| Lieutenant general, | 1,200 |
| Major general, | 350 |
| Brigadier general, | 250 |
| Majors of brigade and Aids de camp, | according to their rank. |
| Colonel, | 150 |
| Lieutenant Colonel, | 75 |
| Major, | 35 |
| Captain, | 20 |
| Lieutenant, | 10 |
| Ensign, | 5 |
| Adjutant, | 10 |
| Quartermaster, | 10 |
| Chaplain, | 10 |

Serjeant,

BIBLE. Massachuset. 1663. Eliot.

Mamvsse Wunneetupanatamwe Up-Biblum God maneeswe Nukkone Testament kah wonk Wusku Testament. Ne quoshkinnumuk nashpe Wuttinneumoh Christ noh asoo-wesit John Eliot.

Cambridge [Mass.]:Printeuoop nashpe Samuel Green kah Marmaduke Johnson.1663.

[832],[356]p. 19½cm.,in case 21cm.

Two columns to the page.

Evans 73 (incl. Evans 64).

Signatures: [-]², A-Lℓℓℓℓ⁴,Mmmmm²; A-L⁴,Aa-Xx⁴ (Xx4 blank), A-N⁴ (N4       blank).

See next card
R59-1409

# NEGONNE OOSUKKUHWHONK *MOSES*,

## Ne asoweetamuk

# GENESIS.

### CHAP. I.

Eike kutchissik a ayum God
Kesuk kah Ohke.

2 Kah Ohke mô matta
kuhkenauunneunkquttinnoo
kah monteagunninno, kah
pohkenum woskeche moonôi, kah Nashauanit popom-
shau woskeche nippekontu.

3 Onk noowau God *b* wequaiaj, kah mô
wequai.

4 Kah wunnaumun God wequai ne en
wunnegen: Kah wutchadchaube-ponumun
God noeu wequai kah noeu pohkenum.

5 Kah wutussoweetamun God wequai Kesukod, kah pohkenum wutussoweetamun
Nukon: kah mô wunnonkoooôk kah mo
mohtompog negonne kesuk.

6 Kan noowau God *c* sepakehtamooudj
nôeu nippekontu, kah chadchapemooudj na-
shauweu nippe wutch nippekontu.

7 Kah ayimn God sepakehtamóonk, kah
wutchadchabeponumunnap nashaueu nippe
agwu, utteyeu agwu sepakehtamóonk, kah
nashaueu nippekontu utteyeu ongkouwe sepakehtamóonk, kah mônkó n nih.

8 Kah wuttissoweétamun God *d* sepakehtamóonk Kesukquash, kah mô wunnonkoooôk, kah mô mohtompog nahohtôeu kesukod.

9 Kah noowau God moémoôidj *e* nippe ut
agwu kesukquashkah pasukqunnu, kah pah-
kemoidj nanabpeu, kah mônkó n u h.

10 Kah wuttissoweétam n God nanabpi
ohke, kah moéémoo nippe wuttissoweetamun
Keitoh, & wunnaumun God ne en wunnegen.

11 Kah noowau God dtannéekej ohke nos-
keht, moikeat ikanneniunáôk ikannéniunath,
& meechimmue mahtugquash meechimmoo-
ok meechimmuonk nish noh pasuk nea te
wuttinnu suonk, ubbuhkunmináôk et
woskeche ohke, kah mônkó n nin.

12 Kah ohke dtannegenup mo ket, kah
mosk t ikanneniunáôk ik neniunnash, nish
noh pasuk neane wuttinnu uonk, kah mah-
tug meechunnáôk, ubbu kunninin nanáôk
wu hogkut nish noh pasuk neane watti nnus-
suonk, kah wunnaumun God ne en wunnegen.

13 Kah mo wunnonkoooôk, kah mo môh-
tompog shwekesukod.

14 Kah noowau God, *f* Wequanantégi-
nuohettich ut wussepakehtamoonganit Kesukquash, & pohshehertich ut nashuuwe kesukod, kah ut nashauwe nukkonut, kah kuk-
kineasuonganuhhettich, kah uttoocheyeu-
hettich, kah kesukodtuoowuhhettich, kah
kodtum noowuhhettich.

15 Kah n nag wequanantéganuóhettich
ut sepakehtamoonganit wequaiumóhettich
tich ohke, onk mô n nih.

16 Kah ayum God nessanath missiyeuash,
wequananteganath, wequananteg mohiag na-
nánumooo kesukod, wequananteg peasik
nananamooomoo nukon, kah anoogiog.

17 Kah upponun God wusse pakehtamoo-
oonganit kesukquash, woh wequohsumwog
ohke.

18 Onk woh *g* wunnananumunneau kesukod kah nukon, kah pohshiémoo nashaueu
wequai, kah nashaueu pohkénum, kah wunnaumun God ne en wunnegen.

19 Kah mô wunnonkoooôk kah mo mohtompog yaou quinukok.

20 Kah noowau God, moonahettich nip-
pekóntu pomómutcheg pomantamwae, kah
puppinshausog pumunahettich ongkouwe
ohket woskeche wussepahkehtamoonganit
kesukquash.

21 Kah kezheau God matikkenunutcheh
Pootáppoh, kah nish noh pomanta noe óâs
noh pompa nayit utteyeug moonacheg nippekontu, nissi noh pasuk neane wuttinnussu-
onk, kah nish n oh coouppohwhunin puppin-
shaath, nish noh pasuk neane wuttinnusuonk,
kah wunnau mun God ne en wunnegen.

22 Kah oonanu noh nahhog God noowau,
Mss.éneetuónittegk, *h* kah muttaanoôk, kah
nuonwapegk nippe ut kehtohhannit, kah pup-
pin shasog mattaanhettich ohket.

23 Kah mo wunpikoo ok kah mo môh-
tompog napanna audea tashik qui nukok.

24 Kah noowau God, Pasnuwaheonch
ohke oâs pomanta nwaeu, nih noh pasuk
neane wuttinnu sin, neetasúeg, pamayéch *g*
     kah

*f* Deut.
4. 19.
Psal.
å 36. 7.

*g* Jer.
31. 35.

*h* Gen.
8. 17.
& 9. 1.

A

**Notes on lectures delivered by Benjamin Rush, M.D., Professor of the Institutes and Practice of Medicine at the University of Pennsylvania, William Steptoe, 1803-05**

*Manuscripts do not have card catalog entries.*

tiously — even as late as the 15 or 20 days — where fresh stimuli have been added to raise the Excitt. — It is however rarely necessary

6. Gestation —

M.M. SS

Genl. Head of Remedies — or such as by acting on the Stomach — Bowels Brain — nerves muscles & skin, equalise the Excit. of the whole System & thereby indirectly destroy onward action in the Uterine vessels by imparting to them a more vigorous & healthy action —

early to bed and early to rise makes a man
early to bed and early to rise makes a man
early to bed and early to rise makes a man
early to bed and early to rise makes a man
early to bed and early to rise makes a man
early to bed and early to rise makes a man
early to bed and early to rise makes a man
early to bed and early to rise makes a man
early to bed and early to rise makes a man
early to bed and early to rise makes a man
early to bed and early to rise makes a man
early to bed and early to rise makes a man
early to bed and early to rise makes a man
early to bed and early to rise makes a man
early to bed and early to rise makes a man
early to bed and early to rise makes a man

STIRLING, WILLIAM ALEXANDER, 1st earl of, 1567?-
1640.
An encouragement to colonies. By Sir William
Alexander, knight ...
London Printed by William Stansby.1624.
3p.*l*.,47p. fold.map. 18cm.
Printer's mark (McK 292) on t.-p.
STC 341; Church 400.
Signatures: A-G⁴ (A1 blank? wanting).
An account of the first settling of the nor-
thern parts of America.

R57-71

# AN
# ENCOVRAGEMENT
## TO COLONIES.

He sending forth of Colonies (seeming a nouelty) is esteemed now to bee a strange thing, as not onely being aboue the courage of common men, but altogether alienated from their knowledge, which is no wonder, since that course though both ancient, and vsuall, hath beene by the intermission of so many ages discontinued, yea was impossible to be practised so long as there was no vast ground, howsoeuer men had beene willing, whereupon Plantations might haue beene made, yet there is none who will doubt but that the world in her infancy, and innocency, was first peopled after this manner.

The next generations succeeding *Shem* planted in *Asia*, *Chams* in *Africke*, and *Iaphets* in *Europe*: *Abraham* and *Lot* were Captaines of Colonies, the Land then being as free as the Seas are now, since they parted them in euery part where they passed, not taking notice of natiues with-

B out

A primer for the use of the Mohawk children, to
acquire the spelling and reading of their own, as
well as to get acquainted with the English, tongue;
which for that purpose is put on the opposite page.
Waerighwaghsawe iksaongoenwa ...
  London,Printed by C.Buckton.1786.
  98p. front.,illus.  13cm.,in case  14cm.
  In this copy the frontispiece is an aquatint by
James Peachey; some copies have a woodcut.
  Sabin 65548.
  Signatures: A-F$^8$,G$^1$.
  Contemp. sheep; in            half brown mor. case.
  Inserted is a photo          graph of the t.-p. of
the 1st ed., Montreal,         1781.
                               R59-1723

326

# P R I M E R,

### FOR THE USE OF THE

# MOHAWK CHILDREN,

To acquire the SPELLING and READING of their own, as well as to get acquainted with the ENGLISH, Tongue; which for that Purpose is put on the opposite Page.

# WAERIGHWAGHSAWE IKSAONGOENWA

Tſiwaondad-derighhonny Kaghyadoghſera; Nayon-deweyeſtaghk ayeweanaghnodon ayeghyàdow Ka-niyenkchàga Kaweanondaghkouh; Dyorheaſ-chàga oni tſinihadiweanotea.

⊙ ⊛ ⊙

*LONDON,*

PRINTED BY C. BUCKTON, GREAT PULTNEY-STREET.

1786.

James Peachey sculp.t 1786

PRISON DISCIPLINE SOCIETY, Boston.
  First annual report of the Board of managers of
the Prison discipline society, Boston, June 2,
1826. Fourth edition.
  Boston:Printed by T.R.Marvin.1827.
  88p. fold.pl.  21cm.
  Signatures: [1]-11$^4$.
  Unbound.

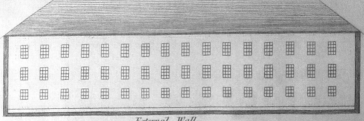

External Wall

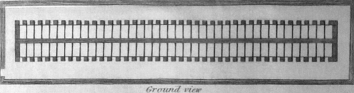

Ground view

Breast-work of Cells.

Scale ¼ inch to 10 feet.

12

to security, solitary confinement, inspection, ventilation, light, cleanliness, instruction, and sickness.

For a Prison securing the important advantages required, we recommend the plan exhibited in this engraving. It represents a building, designed to contain four hundred cells; on the plan of the north wing of the Prison at Auburn, in the State of New York. Retaining the same principle of building, it may be enlarged for a Penitentiary, or diminished for a Jail.

The external wall, in the first figure, is two hundred and six feet long, forty six feet wide and three feet thick. In this wall are three rows of windows, which are four feet by six, except the lower row, which are four feet square. These windows are glazed and secured by a strong grating of iron. They are sufficiently large and numerous to afford perfect ventilation and light to the cells.

The ground view, in the second figure, exhibits the foundation of the cells, and the open area around them. The centre is a solid wall, two feet in thickness, on each side of which the cells are arranged. The walls between the cells are one foot in thickness; those between the cells and the open area, which are broken by the doors, are two feet. The cells are seven feet long, seven feet high, and three and an half feet wide. The only opening from the cell, except the ventilator, is the door, in the upper end of which, is an iron grate, about eighteen by twenty inches. The bars of this grate are round iron, three fourths of an inch in diameter, placed about two inches asunder, leaving orifices smaller than a man's hand. Through this grate all the light, heat, and air, are admitted to the cells. The ventilator which is about three inches in diameter, extends from the back of the cell to the roof of the building. The door of the cell, of which the grate is a part, closes on the inner edge of the wall, leaving a recess between the door and the outer edge of the wall, two feet deep. This recess, in front of each door, increases the difficulty of conversation between the prisoners; pre-

*A*
*f.624g*

SMITH, JOHN, 1580-1631.
... The generall historie of Virginia, New-
England, and the Summer Isles: with the names of
the adventurers, planters, and governours from
their first beginning An$^{o}$: 1584 to this present
1624. With the procedings [!] of those severall
colonies and the accidents that befell them in
all their journeys and discoveries.  Also the
maps and descriptions of all those countryes,
their commodities, people, government, customes,
and religion yet knowne ...
   London.Printed by        I.D. and I.H.for
Michael Sparkes.1624.        See next card
                               R59-1404

*detail, opposite*

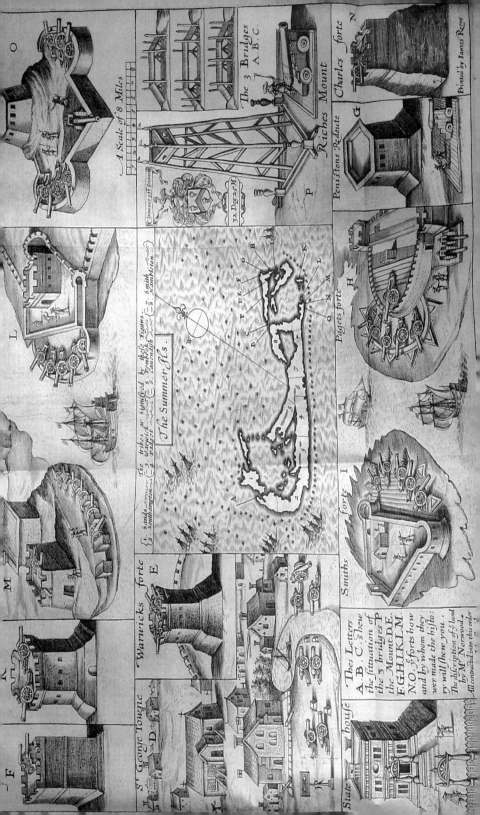

The Summer Isls.

A Scale of 8 Miles

The tribes are signified by these figures
1. Sands          4. Hamilton      7. Smith
2. Unmaroick      5. Cavendish     8. Mainhelton
3. Southampton

St George Towne
Warwicks forte
Smiths forte
State house
Pagets forte
Smiths forte
Charles forte
Penistons Redoute
Riches Mount
The 3 Bridges A.B.C.
Consize off Osburt
32 Degs 5 M.

Thes Letters A. B. C. shew
the situation of
the 3 bridges P
the Mount. D.E.
F.G.H.I.K.L.M.
N.O. forts how
and by whom they
wer made the histo-
ry will shew you.
The discription of Island
by Mr Norwood.
All contracted into this order.

Printed by James Reeve

Liquidation

**Bills of Mortality, London, 1666**

*This book does not yet have a card catalog entry.*

# The Diseases and Casualties this Week.

| | |
|---|---|
| Abortive | 5 |
| Aged | 43 |
| Ague | 2 |
| Apoplexie | 1 |
| Bleeding | 2 |
| Burnt in his Bed by a Candle at St. Giles Cripplegate | 1 |
| Canker | 1 |
| Childbed | 42 |
| Chrisomes | 18 |
| Consumption | 134 |
| Convulsion | 64 |
| Cough | 2 |
| Dropsie | 33 |
| Feaver | 309 |
| Flox and Small-pox | 5 |
| Frighted | 3 |
| Gowt | 1 |
| Grief | 3 |
| Griping in the Guts | 51 |
| Jaundies | 5 |
| Imposthume | 11 |
| Infants | 16 |
| Killed by a fall from the Belfrey at Alhallowes the Great | 1 |
| Kingsevil | 2 |
| Lethargy | 1 |
| Palsie | 1 |
| Plague | 7165 |
| Rickets | 17 |
| Rising of the Lights | 11 |
| Scowring | 5 |
| Scurvy | 2 |
| Spleen | 1 |
| Spotted Feaver | 101 |
| Stilborn | 17 |
| Stone | 2 |
| Stopping of the stomach | 9 |
| Strangury | 1 |
| Suddenly | 1 |
| Surfeit | 49 |
| Teeth | 121 |
| Thrush | 5 |
| Timpany | 1 |
| Tissick | 11 |
| Vomiting | 3 |
| Winde | 3 |
| Wormes | 15 |

|  |  |  |  |  |
|---|---|---|---|---|
| Christned { Males — 95 / Females — 81 / In all — 176 } | Buried { Males — 4095 / Females — 4202 / In all — 8297 } | Plague — 7165 |

Increased in the Burials this Week —————— 607

Parishes clear of the Plague —— 4  Parishes Infected —————— 126

The Assize of Bread set forth by Order of the Lord Major and Court of Aldermen,
A penny Wheaten Loaf to contain Nine Ounces and a half, and three
half-penny White Loaves the like weight.

An account of the robberies committed by John
Morrison, and his accomplices, in and near Philadelphia, 1750. Together with the manner of their
being discover'd, their behaviour on their tryals,
in the prison after sentence, and at the place
of execution.

Philadelphia,Printed [by Anthony Armbruster] in
the year 1750-1.
11,[1],4(i.e.3)p. illus. 18½cm.
Woodcut on t.-p.
Page 3 (2d count) misnumbered 4.
Signed: John Morrison, Francis M'Coy, John Crow,
Elizabeth Robinson.
Evans 6624; Hilde-          burn 1202.
Signatures: [-]⁴,          )( )(⁴.

# AN
# ACCOUNT
## Of the
# ROBBERIES
### Committed by
## JOHN MORRISON,

And his ACCOMPLICES, in and near *Philadelphia*, 1750.
Together with
The *Manner* of their being *discover'd*, their BEHAVIOUR on their
*TRYALS*, in the *Prison* after *Sentence*, and at the *Place* of
Execution.

*Philadelphia*, Printed in the Year 1750-1.

[FRANKLIN, BENJAMIN, 1706-1790.]

A narrative of the late massacres, in Lancaster county, of a number of Indians, friends of this province, by persons unknown. With some observations on the same.

[Philadelphia],Printed [by Anthony Armbruster] in the year M,DCC,LXIV.

31p. 19cm.,in case 20½cm.
Evans 9667; Hildeburn 1992; Vail 556.
Signatures: A-B$^8$.
Inscribed: To Gov$^r$ Bernard from his hum[ble servt.] The Author.

R57-483

Strangers here, with Kindness and Hospitality. Behold the Return we have made them! —— When we grew more numerous and powerful, they put themselves under our *Protection*. See, in the mangled Corpses of the last Remains of the Tribe, how effectually we have afforded it to them!

Unhappy People! to have lived in such Times, and by such Neighbours! —— We have seen, that they would have been safer among the ancient *Heathens*, with whom the Rites of Hospitality were *sacred*. —— They would have been considered as *Guests* of the Publick, and the Religion of the Country would have operated in their Favour. —— But our Frontier People call themselves *Christians!* —— They would have been safer, if they had submitted to the *Turks*; for ever since *Mahomet's* Reproof to *Khaled*, even the *cruel Turks*, never kill Prisoners in cold Blood. These were not even Prisoners: —— But what is the Example of *Turks* to Scripture *Christians?* —— They would have been safer, though they had been taken in actual War against the *Saracens*, if they had once drank Water with them. These were not taken in War against us, and have drank with us, and we with them, for Fourscore Years. —— But shall we compare *Saracens* to *Christians?* —— They would have been safer among the *Moors* in *Spain*, though they had been *Murderers of Sons*; if Faith had once been pledged to them, and a Promise of Protection given. But these have had the Faith of the *English* given to them many Times by the Government, and, in Reliance on that

that Faith, they lived among us, and gave us the Opportunity of murdering them. —— However, what was honourable in *Moors*, may not be a Rule to us; for we are *Christians!* —— They would have been safer it seems among *Popish Spaniards*, even if Enemies, and delivered into their Hands by a Tempest. These were not Enemies; they were born among us, and yet we have killed them all. —— But shall we imitate *idolatrous Papists*, we that are *enlightened Protestants?* —— They would even have been safer among the *Negroes of Africa*, where at least one manly Soul would have been found, with Sense, Spirit and Humanity enough, to stand in their Defence: —— But shall *Whitemen* and *Christians* act like a *Pagan Negroe?* —— In short it appears, that they would have been safe in any Part of the known World, except in the Neighbourhood of the CHRISTIAN WHITE SAVAGES of *Peckstang* and *Donegall!* ——

O ye unhappy Perpetrators of this horrid Wickedness! Reflect a Moment on the Mischief ye have done, the Disgrace ye have brought on your Country, on your Religion, and your Bible, on your Families and Children! Think on the Destruction of your captivated Country-folks (now among the wild *Indians*) which probably may follow, in Resentment of your Barbarity! Think on the Wrath of the United *Five Nations*, hitherto our Friends, but now provoked by your murdering one of their Tribes, in Danger of becoming our bitter Enemies. —— Think of the mild and good Government you have so audaciously insulted; the Laws of your King, your Country,

A true account of the tryals, examinations,
confessions, condemnations, and executions of
divers witches, at Salem, in New-England, for
their bewitching of sundry people and cattel to
death, and doing other great mischiefs to the
ruine of many people about them.  With the strange
circumstances that attended their enchantments:
and their conversation with devils, and other
infernal spirits.  In a letter to a friend in
London ...
  London,Printed for J.Conyers,in Holbourn.[1693?]
  8p.  21cm.
  At end: Salem, 8th. ⌒ month,1692.  C.M.

See next card
R57-339

# A
# True Account

## OF THE
## TRYALS, EXAMINATIONS,
### CONFESSIONS, CONDEMNATIONS,
### and EXECUTIONS of divers

# WITCHES,

## At *SALEM*, in *NEW-ENGLAND*,

### FOR
Their Bewitching of sundry People and Cattel
to Death, and doing other great Mischiefs,
to the Ruine of many People about them.

### WITH
The Strange Circumstances that attended
their Enchantments:

### AND
Their Conversation with Devils, and other
Infernal Spirits.

*In a LETTER to a Friend in* LONDON.

Licensed according to Order.

London, Printed for *J. Conyers*, in *Holbourn*.

The American bloody register: containing a true
and complete history of the lives, last words, and
dying confessions of three of the most noted criminals, that have ever made their exit from a stage
in America, viz. Richard Barrick and John Sullivan,
high way robbers. Together with the dying confess-
ion of Alexander White, a murderer and pirate, who
were executed at Cambridge, (New England) on Thursday, November 18, 1784 ...

Boston:Printed and sold by E.Russell.MDCCLXXXIV.
30,[2]p. illus. 17cm.,in case 20cm. (Bloody
register, no. 1.)

See next card
R59-1616

342

Be not overmuch wicked, neither be thou foolish: Why shouldst
thou die before thy time?

SOLOMON.

READ, CHARLES, 1713(?)-1774.
Copy of a letter from Charles Read, esq; to
the Hon: John Ladd, esq; and his associates,
Justices of the peace for the county of Glouces-
ter.
Philadelphia:Printed and sold by Andrew Steuart,
1764.
8p.  19cm.,in case 20cm.
Printer's mark on t.-p.
Evans 9809; Hildeburn 2050; Sabin 68142.
Signatures: [-]$^4$.

R57-507

*detail, opposite*

*Copy of a Letter from* CHARLES
READ, *Esq; to the Hon.* JOHN LADD,
*Esq; and his Associates, Justices of the*
*Peace for the County of Gloucester.*

GENTLEMEN,

SOME Persons, of good Character, at
*Philadelphia,* having applied to his
Excellency the Governor, for his
Licence for some *Indians,* who have
been always in the *English* Interest, to
reside in your Town, he has been pleased
to grant his Licence, and the Protection
of this Government; by his Order of this
Day, directed to all Officers civil and
military.

The late Outrage committed in *Lancaster,* is such a notorious Violation of
the Rights of Government, and a Crime
of so black a Dye, that I have not the
least Doubt but that the Perpetrators of
it will, in good time, suffer the Punishment the Law inflicts upon Murderers;
for altho' their Consciences may be har-
dened, or they at present in a State of

ters stand on a right footing; their these
Transactions must be enquired into; and
would any Man in his Senses have such
a Cloud hanging over him and his E-
state, which would, by his own Rash-
ness, be subjected to large Demands and
Forfeitures to the Crown?

To have fallen on a Town of the E-
nemy *Indians,* and to have destroyed
them and it, might have terrified the
*Indians,* and lessened the Number of
our Enemies; but such an inhuman
Murder as that at *Lancaster,* can only
serve to convince the World, that there
are among us Persons more savage than
*Indians* themselves. To be cruel in
War, and while the Blood is in a high
Ferment, is frequent; but to assemble
at a Distance, to march many Miles
with Intent, in cool Blood, to butcher
defenceless People, who were placed
where the Magistracy pleased to order
them, was an amazing Depravation of
every Sense of Virtue and Humanity.

Would Wars ever have an End, if

ADAIR, JAMES, trader with the Indians.
  The history of the American Indians; particularly
those nations adjoining to the Missisippi, East and
West Florida, Georgia, South and North Carolina, and
Virginia: containing an account of their origin,
language, manners, religious and civil customs, laws,
form of government, punishments, conduct in war and
domestic life, their habits, diet, agriculture,
manufactures, diseases and method of cure, and
other particulars, sufficient to render it a complete Indian system.  With observations on former
historians, the conduct         of our colony gov-
ernors, superintendents,        missionaries, &c.
                                  See next card
                                  R57-2200

346

## ARGUMENT XV.

The Israelites had CITIES or REFUGE, or places of safety, for those who killed a person unawares, and without design; to shelter them from the blood-thirsty relations of the deceased, or the revenger of blood, who always pursued or watched the unfortunate person, like a ravenous wolf, but after the death of the high-priest they could safely return home, and nobody durst molest him.

According to the same particular divine law of mercy, each of these Indian nations have either a house or town of refuge, which is a sure asylum to protect a man-slayer, or the unfortunate captive, if they can once enter into it. The Cheerake, though now exceedingly corrupt, still observe that law so inviolably, as to allow their beloved town the privilege of protecting a wilful murderer: but they seldom allow him to return home afterwards in safety—they will revenge blood for blood, unless in some very particular case when the eldest can redeem. However, if he should accept of the price of blood to wipe away its stain, and dry up the tears of the rest of the nearest kindred of the deceased, it is generally productive of future ills, either when they are drinking spirituous liquors, or dancing their enthusiastic war dances, a tomohawk is likely to be sunk into the head of some of his relations.

Formerly, when one of the Cheerake murdered an English trader he immediately ran off for the town of refuge; but as soon as he got in view of it, the inhabitants discovered him by the close pursuit of the shrill war-whoop, and for fear of irritating the English, they instantly answered the war cry, ran to arms, intercepted, and drove him off into Tenase-river (where he escaped, though mortally wounded) left he should have entered else reputed holy ground, and thus it had been stained with the blood of their friend; or he had obtained sanctuary to the danger of the community, and the foreign contempt of their sacred altars.

Th[...]

This town of refuge called *Choate*, is situated on a large stream of the Mississippi, five miles above the late unfortunate *Fort-Loudon*,—where some years ago, a brave Englishman was protected after killing an Indian warrior in defence of his property. The gentleman told me, that at his trading house was near to that town of refuge, he had resolved with himself, after some months stay in it, to return home; but the head-men assured him, that though he was then safe, it would prove fatal if he removed thence, so he continued in his asylum still longer, till the affair was by time more obliterated, and he had wiped off all their tears with part of the Muskohge, there was an old beloved town, now reduced to a small ruinous village, called *Koosah*, which is still a place of safety for those who kill undesignedly. It stands on commanding ground, over-looking a bold river, which after running about forty leagues, sweeps close by the late mischievous French garrison *Alebahma*, and down to *Mobille-Strand*, 200 leagues distance, and so into the gulph of Florida.

In almost every Indian nation, there are several *peaceable towns*, which are called "old-beloved," "ancient, holy, or white towns *," they seem to have been formerly "towns of refuge," for it is not in the memory of their oldest people, that ever human blood was shed in them, although they often force persons from thence, and put them to death elsewhere.

## ARGUMENT XVI.

Before the Indians go to WAR, they have many preparatory ceremonies of *purification* and *fasting*, like what is recorded of the Israelites.

In the first commencement of a war, a party of the injured tribe turns out first, to revenge the innocent crying blood of their own bone and flesh, as they term it. When the leader begins to beat up for volunteers, he goes three times round his dark winter-house, contrary to the course of the sun, sounding the war-whoop, singing the war-song, and beating the drum.

* WHITE is their fixt emblem of peace, friendship, happiness, prosperity, purity, holiness, &c. as with the Israelites.

Then

# Installation

**Aaron Levy**
Kloster Indersdorf Orphans (Photographs)

The children in these photographs, reproduced in full later in this book, are from Kloster Indersdorf, a United Nations orphanage established in Germany from 1945-1947. It handled refugees and displaced persons, such as Jews and others previously deported or displaced from Eastern Europe by the Nazis. The assigned if unverifiable name of the orphan has been digitally replaced with an image of his or her own face. The project asks us to consider how we remember or recognize a lost individual or a refugee. These altered photographs are poetic portraits of children needing to be recognized not just by others, but by themselves as well. Our dislocation from these children and from their portraits—a single instant, now more than fifty years old—reveals how little we know even today about their lives.

## Gans & Jelacic Architecture
Refugee Cities (Panels)

This work by Deborah Gans and Matthew Jelacic, reproduced in full earlier in this book, should be read as a direct call "to halt the urbanization of the world through displacement." As quantified by the United Nations, the number of people subject to scenarios of displacement is vast—one in every 297 persons on this planet—including a new category officially recognized by the UN, the Internally Displaced Person, who is forced from home, but not region or country. There are at least twenty-five million refugees—a population equivalent to double the world's largest metropolis. As they wane with attack, wax through immigration, or emerge suddenly in the debased form of the refugee camp, cities register the phenomena of displacement, and displacement describes the temporality and permanencies of cities. Any strategy for housing the displaced ultimately must envision new or recuperated urban cultures.

## Aaron Levy
Posture (Video)

This reworked footage from 1930s German dance culture, in three parts, deals with the issue of mass discipline and conformity through choreography. In the thirties, dance was highly politicized and spiritualized and involved large groups of people engaged in outdoor ecstatic movement. The ideal body is understood here as the result of rigorous cultivation and training—in the service of building utopian communities.

**Katrin Sigurdardottir**
Circuit Cities (Installation)

The work of Katrin Sigurdardottir, because of its scale, advances the illusion that we are in control of our urban spaces. The work playfully presents the viewer with a city so generic and abstract as to be unlivable. This model city empowers us to reimagine our cities with attentiveness to their fragility, hospitality, and dependency on the rationality of the grid. It betrays a fundamental inquisitiveness towards the modular and the non-specific. A model may respond to an imperfect, unfulfilled past; it also seeks to ameliorate a damaged or desolate life. As such, it serves as a prototype for the future: it is a potentiality to be filled, a potentiality too promising to reject.

**Lars Wallsten**
Crimescape (Photographs)

These works by Lars Wallsten are case studies in anonymity. In this series, discarded photographs of crime scenes are projected onto generic public spaces. Today the borders separating our public and private spheres are blurred and perpetually at risk of collapse. These photographs, although seemingly passive, force us to rethink how we process, classify, and ultimately anaesthetize ourselves against the crimes that surround us. The anonymity of the individuals and events that gave rise to these images makes this body of work more dramatic and unsettling than they first appear. Can we envision cities that respond less to fears of violence and violation—and are more inherently hospitable?

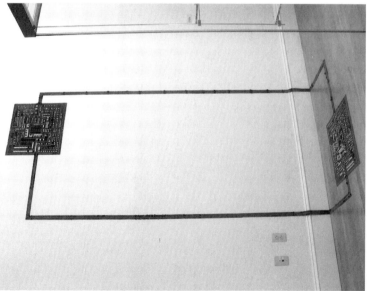

**Kloster Indersdorf**

**Search String: Kloster Indersdorf**

Aaron Levy

Towards the end of the war, the United Nations Relief and Rehabilitation Administration (UNRRA) was established to handle refugees and displaced persons. With the aid of the American Army, UNRRA Team 182 secured an abandoned cloister, Kloster Indersdorf, near what was then the town of Prien am Chiemsee in Bavaria (near Munich, Germany). Kloster Indersdorf maintained a population of some 350 children from 1945 to 1947. Children at Kloster Indersdorf included Jews and others deported or displaced from Eastern Europe by the Nazis and brought to the Reich for extermination, forced labor in concentration camps, or aryanization. Many of the childrens' names had been changed in the process so that they no longer knew their identities. The UNRRA team helped to trace the identities of the children and to arrange for their adoption, return them to their original homelands, or help them emigrate to new countries for settlement. Photographs were taken of the children and published in newspapers to facilitate this process.

The photo archives of the Holocaust Museum in Washington, D.C. contain at least 124 portraits of children from Kloster Indersdorf. The child is often clinically photographed before a white, formless background. The child holds a slate board on which is inscribed his or her given name. Where the child is presumably too young to understand purpose, too weak to hold up the slate, or too injured to support himself or herself, assistance is provided by a hand that enters into the frame from the outside. Alongside their functional purpose as photographic records of survival, aiding reunification, the photographs are strikingly poetic portraits of children needing to be recognized by themselves and others. Here, the act of portraiture attempts to legitimize the "subject" as an individual still worth remembering (in memory), as again being part of a post-war community. Equally important, portraiture marks the individual as amenable to or able to being remembered or recognized.

In the Kloster Indersdorf portraits, the orphan is fundamentally needy, wanting to be recognized by someone or something (i.e. family). The orphan addresses us today through his or her particular estrangement at the time. This photographic address that simultaneously signifies abandonment is perhaps best illustrated by the reliance of the subject upon the name plate. It is worth contemplating whether the subsequent history of the orphans (whether the photographs ultimately aided reunification or not) would alter our relation to the photographs today. The addition of the unverifiable text also encourages doubt regarding the veracity of the visual field. One might ask: "Why hold up one's name? Is the face not enough? Not accurate or memorable?"

It is possible to digitally replace the textual slate with the image of the face, such that the subject is effectively holding a photograph of his or her own face. My motivation for doing so is impelled by the inadequacy of the name (in relation to the image) today to enhance recognition of the individual.

* Exhibited in "Cities Without Citizens" at The Rosenbach Museum & Library, July 8-September 28, 2003. Installation shots are available in Section III (Documentation).

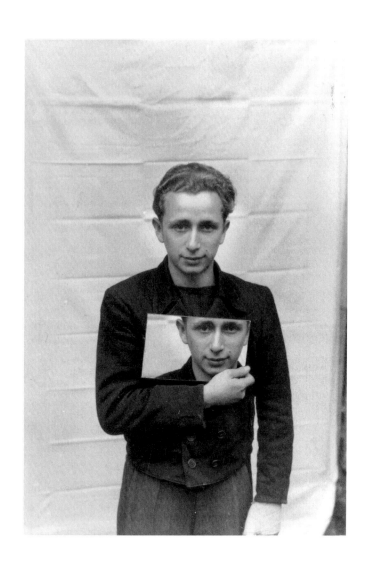

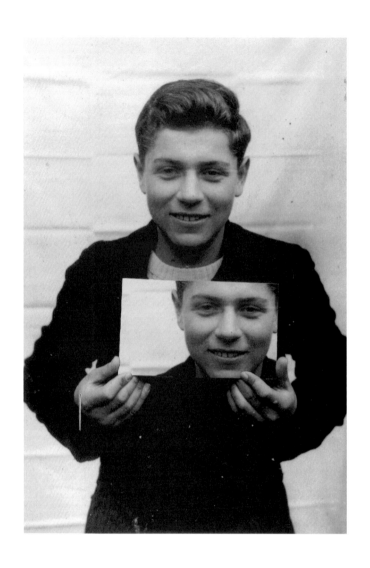

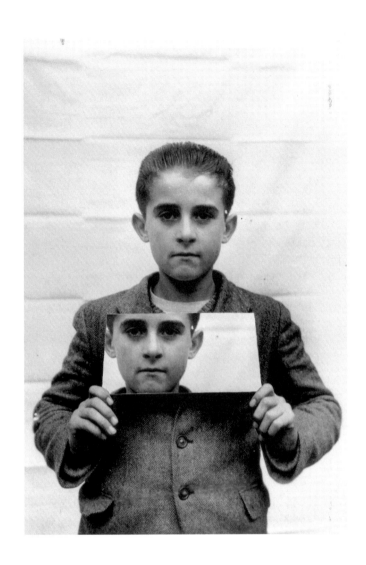

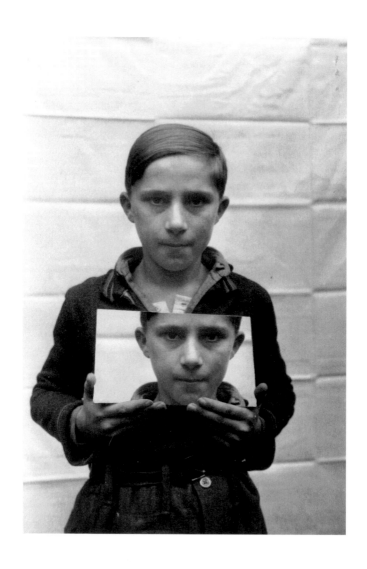

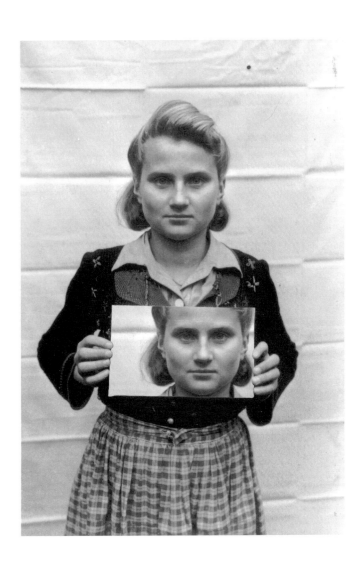

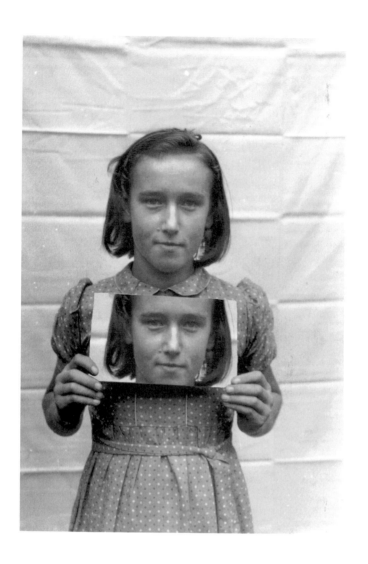

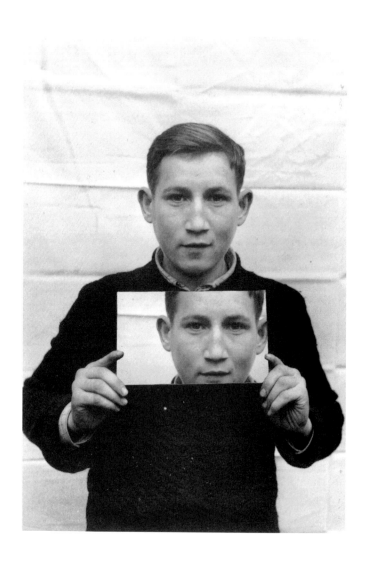

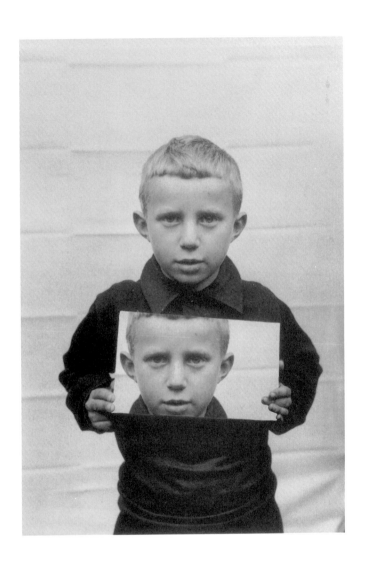

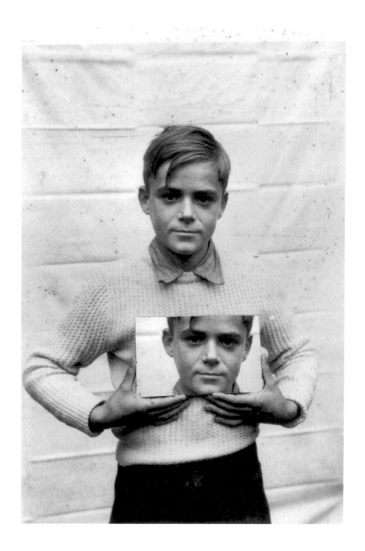

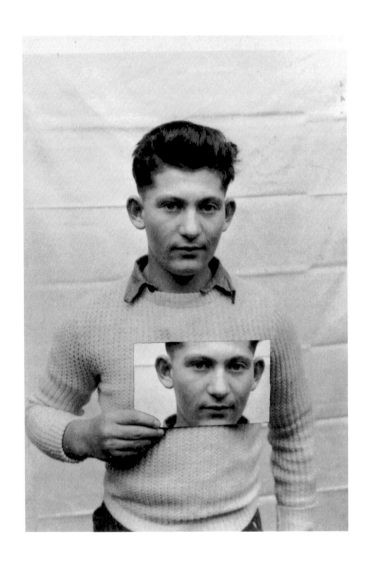

# Inventory

## Settlement

The adventures of Colonel Daniel Boon, [John Filson], Norwich, 1786

Geographiae, Claudius Ptolemaeus, Amsterdam, 1605

Nova Brittania, Robert Johnson, London, 1609

The generall historie of Virginia, John Smith, London, 1624

Information and direction to such persons as are inclined to America..., William Penn, [London, 1684]

A narrative of the troubles with the Indians in New-England, William Hubbard, Boston, 1677

An Enquiry into the causes of the alienation of the Delaware and Shawanese Indians..., [Charles Thomson], London, 1759

A declaration of the state of the colony and affaires in Virginia, [Edward Waterhouse], London, 1622

A true declaration of the estate of the colonie in Virginia, London, 1610

A brief account of the province of Pennsilvania lately granted by the King, [William Penn], London, 1682

A letter from Doctor More...relating to the state and improvement of the province of Pennsilvania..., Nicholas More, [London], 1687

[Agreement to found Aaronsburg with 40,000 acres] Aaron Levy, agreement with Robert Morris and Walter Stewart, 1792

Washington's farewell address, George Washington, New Brunswick, NJ, 1813

Mondus Novus, Amerigo Vespucci, 1504

[Portolan chart of the Atlantic, 1575] Bartolomeu Lasso

Plan of the city of New York, [New York, ca. 1795]

Nicolaus Visscher, Novi Belgii Novaeque Angliae nec non partes Virginiae...[Amsterdam, c. 1655]

[1881] reprint of Thomas Holmes's 1683 map of Philadelphia

## Citizen

Abraham Lincoln, excerpt from the "House Divided" speech, Springfield, IL, 1860

Thomas Jefferson, holograph list of slaves [ca. 1811], Monticello

[Manumission papers], Jon Custis, Williamsburg, VA, 1747

Negroes & Indian Advocate, Morgan Godwin, London, 1860

The people's right to election or Alteration of government in Connecticut, Gershom Bulkeley, Philadelphia, 1689

Declaration by the Representatives of the United Colonies...at Philadelphia, Philadelphia, 1775

Proclamation...present at the execution of John Brown...., Charlestown, West Virginia, 1859

An Essay on the Africans having been subjected to more injuries than the Indians, Benjamin Rush, 1850

Some observations on the situation, disposition, and character of the Indian Natives of this continent, Philadelphia, 1784

**Discipline**

Report of the Commissioners...Exchange of Prisoners, Philadelphia, 1779

A primer for the use of the Mohawk Children..., London, 1786

Mamusse Wunneetupanatamwe Up-Biblum God maneeswe Nukkone Testament kah wonk Wusku Testament, John Eliot, Cambridge, 1663-61

An almanack for the year of Christ 1733..., Philadelphia, 1732

Notes on lectures delivered by Benjamin Rush, M.D., Professor of the Institutes and Practice of the University of Pennsylvania, William Steptoe, 1803-05

First annual report of the Board of managers of the Prison discipline society, Boston, 1826

An encouragement to colonies, William Alexander Stirling, London, 1624

**Liquidation**

Bills of Mortality, London, 1666

A narrative of the late massacres, in Lancaster county...(Ben Franklin's Copy), Philadelphia, 1764

Copy of a letter from Charles Read, esq, to the hon. John Ladd, Charles Read, Philadelphia, 1764

The history of the American Indians..., James Adaire, London, 1775

An account of the robberies committed by John Morrison, and his accomplices, in and near Philadelphia, 1750, Philadelphia, 1750-51

A true account of the trials, examinations, confessions, condemnations, and execution of divers witches, at Salem..., London, 1693

A sermon at the execution of Moses Paul, an Indian, who has been guilty of murder, Samson Occom, New Haven, 1788

More wonders of the invisible world, Robert Calef, London, 1700

The American Bloody Register: Containing a true and complete history of the lives, last words, and dying confessions of [..] noted criminals..., Boston, 1784

Special object in exhibition: Floor-mounted terrestrial globe, 1800

379

REFERENCE MATTER

**Beyond Human Rights**

[1] Hannah Arendt, "We Refugees," *Menorah Journal*, no. 1 (1943): 77.

[2] Arendt, *Imperialism*, Part II of *The Origins of Totalitarianism* (New York: Harcourt, Brace, 1951): 266-98.

[3] Ibid., 290-95.

[4] Tomas Hammar, *Democracy and the Nation State: Aliens, Denizens, and Citizens in a World of International Migration* (Brookfield, Vermont: Gower, 1990).

**Universal Hospitality**

[1] Émile Benveniste, *Le Vocabulaire des institutions indo-européennes* (Paris: Éditions de Minuit, 1969): 360.

[2] Jacques Derrida, *Aporias*, trans. Thomas Dutoit (Stanford: Stanford UP, 1993): 42. Another way to address this structure would be to say that it is "purely historical," but this only displaces and repeats the figure of *aporia* in another location, which now appears in the form of an absent mediator between nature and culture.

[3] Derrida, *Of Hospitality*, trans. Rachel Bowlby (Stanford: Stanford UP, 2000): 55.

[4] Immanuel Kant, *Perpetual Peace, and other essays on politics, history, and morals*, trans. Ted Humphrey (Indianapolis: Hackett Publishing Company, 1983): 103.

[5] Ibid., 102.

[6] Ibid.

[7] Derrida, *Of Hospitality*, 55.

[8] Martin Heidegger, *Introduction to Metaphysics*, trans. Ralph Manheim (New Haven, Yale UP, 1959): 128.

[9] Kant, *Perpetual Peace*, 103.

[10] Derrida, "Une hospitalité à l'infini," in *De l'hospitalité*, ed. Mohammed Seffahi (Paris: Éditions la passe de vente, 2001): 142.

[11] On the subjective qualities attached to relations with strangers, see George Simmel,

"The Stranger in Metropolitan Life," *The Sociology of Georg Simmel*, trans. and ed. Kurt H. Wolff (New York: Free Press, 1964): 405.

[12] Derrida, *Of Hospitality*, 29.

[13] Derrida, "Une hospitalité à l'infini," 126.

[14] Kant, *Perpetual Peace*, 103.

[15] Ibid.

[16] Ibid., 105.

## The Home of Shame

[1] Walter Benjamin, "Paris, Capital of the Nineteenth Century," in *Reflections*, ed. Peter Demetz, trans. Edmund Jephcott (New York: Schocken, 1978): 150.

[2] Oliver Wendell Holmes, "The Stereoscope and the Stereograph," in *Classic Essays on Photography*, ed. Alan Trachtenberg (New Haven: Leete's Island Books, 1980): 72.

[3] Ibid., 73.

[4] Michel Foucault, "Photogenic Painting," in *Photogenic Painting*, trans. Dafydd Roberts (London: Black Dog Publishing, 1999): 85.

[5] Ibid.

[6] Ibid., 87.

[7] Ibid.

[8] Ibid.

[9] Giorgio Agamben, *Remnants of Auschwitz: The Witness and the Archive*, trans. Daniel Heller-Roazen (New York: Zone Books, 2002): 120-1.

[10] Maurice Blanchot, *The Instant of My Death*, trans. Elizabeth Rottenberg (Stanford: Stanford UP, 2000): 8-9.

[11] Blanchot, *The Step Not Beyond*, trans. Lynette Nelson (Albany: Suny Press, 1992): 76.

[12] Jacques Derrida, *Demeure: Fiction and Testimony*, trans. Elizabeth Rottenberg (Stanford: Stanford UP, 2000): 33.

[13] Ibid., 33.

[14] Ernst Bloch, "Sledding at Eye Level," in *Literary Essays*, trans. Andrew Joron, et al (Stanford: Stanford UP, 1998): 191.

[15] Eduardo Cadava, *Words of Light: Theses on the Photography of History* (Princeton: Princeton UP, 1997): 61.

[16] Bloch, "Sledding at Eye Level," 191.

[17] Derrida, *Archive Fever: A Freudian Impression*, trans. Eric Prenowitz (Chicago: U of Chicago P, 1996): 11.

[18] Roland Barthes, *Camera Lucida: Reflections on Photography*, trans. Richard Howard (New York: Hill and Wang, 1981): 14.

[19] Ibid., 10-11.

[20] Agamben, *Remnants of Auschwitz*, 106.

## Harlem

[1] In the acknowledgements to Alice Attie, *Harlem on the Verge* (New York: Quantuck Lane, 2003), 119, Attie has noted some of the places I took her photos, but has missed these three. All the Attie photographs in this article are included in that book.

[2] Wang Kar-wei's film *Chungking Express* (1994) stages this by robbing well-established cinematic idiom—French New Wave, American noir, and gangster movies—of all the expected semantic charge. On the Cultural Studies front, Ackbar Abbas' work comments most extensively on this cultural denuding: "Hyphenation: The Spatial Dimensions of Hong Kong Culture" in *Walter Benjamin and the Demands of History*, ed. Michael P. Steinberg (Ithaca: Cornell UP, 1996): 214-231; "Hong Kong: Other Histories, Other Politics" *Public Culture* Vol. 9.3 (Spring 1997): 293-313.

[3] *Journey to the East '97* (Hong Kong: HKUST Center for the Arts, 1997): 92.

[4] Gilbert Osofsky, *Harlem: The Making of a Ghetto* (1966; rpt. Chicago: Ivan R. Dee, 1996): 71. I am grateful to Brent Edwards for sharing some references. Some of the prose is a paraphrase of the Encyclopedia Britannica entry.

[5] For an unsentimental account of this, see Jervis Anderson, *This Was Harlem: 1900-1950* (New York: Noonday, 1981).

[6] Robin Kelley, "Disappearing Acts: Capturing Harlem in Transition," in *Harlem on the Verge*, 9-17.

[7] Aaron Levy, *Cities Without Citizens: Statelessnes and Settlements in Early America*, Rosenbach Museum & Library (Philadelphia), July 8-September 28, 2003.

[8] W.E.B. DuBois, *The Souls of Black Folk* (Boston: Bedford, 1997): 38.

[9] Derrida speaks of "teleopoiesis" in *Politics of Friendship,* trans. George Collins (New York: Verso, 1997). I have connected it to cultural work in "Deconstruction and Cultural Studies: Arguments for a Deconstructive Cultural Studies," in Nicholas Royle, ed. *Deconstructions* (Oxford: Blackwell, 2000): 14-43.

[10] These words are somewhat modified in the head note to the acknowledgements to *Harlem on the Verge*, 119.

[11] Cited in Derrida, "Différance," in *Margins: of Philosophy*, trans. Alan Bass (Chicago: U of Chicago Press, 1982): 14.

[12] This is the main argument of Spivak, *Imperatives to Re-Imagine the Planet/Imperative zur Neuerfindung des Planeten*, ed. Willi Goetschel (Passagen: Vienna, 1999).

[13] Amy Finnerty, "Outnumbered: Standing Out At Work," *New York Times.* 7/16/00, 63. Mr. McDonald, you may have "decided Derridean deconstruction wasn't for me," but this liberating statement, standing alone in an issue full of clichés, shows that you can't take the Yale out of Erroll.

[14] If one credited the Lacanian narrative, this would be a kind of group mirror stage, to be superseded by the symbolic (Jacques Lacan, "The Mirror Stage," in *Ecrits*, trans. Alan Sheridan (New York: Norton, 1977): 1-7. I can hang in with this kind of generalized psychoanalytic talk, only as long as it remains general.

[15] To see how this ruse works for constitutions, see Jacques Derrida, "Declarations of Independence," trans Thomas Keenan, in *New Political Science* 15 (Summer 1986): 7-15; and *For Nelson Mandela*, ed. Jacques Derrida and Mustapha Tlili (New York: Seaver Books, 1987).

[16] James Weldon Johnson, *Black Manhattan* (New York: Da Capo, 1991): 161.

[17] This is Edward Soja's term for that sort of living together that is the motor of history. (Soja, *Postmetropolis: Critical Studies of Cities and Regions* (Malden, MA: Blackwell,

2000): 12-18).

[18] A case in point would be John Hutnyk's brilliant book *The Rumour of Calcutta: Tourism, Charity and the Poverty of Representation* (London: Zed Books, 1996), that talks a lot about writing. But the inscriptions of Kolkata remain illegible to him. Michael Douglas's marvelous video *Tramjatra* (presented at Conference on New Directions in the Humanities, University of the Aegean, Greece, July 5, 2003) could not accommodate the complex irony of the Bengali, Indian, and Calcuttan material captured by his technical equipment.

[19] Attie, *Harlem On the Verge*, 14.

[20] *Harlem Song* By George C. Wolf, Dir. George C. Wolf, Apollo Theatre, New York, July 8—December 29, 2002. Alain Locke, *The New Negro* (New York: Atheneum, 1970). Of the many television programs, PBS's "A Walk through Harlem" is the most exemplary.

[21] Michael Henry Adams, "Harlem Lost and Found," Museum of the City of New York, May 3, 2003-January 4, 2004.

[22] Emmanuel Levinas, *Totality and Infinity*, trans. Alphonso Lingis (Pittsburgh: Duquesne Univ. Press, 1969): 169-170.

[23] Immanuel Kant, *Critique of the Power of Judgment*, trans. Paul Guyer and Eric Matthews (Cambridge: Cambridge UP, 2000): 141. See also Spivak, *A Critique of Postcolonial Reason: Toward a History of the Vanishing Present* (Cambridge: Harvard UP, 1999): 11, n.18.

[24] DuBois, *Darkwater: Voices From Within the Veil* (Millwood, N.Y.: Kraus-Thomson, 1975): 88; emphasis mine. Marx, "The Eighteenth Brumaire of Louis Bonaparte," in *Surveys From Exile*, trans. Ben Fowkes (New York: Vintage, 1974): 239. Upon the issue of the role of the international civil society in today's world, I have a serious difference with my long-term ally and dear friend Homi Bhabha. I hope to discuss this with him next month. The passage from DuBois is cited in Bhabha, "Democracy De-realized," in Okwui Enwezor, et al. eds., *Democracy Unrealized: Documenta 11-Platform 1* (Ostfildern-Ruit: Hatje Cantz, 2002): 360. The full passage is "in future democracies the toleration and encouragement of minorities and the willingness to consider as 'men' the crankiest, humblest and poorest and blackest peoples, must be

the real key to the consent of the governed" (*Darkwater*, New York: AMS Press, reprinted from the 1920 edition, 1969, 153). The ellipses should be noticed. DuBois's piece is indeed about "the old cry of privilege, the old assumption that there are those in the world who know better what is best for others than those others know themselves, and who can be trusted to do their best...They say of persons and classes: 'They do not need the ballot'"(140-141). I am making the point that self-selected moral entrepreneurs fit this description. I will not comment here on the folly of drawing in the Levinas of *Otherwise than Being* to endorse that role. DuBois's use of the feminine metaphor in the subtitle of his book also bears further inquiry.

[25] See for instance, Kieran Allen, "Immigration and the Celtic Tiger," in Gareth Dale and Mike Cole, eds. *The European Union and Migrant Labor* (New York: Berg, 1999): 91-111 and Khalid Koser and Melisa Salazar, "Ireland," in Steffen Angenendt, ed. *Asylum and Migration Policies in the European Union* (Berlin: DGAP, 1999): 217-227. I thank Benjamin Conisbee Baer for inspired research assistance.

[26] Nina Siegal "A Legendary Bookstore Gets a Last-Minute Lease on Life" *New York Times* Section 14, 9, 30/7/00. Full reference to *Nation* article forthcoming. See also Kathleen McGowan "Fish Store Buys Bakery, Harlemites Say Deal Stinks" *City Limits Weekly* 22/5/00, from webpage.

[27] Djebar, *Women of Algiers in their Apartment* (Charlottesville and London: U of Virginia Press, 1992): 141, translation modified.

[28] J. LaPlanche and J.-B. Pontalis *The Language of Psycho-analysis*, trans. Donald Nicholson-Smith (New York: W.W. Norton, 1973): 447-449 provides a list of the documentation to follow.

[29] Jim Rasenberger, "City Lore; A Lost City, Frozen in Time," *The New York Times* (Jul 30, '00), web access. The following two quotations are from the same source.

[30] "Eco-Illuminations: The Art of Cynthia Mailman," Staten Island Institute of Arts and Sciences, September 23, 2000-December 31, 2000.

[31] Henry Staten, unpublished communication.

[32] Printout given at the museum; emphasis mine.

[33] Henry John Drewal and John Mason, eds. *Beads Body and Soul: Art and Light in the Yorùbá Universe* (Los Angeles: Fowler Museum, 1998): 278.

[1] Samuel Beckett, "The Capital of the Ruins", in *As the Story Was Told* (London: John Calder, 1990): 27-8; and "First Love", in *First Love and Other Shorts* (New York: Grove Press, 1974): 21.

[2] E. Estyn Evans, *Irish Folk Ways* (London: Routledge and Kegan Paul, 1957): 18.

[3] R.A.S. Macalister, *The Archaeology of Ireland* (1949), cited in Evans, *Irish Folk Ways*, 12.

[4] On the history of symbolist aesthetics, see Benjamin, *The Origin of German Tragic Drama*, trans. John Osborne, intro. George Steiner (London: Verso, 1990): 159-167.

[5] Benjamin, *Origin of German Tragic Drama*, 186.

[6] On the importance of these two disciplines in particular, among the array of governmental discourses, see David Lloyd, "The Memory of Hunger," in David Eng and David Kazanjian, eds., *Loss: The Politics of Mourning* (Berkeley: U of California Press, 2002): 205-228.

[7] Karl Marx, *Capital: A Critique of Political Economy*, Vol. I, ed. Frederick Engels, trans. Samuel Moore and Edward Aveling (London: Lawrence and Wishart, 1954): 658.

[8] Marx, *Capital* I, 664-5.

[9] Max Horkheimer and Theodor W. Adorno, *Dialectic of Enlightenment*, trans. John Cumming (New York: Continuum, 1972): 9-13.

[10] Adorno and Horkheimer, *Dialectic of Enlightenment*, 6.

[11] Ashis Nandy, *The Intimate Enemy: Loss and Recovery of Self under Colonialism* (Oxford: Oxford UP, 1983): 57-9.

[12] Estyn Evans, *Irish Folk Ways*, 29-30.

[13] Ibid., 30.

[14] Alanna O'Kelly, *No Colouring Can Deepen the Darkness of Truth* from the series "The Country Blooms....A Garden and a Grave", 1992-1995. This video installation was one element of O'Kelly's joint exhibition with Frances Hegarty at the San Francisco Art Institute, March-May 1997, *Deoraiocht/Displacement*.

[1] This passage is taken from one of George Jackson's prison letters. Dated April 4, 1970, the letter can be found in *Soledad Brother: The Prison Letters of George Jackson* (Chicago: Lawrence Hill Books, 1994): 233-34.

[2] I am indebted here, and in the rest of this paragraph, to Saidiya Hartman's discussion of a memory born from violence and loss in *Scenes of Subjection: Terror, Slavery, and Self-Making in Nineteenth-Century America* (New York: Oxford UP, 1997): 72-74.

[3] I am indebted here to Derrida's discussion of the relations among capital, ghosts, and mourning in his *Specters of Marx: The State of the Debt, the Work of Mourning, & the New International*, trans. Peggy Kamuf (New York: Routledge, 1994), especially chapters 1 and 2.

[4] See Genet's *The Prisoner of Love*, trans. Barbara Bray (Middletown, CT.: Wesleyan UP, 1992 [1986]): 259.

[5] See Emerson's "Fate," in *The Complete Works of Ralph Waldo Emerson*, ed. Edward Waldo Emerson, 12 vols, Centenary Edition (Boston: Houghton, Mifflin and Company, 1903-04): VI, 16-17. All references to Emerson's writings are to this edition, unless otherwise noted, and will be cited by volume number and page.

[6] See Cavell, "Emerson's Constitutional Amending: Reading 'Fate,'" in *Philosophical Passages: Wittgenstein, Emerson, Austin, Derrida* (Cambridge: Blackwell Publishers, Inc., 1995): 14.

[7] See *The Journals and Miscellaneous Notebooks of Ralph Waldo Emerson*, ed. William H. Gilman, et al, 16 vols. (Cambridge: Harvard UP, 1960- ): XIII, 114. All references to Emerson's journals are to this edition, and will be cited by volume number and page.

[8] Cavell, "Emerson's Constitutional Amending," 18.

[9] See *Emerson's Antislavery Writings*, ed. Len Gougeon and Joel Myerson (New Haven, CT.: Yale UP, 1995): 9. Future references to this collection of writings will be cited as *AS* and page number.

[10] See "Annexation," in the *Democratic Review* 17 (July and August 1845): 5.

[11] See "The Great Nation of Futurity," in the *Democratic Review* 16 (November 1839): 426-430.

[12] See Sundquist, "The Literature of Expansion and Race," in *The Cambridge History of American Literature, Vol. 2, 1820-1865*, ed. Sacvan Bercovitch (Cambridge: Cambridge UP, 1995): 128 and 182.

[13] Cited in Nicoloff, *Emerson on Race and History*, 134.

[14] This passage is from a letter of Samuel A. Cartwright to William S. Forwood. Dated February 13, 1861, it is cited in *The Ideology of Slavery: Proslavery Thought in the Antebellum South, 1830-1860*, ed. Drew Gilpin Faust (Baton Rouge: Louisiana State UP, 1981): 15.

[15] See Nott, *Two Lectures on the Connection between the Biblical and Physical History of Man* (Mobile: Bartlett and Welford, 1849): 36.

[16] Nott and Gliddon, *Types of Mankind: Or, Ethnological Researches based upon the Ancient Monuments, Paintings, Sculptures, and Crania of Races, and upon their Natural, Geographical, Philological, and Biblical History: Illustrated by Selections from the Inedited Papers of Samuel George Morton, M. D., (Late President of the Academy of Natural Sciences at Philadelphia) and by Additional Contributions from Prof. L. Agassiz, LL.D.; W. Usher, M.D.; and Prof. H. S. Patterson, M.D.* (Philadelphia: Lippincott, Grambo & Co., 1854): 79.

[17] Ibid., 53.

[18] Whitman, *Walt Whitman: Complete Poetry and Collected Prose*, ed. Justin Kaplan (New York: The Library of America, 1982): 1170.

[19] I am indebted in this discussion of Emerson's relation to geology to Joseph G. Kronick's *American Poetics of History: From Emerson to the Moderns* (Baton Rouge: Louisiana State UP, 1984), especially chapter 2.

[20] Chambers, *Vestiges of the Natural History of Creation* (London: John Churchill, 1845; Third Edition): 58.

[21] See Emerson, *The Early Lectures of Ralph Waldo Emerson*, ed. Stephen Whicher, Robert E. Spiller, and Wallace E. Williams, 3 vols. (Cambridge, MA.: Harvard UP, 1961): I, 18. Subsequent references to these lectures will be cited by volume number and page.

[22] See Harris, *The Pre-Adamite Earth: Contributions to Theological Science* (Boston: Gould, Kendall & Lincoln, 1850): 69.

[23] See *The Pre-Adamite Earth*, 68 and 71. In Lyell's words, geology teaches us that "the successive destruction of species must now be part of the regular and constant order of Nature." See Charles Lyell, *Principles of Geology*, 2 vols. (Chicago: U of Chicago P, 1990), II: 141. This edition is a reprint of *Principles of Geology, being an attempt to explain the former changes of the earth's surface, by reference to causes now in operation* (London: John Murray, 1830).

[24] Thoreau, *Walden and Civil Disobedience*, ed. Owen Thomas (New York: W. W. Norton and Company, Inc., 1966): 203.

[25] See *Principles of Geology*, I: 157.

[26] Ibid., II: 141 and 156.

[27] See Patricia Seed, *Ceremonies of Possession in Europe's Conquest of the New World, 1492-1640* (Cambridge: Cambridge UP, 1995), especially pages 16-40. I am grateful to Al Raboteau for directing me to this text.

[28] Ibid., 32.

[29] See Skaggs, *The Great Guano Rush: Entrepreneurs and American Overseas Expansion* (New York: St. Martins, 1994): 1-2.

[30] On this point, see Avery Odell Craven's excellent *Soil Exhaustion as a Factor in the Agricultural History of Virginia and Maryland, 1606-1860* (Urbana, IL.: U of Illinois P, 1925), especially pages 9-53.

[31] Gray uses this phrase in a discussion of the importance of guano to the Cotton Belt in particular. See his *History of Agriculture in the Southern United States To 1860*, 2 vols. (New York: Peter Smith, 1941): II, 701.

[32] Skaggs, *The Great Guano Rush*, 10. See also "Inspection Laws," in *The Southern Planter* 16 (March 1856): 80-90.

[33] For a detailed account of this "test by burning," see Solon Robinson's *Guano: A Treatise of Practical Information for Farmers; Containing Plain Directions on How to Apply Peruvian Guano to the Various Crops and Soils of America, with a brief synopsis of its history, locality, quantity, method of procuring, prospect of continued supply, and price; analysis of its composition, and value as a fertilizer, over all other manures* (NY:

Theodore W. Riley, 1853): 69-70.

34 Fillmore, "First Annual Message," in *State of the Union Messages of the Presidents, 1790-1966*, ed. Fred L. Israel, Vol. I, 1790-1860 (New York: Chelsea House, 1966): 797.

35 See the *U. S. Congressional Globe* (34th Congress, 1st Session, July 22, 1856): 1296.

36 See Skaggs, *The Great Guano Rush*, 71.

37 See her "Coolies, Shopkeepers, Pioneers: The Chinese of Mexico and Peru (1849-1930)," in *Amerasia* 15.2 (1989): 92.

38 Ibid., 108.

39 See Melville, "The Encantadas, or Enchanted Isles," in *The Piazza Tales and Other Prose Pieces, 1839-1860* (Evanston and Chicago: Northwestern UP and the Newberry Library, 1987), especially pp. 134-37; Thoreau, *Walden and Civil Disobedience*, 3; Douglass, "What to the Slave is the Fourth of July?: An Address Delivered in Rochester, New York, on 5 July 1852," in *The Frederick Douglass Papers, Series One: Speeches, Debates, and Interviews, Volume 2: 1847-54*, ed. John W. Blassingame (New Haven: Yale UP, 1982): 373; and Faulkner, *Absalom, Absalom!* (New York: Vintage Books, 1990): 201-02.

40 See *Selections from the Letters and Speeches of the Hon. James H. Hammond, of South Carolina* (New York: John F. Trow & Co., 1866): 317-18.

41 Ibid., 318-19.

42 See Sundquist, "The Literature of Expansion and Race," 245.

43 Karl Marx, *Poverty of Philosophy* (Moscow: Foreign Languages Publishing House, 1955 [1847]): 112.

44 Hamacher, "One 2 Many Multiculturalisms," trans. Dana Hollander, in *Violence, Identity, and Self-Determination*, ed. Hent de Vries and Samuel Weber (Stanford UP, 1997): 301.

45 Ibid., 301.

46 Ibid., 304.

47 Benjamin, "Theses on the Philosophy of History," in *Illuminations: Essays and Reflections*, trans. Harry Zohn, ed. Hannah Arendt (New York: Schocken, 1969): 255.

[1] Robert F. Drinan, S.J., *The Mobilization of Shame: A World View of Human Rights* (New Haven: Yale UP, 2002).

[2] B.V.A. Roling, "Aspects of the Criminal Responsibility for Violations of the Laws of War" in *The New Humanitarian Law of Armed Conflict*, ed. Antonio Cassese (1979): 199-200. Thanks to Ewen Allison for the citation.

[3] David K. Shipler, "Soviet is Assailed Over Emigration," *New York Times*, March 20, 1983, A4.

[4] Louis Henkin, "Human Rights: Ideology and Aspiration, Reality and Prospect," in *Realizing Human Rights: Moving from Inspiration to Impact*, ed. Samantha Power and Graham Allison (New York: St. Martin's Press, 2000): 24.

[5] Bill Steigerwald, "Human rights and wrongs," *Pittsburgh Tribune*, March 29, 2003.

[6] "Workshop On Science And Human Rights. Sharing Information And Building Skills: Tools For Casework, Thursday, May 17, 2001, AAAS, Washington, DC." <http://mailman.aaas.org/pipermail/per/2001-May/000002.html>

[7] See Alex de Waal, "Becoming Shameless: The failure of human-rights organizations in Rwanda," *Times Literary Supplement*, February 21, 1997, 3-4; and Stanley Cohen, "Government Responses to Human Rights Reports," *Human Rights Quarterly* 18.3 (1996): 517-543.

[8] Quoted in Brian Lowry and Elizabeth Jensen, "The 'gee whiz' war," *Los Angeles Times*, March 28, 2003.

[9] To his credit, on the contrary, Nuruddin Farah includes this in his new account, *Links* (Cape Town: Kwela, 2003): 239-240, 245.

[10] Anon., "Mission Profile: Operations PROVIDE RELIEF and RESTORE HOPE, Somalia, 1992-1995." <http://www.specialoperations.com/Operations/Restore_Hope/Operation1.htm>

[11] Michael Gordon, "TV Army on the Beach Took U.S. by Surprise," *New York Times*, December 10, 1992, A18.

[12] Quoted in Seymour Topping, "Suspend Hostilities," *Columbia Journalism Review*, March/April 1998.

[13] Charles W. Ricks, "The Military-News Media Relationship: Thinking Forward," December 1, 1993 <http://www.carlisle.army.mil/ssi/pubs/1993/media/media.htm>

[14] Richard Dowden, "TV brings US grim news of Mogadishu," *The Independent*, October 7, 1993, 10.

[15] Calin Neacsu, "Kosovo rebels under fire after Milosevic rejects NATO again," *Agence France Presse*, March 11, 1999.

[16] Anne Thompson, *Associated Press AP Worldstream*, March 14, 1999; Sunday 12:56 ET.

[17] Julius Strauss, "Serbs unleash 'scorched earth' policy on Kosovo," *The Daily Telegraph* (London), March 14, 1999, 9. My emphasis.

[18] Reuters, March 14, 1999.

[19] Carlotta Gall, "For Villages Of Kosovo, War Is Part Of Daily Life," *New York Times*, March 16, 1999, A10.

[20] John Keats, "This living hand, now warm and capable," in *The Complete Poems*, ed. John Barnard (New York: Penmuin, 1977): 459.

[21] Boris Buden, "Saving Private Havel," *Arkzin/ Bastard Global Edition* (Zagreb, May/June 1999). <http://amsterdam.nettime.org/Lists-Archives/nettime-l-9904/msg00325.html>

**Displacement: The *RealPolitik* of Utopia**

[1] For an analysis of cold war politics, see Roberta Cohen and Francis Deng, *Masses in Flight* (Washington, D.C.: Brookings Institute Press, 1998): 1-5.

[2] Immanuel Wallerstein, *The End of the World as We Know It* (Minneapolis: U of Minnesota P, 1999): 81. Also, Saskia Sassen, *Globalization and Its Discontents: Essays on the New Mobility of People and Money* (New York: The New Press, 1998).

[3] Roberta Cohen and Francis Deng, *Masses in Flight*, 1-5. Also, UNHCR, *Refugees by Numbers* (New York: United Nations Publications, 2001).

[4] Conversation with Erin Mooney, Assistant Director, Bunche Institute, Graduate Center City University of New York.

[5] Eva Huseby-Darvas, "Refugee Women from Former Yugoslavia in the Camps of Rural Hungary," in Joel Halpern and David Kideckel, eds. *Neighbors at War; Anthropological Perspectives on Yugoslav Ethnicity, Culture and History* (University Park, PA: Penn State UP, 2000): 340-57.

[6] Engineering and Environmental Services Section UNHCR, *Refugee Operations and Environmental Management, Selected Lessons Learned* (New York: UNHCR, 2001), p1. http//www.unhcr.ch

[7] *Environment in the UNHCR*, 5.2, December 2000, ("http://www.unhcr.ch," 7).

[8] Ibid., 9.

[9] For the origins of permaculture in Australia in the 1970's and present experiments, see *Sustainable Communities,* ed. Hugh Barton (London: Earthscan, 2000).

[10] Engineering and Environmental Services Section UNHCR, *Refugee Operations and Environmental Management*, 46-90.

[11] *Environment in the UNHCR*, 4.

[12] Brian Milani, *Designing the Green Economy* (New York: Rowman and Littlefield, 2000).

[13] Julie Mertus, ed. *The Suitcase: Refugee Voices from Bosnia and Croatia* (Berkeley: U of California P, 1997): 71.

[14] Larissa Lomnitz, "The Social and Economic Organization of a Mexican Shanty Town," in Josef Gugler, ed. *Cities in the Developing World: Issues, Theory, Policy* (Oxford: Oxford UP) p.207. In Cerrada del Condor a town of 177 families there are two water facets; 80 percent of the population uses a gully for a latrine; 33 percent of households have a television.

[15] Scott Andersen, "The Curse of Blood and Vengeance," *The New York Times Magazine*, December 26, 1999.